New Perspectives on Yugoslavi

Twenty years after it ceased to exist as a multinational federation, Yugoslavia still has the power to provoke controversy and debate. Bringing together contributions from 12 of the leading scholars of modern and contemporary South East Europe, this volume explores the history of Yugoslavia from creation to dissolution.

Drawing on the very latest historical research, this book explains how the country came about, how it evolved and why, eventually, it failed. From the start of the twentieth century, through the First World War, the interwar years and the Second World War, to the road to socialism under President Tito and the wars of Yugoslav succession in the 1990s, this volume provides up to date analysis of the causes and consequences of a range of events that shaped the development of this remarkable state across its various iterations. The book concludes by examining post-conflict relations in the era of European integration.

Traversing 90 years of history, this volume presents a fascinating story of how a country that once served as the model for multi-ethnic states around the world has now become a byword for ethno-national fragmentation and conflict.

Dejan Djokić is Senior Lecturer in History at Goldsmiths, University of London. His publications include *Elusive Compromise: A History of Interwar Yugoslavia* (2007) and *Nikola Pašić and Ante Trumbić: The Kingdom of Serbs, Croats and Slovenes* (2010).

James Ker-Lindsay is Eurobank EFG Senior Research Fellow on the Politics of South East Europe at the London School of Economics and Political Science. He is also the author of *Kosovo: The Path to Contested Statehood in the Balkans* (2009).

New Perspectives on Yugoslavia

Key Issues and Controversies

Edited by
Dejan Djokić and James Ker-Lindsay

LONDON AND NEW YORK

First edition published 2011
by Routledge
2 Park Square, Milton Park, Abingdon, Oxon OX14 4RN

Simultaneously published in the USA and Canada
by Routledge
270 Madison Avenue, New York, NY 10016

Routledge is an imprint of the Taylor & Francis Group, an informa business

© 2011 Dejan Djokić and James Ker-Lindsay for selection and editorial matter;
individual chapters, the contributors

Typeset in Garamond by Taylor and Francis Books
Printed and bound in Great Britain by TJ International Ltd, Padstow, Cornwall

British Library Cataloguing in Publication Data
A catalogue record for this book is available from the British Library

Library of Congress Cataloging in Publication Data
A catalog record for this book has been requested

ISBN 13: 978-0-415-49919-4 (hbk)
ISBN 13: 978-0-415-49920-0 (pbk)
ISBN 13: 978-0-203-84601-8 (ebk)

Contents

Maps

Acknowledgements

We wish to thank our two editors at Routledge: Alison Yates, who commissioned the book, and Emily Kindleysides, who carried it through to completion. They have both shown support and enthusiasm for the project from the very beginning and we hope the book has not disappointed them.

Dejan would like to thank his colleagues in the Department of History at Goldsmiths, University of London, for creating a stimulating and friendly environment in which working on this and other research projects was a pleasure, despite considerable teaching and administrative commitments. Likewise, James would like to thank his colleagues at the Hellenic Observatory, LSE, and to the Institute for Defence Analysis (IAA) in Athens, which so generously provided funding for his senior research fellowship at the School in 2008–9.

DDj & JK-L
London, 28 June 2009

About the Contributors

About the Editors

Dejan Djokić is Senior Lecturer in History and Director of the Centre for the Study of the Balkans at Goldsmiths, University of London. He has also taught at Nottingham University, Birkbeck, University of London and UCL School of Slavonic and East European Studies and held fellowships at Columbia University and the Woodrow Wilson International Center for Scholars. His main publications include *Yugoslavism: Histories of a Failed Idea, 1918–1992* (2003, editor), *Elusive Compromise: A History of Interwar Yugoslavia* (2007) and *Nikola Pašić and Ante Trumbić: The Kingdom of Serbs, Croats and Slovenes* (2010).

James Ker-Lindsay is Senior Research Fellow in the Politics and International Relations of South East Europe at the London School of Economics and co-convenor of the British International Studies Association (BISA) Working Group on South East Europe. His main publications include *EU Accession and UN Peacemaking in Cyprus* (2005), *Crisis and Conciliation: A Year of Rapprochement between Greece and Turkey* (2007) and *Kosovo: The Path to Contested Statehood in the Balkans* (2009).

About the Contributors

Florian Bieber is Professor in Southeast European Studies at the University of Graz. Prior to this he lectured in East European Politics at the University of Kent and has held visiting posts at Cornell University and the London School of Economics. Among other works, he is the author of *Post-war Bosnia: Ethnicity, Equality and Public Sector Governance* (2007) and is editor-in-chief of *Nationalities Papers* and associate editor of *Southeastern Europe*.

Mark Cornwall is Professor of Modern European History and Head of the Department of History at the University of Southampton. His main publications include *The Undermining of Austria-Hungary: The Battle for Hearts and Minds* (2000), *The Last Years of Austria-Hungary: A Multi-National*

Experiment in Early Twentieth Century Europe (2002, editor), and *Czechoslovakia in a Nationalist and Fascist Europe, 1918–1948* (2007, co-editor).

Jasna Dragović-Soso is Senior Lecturer in International Relations at Goldsmiths, University of London. Her publications include '*Saviours of the Nation': Serbia's Intellectual Opposition and the Revival of Nationalism* (2002) and *State Collapse in South-Eastern Europe: New Perspectives on Yugoslavia's Disintegration* (2007, co-editor).

Tomislav Dulić is a research fellow at the Hugo Valentin Institute, Uppsala University. His publications include *Utopias of Nation: Local Mass Killing in Bosnia and Herzegovina, 1941–42* (2005) and *Balkan Currents: Essays in Honour of Kjell Magnusson* (2005, co-editor).

Eric Gordy is Senior Lecturer in the Politics of South East Europe and Director of the Centre for South East European Studies at the School of Slavonic and East European Studies, University College London. He is the author of *The Culture of Power in Serbia: Nationalism and the Destruction of Alternatives* (1999).

Dejan Jović is Lecturer in Politics and Director of the Centre for European Neighbourhood Studies at the University of Stirling. He is the author of *Yugoslavia: A State that Withered Away* (2009) and guest editor of several special issues of the *Journal of Southern Europe and the Balkans*.

John Paul Newman is post-doctoral research fellow at University College Dublin. He is working on a social and cultural history of the Kingdom of Serbs, Croats, and Slovenes which focuses on the cultural demobilization of former soldiers.

Stevan K. Pavlowitch is Emeritus Professor of History at the University of Southampton. His main publications include *The Improbable Survivor: Yugoslavia and its Problems, 1918–1988* (1988), *Tito: Yugoslavia's Great Dictator* (1992), *A History of the Balkans, 1804–1945* (1999), *Serbia: The History behind a Name* (2002), and *Hitler's New Disorder: The Second World War in Yugoslavia* (2008).

Connie Robinson is Lecturer in the Department of Sociology at Central Washington University. She is currently working on a historical and social movement analysis of the activities of the Yugoslav Committee during the First World War.

Nebojša Vladisavljević is Associate Professor in the Faculty of Political Science at the University of Belgrade. Prior to this he was Tutorial Fellow in the Department of Government at the London School of Economics. He is the author of *Serbia's Antibureaucratic Revolution: Milošević, the Fall of Communism and Nationalist Mobilization* (2008).

Note on Spelling and Pronunciation

All former Yugoslav personal and place names are in their original spelling, unless there exist commonly accepted Anglicised spellings. Therefore, it is Belgrade, not Beograd, King Alexander, not Aleksandar, and Prince Paul, not Pavle.

The following is a brief guide to pronunciation in the language formerly known as Serbo-Croat and in the Slovene:

c – 'ts' as in nets
č – 'ch' as in charming
ć – softer than č, close to 'tu' as in tuna
dj (also spelled as đ) – 'j' as in juice
dž – harder than 'dj', 'j' as in jogging
j – 'y' as in Yugoslavia
lj – similar to 'lia' as in parliament
nj – 'n' as in new
r – pronounced similarly to the Scottish rolling 'r'
š – 'sh' as in shy
ž – 'su' as in pleasure

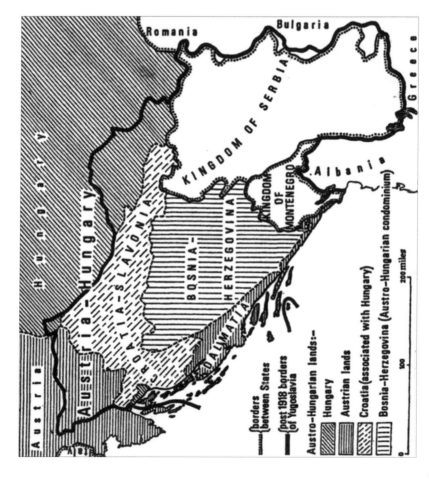

Map 1 The Yugoslav lands on the eve of the First World War.

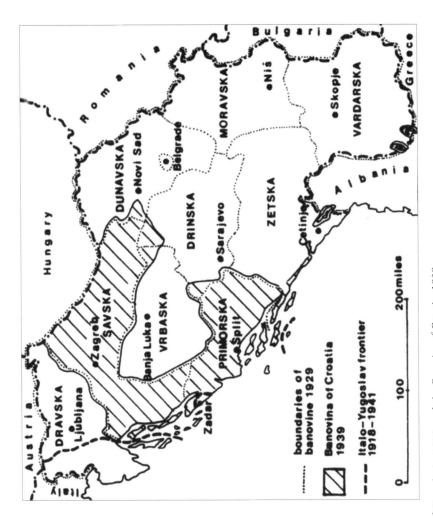

Map 2 The *Banovine* of Yugoslavia, 1929, and the *Banovina* of Croatia, 1939.

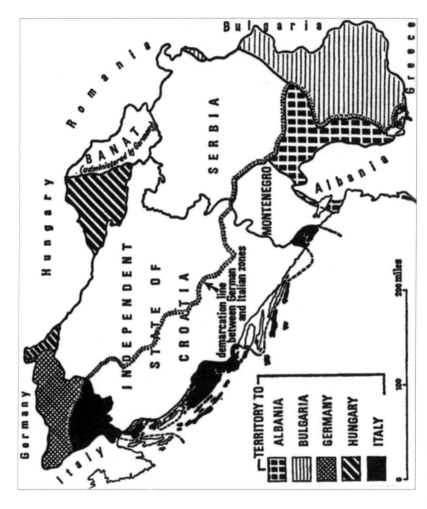

Map 3 The territory of Yugoslavia during the Second World War.

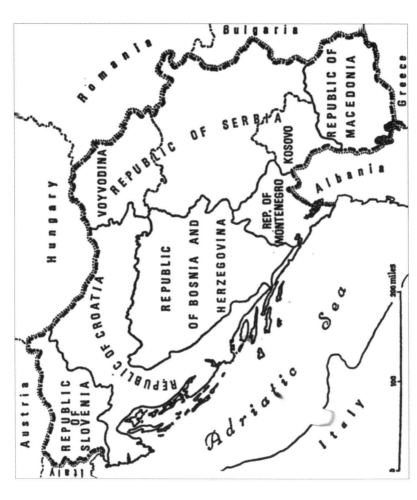

Map 4 The federated units of Yugoslavia after 1945.

Introduction

Dejan Djokić and James Ker-Lindsay

Yugoslavia was more than a country – it was also an idea.[1] This perhaps explains why the mere mention of the common South Slav state, 20 years after it has ceased to exist, is still capable of stirring up intense emotions. Yugoslavia, especially Tito's socialist federation, was often regarded as an idyll, both inside and outside of the country. It was an example of how a shared vision, based on ethnic and linguistic proximity and inspired by a united purpose, could bring together cultural, religious and regional differences to create a single, united polity. It was something to be celebrated, although Yugoslavia's problems were clear even to many of its most enthusiastic supporters.[2] Even today, the Yugoslav concept has its adherents and admirers. The phenomenon of 'Yugonostalgia', so prevalent in parts of the former Yugoslavia, can in part be interpreted as a continuing expression of the power of the idea.[3]

However, there are different views. Far from being an example to be emulated, Yugoslavia was an abhorrent construction. It subjugated the free expression of national identities, forcing diverse groups of people to live together within a state that was doomed to failure.[4] Indeed, such is the backlash against the very idea that any suggestion of greater regional co-operation, as one often hears from the European Union, is sometimes fiercely resisted as an attempt to create a new Yugoslavia.[5]

A debate continues over these competing interpretations, both at a popular level and among intellectual and political elites.[6] Was Yugoslavia a good idea brought down by petty nationalism, or did national identity and self-determination triumph over an authoritarian central authority? The answer is less than clear. The historical record indicates that both positions have their merits and weaknesses. As is so often the case, reality is not black and white. Trying to provide definitive direct answers to these questions is rather futile. More to the point, it is a diversion from a set of far more interesting questions that, in their own way, can go a long way towards answering the fundamental conundrum about the merits of the Yugoslav idea: how did Yugoslavia emerge; how did it develop and evolve; and why and how did it fail?

The book is a product of these very questions. It explores, from below and above, former Yugoslavia at various points throughout its history, from the early twentieth century until its final demise at the start of the twenty-first. Thus it follows a course of events from the emergence of Yugoslavism as a political project prior to the start of the First World War to the formation of the Kingdom of Serbs, Croats, and Slovenes in December 1918 – the first incarnation of a united South Slav state that would be renamed into the Kingdom of Yugoslavia a decade later – and the intrigues that permeated the country during the interwar period. Thereafter, it examines the bloody events that befell Yugoslavia during the Second World War before concentrating on the emergence of the country as a socialist federation led by Marshal Tito. It then looks at the factors that contributed to the collapse of Yugoslavia in the 1990s, which led to some of the most bitter and brutal conflicts of the late twentieth century, and the declaration of independence by Kosovo, which many observers viewed as the final end of the break up of Yugoslavia. Finally, it seeks to examine how the peoples of the former Yugoslavia have sought to come to terms with the legacy of the past and their shared history. Encapsulated within this span of history is a fascinating story of a country that once served as the model for multiethnic states around the world, but has now become a byword for ethno-national fragmentation and conflict.

Despite the idealizations and notoriety that surround Yugoslavia, the country remains little understood. Certainly, the literature on former Yugoslavia is vast – largely due to the interest among scholars and research students about the disintegration and the subsequent wars.[7] However, for all the attention former Yugoslavia received in the 1990s, there have in fact been very few books that have traced the full spread of the country's history. Most books on the subject tend to neglect history, especially the history of the country prior to the end of the Second World War – a rather paradoxical situation given that many authors also agree that the misuse of history by political leaders and nationalist intellectuals, as well as confusion among 'ordinary' people regarding the distinction between history and historical myths, have played an important role in the disintegration of Yugoslavia. Thus, a better understanding of history in general – and specific key periods, incidents and developments, in particular – is absolutely vital if one is to gain a clearer understanding of more recent events.[8]

This volume is no conventional history book. Rather than take a standard linear approach and present a broad brush 'History of Yugoslavia', the book instead explores Yugoslav history by concentrating on previously understudied or neglected issues that can inform the debate on why and how Yugoslavia came about, how it was perpetuated and why, ultimately, it failed. Drawing on contributions from leading scholars of modern and contemporary South East Europe, and utilizing the latest archival research and the most up to date analysis and interpretations of the causes and consequences of a range of events that shaped the development of Yugoslavia, this work traces the evolution of Yugoslavia across its various iterations – from its genesis to extinction – by exploring a number of key issues and controversies that, in their own ways, contributed to the 'bigger picture'. Yugoslav history is therefore told from the perspective of a number of important questions that may be seen as being of central importance to the story of former Yugoslavia.

Naturally, this approach has resulted in a diverse variety of contributions, ranging across seemingly not directly related topics. However, uniting them all are certain themes that recur throughout the book. For example, while high politics not unexpectedly features prominently in the work, the role of grassroots politics is explored in many of the contributions. As is shown, the history of Yugoslavia was not just shaped by political leaders, acting both within and outside of the country, but also by the people of Yugoslavia. Indeed, at points there were obvious tensions between the two. A constant theme that runs throughout the book, and is dealt with in almost every chapter, is the question of nationalism and national identity. How were the people of Yugoslavia told to see themselves? And how did they actually see themselves? Another major theme that emerges is the consequences of war and the process of reconciliation. It is not just today that the people of the former Yugoslavia have to come to terms with the bitter legacy of conflict; it was also a key issue that needed to be addressed in the first years of the Yugoslav kingdom and of the socialist republic. At the same time there is the question of external actors and the role they played. While there is perhaps a tendency sometimes to place too much emphasis on the part played by 'great powers' and outside forces, the history of Yugoslavia – especially at its formation and its dissolution – intimately involved what is commonly referred to today as the 'international community'. These themes arise time and time again throughout the work, providing common strands that in turn help to address the core questions that lie at the heart of the book.

Structure of the book

The book deals with a range of specific themes, but is set out in broadly chronological order following the evolution of Yugoslavia from its foundation to its dissolution and the aftermath. In Chapter 1, Connie Robinson explores the role of the Yugoslav Committee in the formation of a South Slav state. As she explains, in order to succeed, the Yugoslav movement, and specifically the Yugoslav Committee, had to negotiate a complex network of international state and non-state actors as well as a web of military alliances institutionalized by Great Power diplomacy and treaty-making. The Yugoslav Committee's strategy was therefore centred on a sustained advocacy programme, which included the production of publications, in order to gain international support for the creation of Yugoslavia. By analyzing these publications and speeches, one can see the way in which the Committee attempted to create symbolic alliances between the Yugoslav nation and the Allied countries, in this case Britain, in order to gain international recognition as a nation and as a state.

While recent historiography on Yugoslavia has naturally focused on its demise, Mark Cornwall, in Chapter 2, seeks to revisit the question of its creation in the turmoil of the First World War. In most histories of early Yugoslavia, the emphasis is usually placed on Serbia's key role in perpetuating the Yugoslav mission and bringing it to fruition in 1918. In contrast, he stresses the equal importance of uncovering grassroots Yugoslav agitation within the regions of the Habsburg monarchy as a way of understanding the serious difficulties that the new state would face. It moves, in line with recent trends in 'cultural history' of the Great War, to investigate the mentalities of those many individuals in 'Slovenia', Dalmatia, Croatia and Bosnia, who by 1918 could ostensibly shift their allegiance away from the Habsburg Monarchy towards some new state entity. The chapter highlights the crucial role of Slovene grassroots agitation, the so-called 'declaration movement' of 1917–18, which spread out of the Slovene lands into Dalmatia and set a vibrant example to politicians and clergy in Croatia and Bosnia. It was a fresh popular mobilization that acted as a kind of plebiscite for some new 'Yugoslavia'. But while Habsburg legitimacy in 1918 was tested and found wanting, the support for a Yugoslav alternative was nevertheless still uneven and variegated. As a result, those lands and peoples entering the new state did so with diverse aspirations, many of which were based on short-term anxieties from the wartime period.

Following on from this, John Paul Newman, in Chapter 3, explores how the peoples of the new Yugoslavia came to terms with the aftermath of the First World War. The magnitude of the impact of the Great War in the First Yugoslavia cannot be overstated. It permeated society, politics, and culture throughout the interwar period; especially in the decade immediately after the conflict. By studying the question of disabled veterans, he shows how a society came to terms with the aftermath of total war and struggled to define a social policy which was responsive to veterans' sense of entitlement. The widening disparity between what the state had promised and what it delivered in terms of welfare created a sense of disillusionment amongst former soldiers and fits into a wider, regional narrative of the failure of democratic process after 1918. Significantly, the chapter also shows that contrary to what one might expect, the ex-soldiers should be differentiated in terms of the armies in which they had fought during the war – namely Serbian or Habsburg – rather than in terms of their specific nationality.

Dejan Djokić also challenges, in Chapter 4, the 'ethnic approach' to the history of interwar Yugoslavia. Although the chapter acknowledges that ethnic politics and Serb-Croat conflict formed an important dimension of the interwar politics, the period may be better understood as a complex interplay between inter-ethnic, intra-ethnic and intra-party rivalries and alliances. The contest between Serb nationalism and Serb-dominated state institutions that emerged in the second half of the 1930s is the chapter's central theme. Serb national mobilization had begun even before Croatia was granted autonomy in 1939. As he argues, the commonly accepted interpretation of First Yugoslavia as a Serb-dominated state is largely a correct one, but it does not explain developments such as the Serb dissatisfaction with Yugoslavia in the 1930s. The 'Croat question' emerged by the early 1920s primarily as a reaction to state centralism. The 'Serb question' of the late 1930s was to a large extent a response to the devolution of central power. While Yugoslavia could not have been saved from the Axis invasion in 1941, would the country's experiences during the Second World War have been so violent, and could the government-in-exile have functioned more effectively, without the legacy of the interwar period?

Chapters 5 and 6 examine the Second World War and its effects on Yugoslavia. In his contribution, Tomislav Dulić notes how the mass killings that were perpetrated in Yugoslavia during the Second World War have played a pivotal role in reinforcing stereotypes about the Balkan peoples as being particularly prone to irrational violence. A careful analysis shows that the *četnik* and *ustaša* campaigns of 'ethnic homogenization' were in fact based on 'modern' patterns of thought, including nationalism, fascism and racism. The differences are attributable to the fact that the *ustašas* controlled a state with a modern bureaucratic apparatus and means of coercion that were vastly superior to those that the *četniks*, a loosely connected network of guerilla groups, had at their disposal. Meanwhile, at the local level, the most notable difference between *ustaša* and *četnik* mass killings is that the *ustašas* appear to have sub-divided the killings into distinct phases more frequently than the *četniks*, who instead used murder, pillaging and arson as a way of signaling to the victims that they had to leave. Even if these differences mattered little for the victims, they illustrate that structural preconditions and conceptual differences may have at least some effects on the ground.

Stevan Pavlowitch explores the period from a very different perspective. He shows that just like all other allied governments exiled in London during the Second World War, the Yugoslav government had problems in affirming its legitimacy. The government put together on the eve of the Axis invasion was a disparate if widely representative collection of party leaders and other personalities, but not a working team. Once in London, the government was faced with a range of unresolved prewar problems hideously magnified by multiple and chaotic enemy occupation, and by ethnic and ideological conflict. Ultimate legitimacy still rested on an 18-year-old monarch. No team spirit existed between Serbs and Croats, or even between Serbs themselves. Unable to provide guidance or to toe the British line, the government lost prestige, in British as well as in Yugoslav eyes. Its only policy was to wait and see as each faction came to believe that which fed its wishful thinking. Lost in the fog of Allied London, exiled Serb, Croat and Slovene leaders were used and eventually dismissed by the British, who were fighting their own war in uneasy alliance with the USA and the USSR, and who were anxious to reach a working compromise on a restored Yugoslavia, which they came to believe they had found in Tito's Partisan movement.

Tito and the Communist Party reunited Yugoslavia in 1945, but divisions caused by a brutal ethnic and ideological conflict that included elements of resistance, collaboration, civil war and war of liberation, and claimed around 1 million dead, remained long after the war was over. How did socialist Yugoslavia deal with the past and how did it emerge as a relatively prosperous and stable multiethnic federation? Dejan Jović's chapter deals with this question, by concentrating on Croatia, where wartime scars were arguably deepest in the whole of former Yugoslavia. Ethnic (Serb-Croat) and ideological (Partisan-*ustaša-četnik*) divisions were suppressed by the new regime, but, as Jović argues, the repression was only initial, largely ideologically motivated, and was not the sole factor that kept Yugoslavia – and indeed Croatia – together. Tito and the Party created a new Yugoslavia, based on 'brotherhood and unity' and a finely tuned balance of power between the federal republics. In such a Yugoslavia, far from being suppressed and placed in an inferior position (as is today sometimes argued), Croatia enjoyed a status equal to other republics. Jović convincingly shows that socialist Yugoslavia enjoyed a wide support in Croatia, largely because Tito's concept of socialism fulfilled two main goals of the Croatian national movement of the early twentieth century: republicanism and federalism. At the same time, however, Tito was not a Croat nationalist: he simply created a system that offered, at least for a while, something to everybody, including the Croats. The concluding part of the chapter analyzes the end of socialism and radicalization of Croat politics.

The following three chapters all explore different aspects of the dissolution of Yugoslavia, which started after Tito died and the system he helped create began to lose legitimacy. Why did Yugoslavia disintegrate and what were the consequences of the disintegration and wars of the 1990s? Nebojša Vladisavljević notes in Chapter 8 that while the break up of Yugoslavia triggered a long and heated debate among scholars, the focus has largely been on the political and cultural elites in Yugoslavia and the personalities of key political leaders. Popular politics is conspicuously absent in the literature. This is particularly surprising since the mobilization of ordinary people across Yugoslavia in the late 1980s went well beyond popular protests in Eastern Europe and the Soviet Union in terms of numbers of participants, its geographical scope and the dramatic political implications. Examining developments from below, Vladisavljević looks at several key episodes of extended grassroots protest in the second half of the 1980s, most notably the mobilization of Kosovo Serbs, protests by industrial workers and the 'antibureaucratic revolution' – a series of large rallies and demonstrations of various groups, strongly backed by Slobodan Milošević. In doing so, he shows how the main unintended consequence of popular politics was a high level of conflict, which proved highly destabilizing in a very diverse multinational society at a time when Yugoslavia's complex political institutions became dysfunctional and the old power structure was imploding.

Continuing on, Florian Bieber also explores the role of popular politics. He too seeks to draw attention away from the strong focus on political leaders in the discussions about warfare and conflict in the post-Yugoslav space in the 1990s and instead focus on politics from below. Specifically, he explores the link between nationalism and democratization in Serbia and challenges the suggestion that nationalism and democracy fell within the exclusive realms of the regime and opposition respectively. As he explains, it was far more complex than this. Contrary to conventional wisdom, it was not the popularity of nationalism that helped the regime and thus delayed democratization. Instead, it was the divisive nature of the 'national question' that proved to be problematic. As is shown, despite the fact that a 'national issue' presupposes national unity, it in fact rendered substantial political co-operation among opposition parties difficult, if not impossible, for a decade.

In Chapter 10, James Ker-Lindsay addresses the question of Kosovo and explores the role of external actors. In 1998, when Kosovo came to international attention, the prevailing view was that the solution to the conflict should be based on autonomy. Indeed, even after the NATO intervention and the establishment of international administration, in 1999, some form of self-government remained the preferred outcome for the international community. However, by late-2005, when status talks were launched, independence was widely seen to be the only viable option. Calls for the political compromise had been abandoned as Western leaders increasingly referred to Kosovo as the final chapter in the disintegration of Yugoslavia. As Ker-Lindsay shows, this transformation in views, and the justification for independence, was less a product of a fundamental reappraisal of the legal basis for self-determination in the Western Balkans – and beyond – than a pragmatic response to an increasingly unstable situation on the ground that emerged after the establishment of a UN administration in the province. In this sense, just as external actors had played such an important role during the emergence of a united, internationally recognized Yugoslav state in 1918–19, and had played a major part in shaping its socialist future at the end of the Second World War and its aftermath, so they were also key participants at its very end.

The final contribution explores how the peoples and former republics of Yugoslavia are coming to terms with their past and how this is shaping relations in the region after the wars of the 1990s. Jasna Dragović-Soso and Eric Gordy draw an assessment of transitional justice in the post-Yugoslav lands. As they show, in addition to the establishment of the International Criminal Tribunal for the Former Yugoslavia at the Hague in 1993, which has rendered opinions on matters with broader global implications, domestic institutions have emerged to try cases of international humanitarian law. However, efforts to establish state-sponsored and civil-society based truth commissions have, for the most part, not got off the ground. As Dragović-Soso and Gordy argue, this record of failure can be traced to a lack of domestic political will, uncertain and sometimes heavy-handed international involvement, and a lack of fit between legal mechanisms and the social goals with which they are associated.

Notes

1 For a recent study exploring the history and evolution throughout the twentieth century of Yugoslavist ideas see D. Djokić (ed.), *Yugoslavism: Histories of a Failed Idea, 1918–1992* (London: Hurst, 2003).

2 See A. Djilas, 'Funeral Oration for Yugoslavia: An Imaginary Dialogue with Western Friends', in Djokić (ed.), *Yugoslavism*, pp. 317–33, St. K. Pavlowitch, 'Yugoslavia: The Failure of a Success', *Journal of Southern Europe and the Balkans*, vol. 1, no. 2 (November 1999), pp. 163–70, and numerous writings by Desimir Tošić, for rare examples of works that find balance between being critical of Yugoslavia's shortcomings and at the same time acknowledging the creation of a common South Slav state as an important achievement, the demise of which is to be lamented.

3 'Yugonostalgia' is perhaps best manifested in commercial and critical success across former Yugoslavia of two books that deal with popular memory of everyday life, culture and music during the socialist period: I. Adrić et al. (eds), *Leksikon Yu Mitologije* (Belgrade and Zagreb: Rende and Postscriptum, 2004) and P. Janjatović, *Ex Yu Rock Enciklopedija, 1960–2006*, 2nd revised ed. (Belgrade: Author, 2006). See also N. Lindstrom, 'Yugonostalgia: Restorative and Reflective Nostalgia in Former Yugoslavia', *East Central Europe*, vol. 32, no. 1–2, 2005, pp. 227–38; and Z. Volčič, 'Yugo-Nostalgia: Cultural Memory and Media in Former Yugoslavia', *Critical Studies in Media Communication*, vol. 24, no. 1, March 2007, pp. 21–38. More recently, nostalgia for Tito has emerged as a major feature of Yugonostalgia. See P. Popham, 'Bringing back Tito', *The Independent*, 1 March 2008; and M. Velikonja, *Titostalgia: A Study of Nostalgia for Josip Broz* (Ljubljana: Mirovni inštitut, 2008). 'Yugonostalgia' is, of course, part of a wider phenomenon of nostalgia for socialism across the former Eastern Bloc. See S. Boym, *The Future of Nostalgia* (New York: Basic Books, 2001) and M. Todorova and Z. Gille (eds), *Post-Communist Nostalgia* (Oxford: Berghahn, 2010).

4 Such arguments may be found even in the works of leading historians of Yugoslavia, such as Ivo Banac, author of the classic and passionately argued *The National Question in Yugoslavia: Origins, History, Politics* (Ithaca, NY: Cornell University Press, 1984). Professor Banac appears to have modified his views since the publication of the book; see, for example, Omer Karabeg's interview with Banac, Dubravko Lovrenović and Latinka Perović, 'O raspadu Jugoslavije' [About the dissolution of Yugoslavia], 27 February 2008, available at the Serbo-Croat website of Radio Free Europe (http://www.slobodnaevropa.org/content/article/ 1045353.html/). The title of Sabrina Ramet's *Balkan Babel: The Disintegration of Yugoslavia, From the Death of Tito to the Fall of Milošević*, 4th ed. (Boulder, Co: Westview Press, 2002), suggests the author's main argument.

5 See, for example, A. Mitić, 'Western Balkans: Too much Yugoslavia or too little EU?' *Transitions Online*, 6 February 2006. A recent suggestion by Vida Ognjenović, an eminent author and president of the Serbian PEN, that regional PEN centres should consider merging into one, caused a polemic in Croatia and Serbia, after it was strongly rejected by her Croatian counterpart, Zvonko Maković, on the grounds that it smacked of yet another attempt by Belgrade to establish regional domination. See Milica Jovanović's interview with Maković, 'Balkanski PEN kao nova srpska fantazija', *e-novine*, 15 October 2008 (http://www.e-novine.com/sr/kultura/clanak.php?id=17909/), and critical reaction to Maković's view by Miljenko Jergović ('Balkanski PEN nije sadnja tikava sa Srbima', 14 October 2008, http://www.e-novine.com/sr/kultura/clanak.php?id=17890/) and Boris Dežulović ('Strah od Jugoslavije', 25 October 2008, http://www.e-novine.com/sr/kultura/ clanak.php?id=18293/), two eminent Croatian writers.

6 A conversation with a taxi driver in any part of former Yugoslavia is likely to offer an insight into popular perceptions about Yugoslavia's merits and flaws, that usually include a seemingly self-contradictory sorrow for 'good old times' and complaints about domination, separatism, and treachery of an 'Other'. For the views of historians and public figures see, for example, P. J. Marković, 'Lični stav: Za i protiv stvaranja Jugoslavije. Država bez

gradjana', *Vreme*, 4 December 2008; O. Karabeg's interview with L. Perović, I. Banac, and D. Lovrenović, op. cit.; and Z. Latinović, 'Zašto su Srbi neizlečivi Jugosloveni?', *NIN*, 25 October 2007. See also D. Djokić, 'Sukob sa Istorijom: Neka razmišljanja o odnosu prema prošlosti u post-socijalističkoj Srbiji', *Reč*, no. 75.21, December 2007, pp. 41–60.

7 For a list of the most important recent overviews of the literature on the disintegration of Yugoslavia see Nebojša Vladisavljević's chapter in this book, note 1.

8 There are some notable exceptions among numerous works published in English since 1991, such as: J. B. Allcock, *Explaining Yugoslavia* (London: Hurst, 2000); L. Benson, *Yugoslavia: A Concise History* (Basingstoke: Palgrave, 2001); M. K. Bokovoy, C. Lilly and J. Irvine (eds), *State-Society Relations in Yugoslavia, 1945–1992* (New York: St. Martin's Press, 1997); M. K. Bokovoy, *Peasants and Communists: Politics and Ideology in the Yugoslav Countryside, 1941–1953* (Pittsburgh: University of Pittsburgh Press, 1998); A. Djilas, *The Contested Country: Yugoslav Unity and Communist Revolution, 1919–1953*, 2nd ed. (Cambridge, MA: Harvard University Press, 1996); J. Irvine, *The Croat Question: Partisan Politics in the Formation of the Yugoslav Socialist State* (Boulder, CO: Westview Press, 1992); John R. Lampe, *Yugoslavia as History: Twice There Was a Country*, 2nd ed. (Cambridge: Cambridge University Press, 2000); C. Lilly, *Power and Persuasion: Ideology and Rhetoric in Communist Yugoslavia, 1944–1953* (Boulder, CO: Westview Press, 2001); N. Malcolm, *Bosnia: A Short History* (London: Macmillan, 1994), and *Kosovo: A Short History* (London: Macmillan, 1998); St. K. Pavlowitch, *Hitler's New Disorder: The Second World War in Yugoslavia, 1941–1945* (London: Hurst, 2008); S. Ramet, *The Three Yugoslavias: State-Building and Legitimation, 1918–2005* (Indiana and Washington, DC: Indiana University Press and Woodrow Wilson Center Press, 2006) – although Ramet's book dedicates proportionally the largest space to post-1991 events and is, essentially, an update of her earlier work *Balkan Babel*, op. cit.; S. Trew, *Britain, Mihailović and the Chetniks, 1941–42* (Basingstoke: Macmillan, 1998); A. B. Wachtel, *Making a Nation, Breaking a Nation: Literature and Cultural Politics in Yugoslavia* (Stanford, CA: Stanford University Press, 1998); and H. Williams, *Parachutes, Patriots and Partisans: The Special Operations Executive and Yugoslavia. 1941–1945* (London: Hurst, 2004). L. J. Cohen and J. Dragović-Soso's edited volume, *State Collapse in South-Eastern Europe: New Perspectives on Yugoslavia's Disintegration* (West Lafayette: Purdue University Press, 2008), includes chapters that deal with the pre-1945 history.

1 Yugoslavism in the Early Twentieth Century

The politics of the Yugoslav Committee

Connie Robinson

While the immediate conditions allowing for the creation of Yugoslavia were directly related to the outcome of the First World War and were not anticipated, Yugoslavism was a recognizable discourse that had framed political action and cultural initiatives for much of the nineteenth century and early twentieth century.[1] Starting with Ljudevit Gaj's Illyrian movement in the 1830s, the South Slav intellectual and political elite within the Habsburg Monarchy sought to unite diverse groups into a single 'nation' large enough to assert a claim for political autonomy within the Monarchy or political independence in a new state, either alone or together with Serbia. Despite its difficulties in competing with alternative nationalisms, perhaps the greatest obstacle for Yugoslavism and the Yugoslav movements was the challenge that it posed to the Habsburg Monarchy as any version of the desired Yugoslav state meant a loss of territory and power for the Monarchy. This placed the Yugoslav movement and the probability of its success or failure within an international context structured by power relations within Austria-Hungary and by its relationships with other states. The First World War provided the opportunity to challenge the power of Austria-Hungary and allowed national movements such as the Yugoslav, Czechoslovak, and Polish movements to press for independence from the Monarchy and establish independent and sovereign states. On behalf of the Yugoslavs, the Yugoslav Committee sought to negotiate the complex geopolitical and international context created by the outbreak of war in order to challenge Austria-Hungary and to gain support for an internationally recognized nation-state.

The Yugoslav Committee and the formation of Yugoslavia in 1918 provides an excellent case study in which to examine ways that a state-seeking national movement seeks to gain support for the establishment of an internationally recognized nation-state. State-seeking national movements often use nationalism as a way of building and mobilizing support for its goals. Nationalism should be seen in part as a discourse that draws upon available symbols and images to create a new historical narrative capable of conferring legitimacy upon a particular national movement and/or its goals by both its international and domestic audiences. Importantly, by addressing international audiences, the movement actors aim to create symbolic alliances with other nations and states as they navigate an international context structured by military and political relationships between states and reinforced by treaty-making and international law.[2]

At the outbreak of the First World War, the Yugoslav Committee was formed to lobby for public international support of unification of all South Slavs within one independent state. Headed by Ante Trumbić, a politician from Split and co-founder of the Croat-Serb Coalition, the Yugoslav Committee included politicians, journalists, attorneys, and professors from Dalmatia, Slovenia, Istria, and Bosnia as well as members of emigrant communities in the United States and South America. The Yugoslav Committee received diplomatic and some financial support from Prime Minister Nikola Pašić and the Serbian government, although the relationship between the Committee and the government grew increasingly contentious as the war progressed. The Yugoslav Committee could utilize access provided by their émigré status to appeal directly to the Allies to facilitate their goals of national unity and independence. Their stated purpose was to prepare international public opinion for the possible unification of the South Slavs in a new state. To assist in their advocacy efforts, the Yugoslav Committee published *The Southern Slav Bulletin* and other publications. By utilizing certain myths, symbols, and historical narratives within their publications, the Yugoslav Committee sought to create symbolic alliances between the Yugoslav nation and the Allied nations in order to build international support for the establishment of Yugoslavia.

Yugoslavism in the nineteenth and early twentieth centuries

In their publications, the Yugoslav Committee drew upon the Yugoslavism of the nineteenth century which had relied upon cultural and linguistic similarities to provide a basis for political representation and/or political autonomy within the Habsburg political structures. During the nineteenth century, Yugoslavism and the Yugoslav national movements had to negotiate a complex and dynamic power structure within the Habsburg Monarchy and Austria-Hungary after 1867. The strength of the Monarchy prompted the Yugoslav national movements to focus on fostering a sense of cultural unity to serve as the basis of political reform within the existing state structure and political institutions and at most promoted trialism as an appropriate vehicle for national self-determination and governance.

The basic tenets of Yugoslavism were first elaborated in the 1830s as part of the Illyrian movement led by Ljudevit Gaj in Zagreb, Croatia and its immediate environs. The term 'Illyrian' is derived from the original inhabitants of the Balkan peninsula and was revived by Napoleon when he established the Illyrian provinces from 1809 to 1813. The Illyrianists chose it because it invoked a continuity with the past but more importantly, it was a neutral label that allowed them to avoid politically sensitive associations with the 'Croatian,' 'Serbian,' and 'Slovenian' identities used by their respective national movements. Adopting Herder's conception of romantic nationalism, the Illyrianists argued that the South (Jugo-) Slavs shared a common ethnic origin and spoke variants of the same language. They chose the *štokavski* dialect spoken in most of Croatia, Serbia, and Bosnia-Herzegovina to serve as the basis for a standard literary language. To introduce Illyrian as a basis for national unity, Gaj and his co-Illyrianists published journals such as *Danica Ilirska* (Illyrian Morning Star) and *Kolo* (literally, a folk dance) and founded Matica Ilirska, a national cultural society. The Illyrianists later co-founded the Illyrian Party but the movement collapsed as Austria regained control after the events of 1848.[3]

Yugoslavism resurfaced in the work of Bishop Josip Strossmayer and Franjo Rački, a canon and historian. For Strossmayer and Rački, the Serbs and Croats were one nation with two names; they viewed Yugoslavism as a way of unifying all South Slavs into one unit.[4] They recognized the uniqueness of Serbian and Croatian cultures but stressed that Serbs and Croats must work together to resist Ottoman and Habsburg domination. Thus, cultural unity was a necessary precursor to political unity in a common state.[5] Strossmayer and Rački founded several cultural institutions such as the Yugoslav Academy of Arts and Sciences and the University of Zagreb, co-founded a new National Party, and actively participated in the political life of Zagreb, Budapest, and Vienna as they worked towards political unity in an independent state.[6]

The Illyrian movement under Gaj and the Yugoslav movement under Strossmayer and Rački both achieved a certain amount of success as measured through the successful establishment of reading circles and cultural societies; publication of periodicals, grammars, and other literary works; and the establishment of key cultural institutions. All were formed with the express purpose of fostering cultural unity of the South Slavs. However, when both movements attempted to cross from the cultural into the political, i.e. when they founded political parties and more overtly challenged the status quo, they met resistance not only from the imperial authorities but from their fellow South Slavs who sought autonomy and independence according to differing conceptions of the political nation.

Importantly, Illyrianism and Yugoslavism as formulated by Gaj and Strossmayer found little support among Serbs in both Austria-Hungary and in Serbia proper. Since 1804, Serbian revolutionaries had been contesting the power of the Ottoman Empire and at first achieved autonomy and later independence. Serbian elites feared that Illyrianism and Yugoslavism would strengthen the power and influence of the Habsburg Monarchy, the Catholic Church, and Croatia among the South Slavs, and saw the Yugoslav movement as a vehicle for Croatian national expansion.[7] Yugoslavism was attractive only as a way to complete the unification of all Serbs into one political unit. Instead, bolstered by their successes, the Serbian elite saw Serbia as the 'Piedmont' which would lead the drive for unification of all Serbs and all South Slavs with Serbia proper.[8]

By the beginning of the twentieth century, another conception of the Yugoslav nation was developing.[9] This new Yugoslavism sought to promote a national unity that did not rely on linguistic or cultural similarities but offered a political framework that could both challenge the primacy of Austria and Hungary and incorporate the progressive ideals offered by new social and political movements emanating from Europe and gradually gaining currency in South Slav lands.[10] Starting in the 1890s, the concept of *narodno jedinstvo* (national oneness) of the Croats and Serbs gained social and political currency as students, intellectuals, and politicians became increasingly aware of the need for political change, specifically changing the basis for political participation from collective to individual rights. Supporters of *narodno jedinstvo* believed that cultural unity and integration between the Serbs and Croats was necessary in order to provide the basis for political unity but also recognized the cultural distinctiveness of the constituent parts and asserted political equality of all members in the Yugoslav nation. They blamed foreign intrigue and domination for any divisions that had arisen among the South Slavs.[11]

Building on the work of the student movements and frustration at the divisive policies of Count Károly Khuen-Héderváry, *ban* (governor) of Croatia, the 'New Course' was first formulated in 1903 and the Croat-Serb Coalition was founded in 1905. These initiatives represent one of the first instances in which there was real political collaboration between Serbs and Croats within Austria-Hungary. Frano Supilo and Ante Trumbić, two of the founding members of the future Yugoslav Committee, along with Pero Čingrija and Josip Smodlaka, formulated the New Course in such a way to take advantage of dissatisfaction among the Hungarian opposition parties and gain their support for political manoeuvres against the Austrian authorities and the unification of Dalmatia with Croatia.[12] As Trumbić outlined in a speech to the Dalmatian Sabor, German civilization posed a threat to all non-Germans – in other words Serbs, Croats, and Magyars – living in the Monarchy and it was necessary to push aside differences and focus on the real problem, German expansion.[13] This discourse would reappear in the publications of the Yugoslav Committee during the First World War. The New Course became a political platform when the Croat-Serb Coalition, a group of Serb and Croat political parties, published a manifesto that pushed political action in support of Yugoslav unity in which they stressed the solidarity of Serbs and Croats and asserted the principle of national self-determination.[14] In 1905, the Croat-Serb Coalition won elections to the Dalmatian *Sabor* (assembly) and in 1906 to the Croatian *Sabor*. It would retain its dominance in local politics until 1914 and its members would remain politically active in interwar Yugoslavia.[15]

In Serbia, political life focused on opposition to Serbia's political, military, and economic dependence upon Austria-Hungary. Since the 1880s, after Serbia's independence and its entry into the European economy, Serbia had become a client state of Austria-Hungary as all exports from Serbia had to cross through its territories to reach European markets. Austria-Hungary demanded 'most-favored-nation' status in terms of tariffs for its products but in turn, subjected Serbian exports to high customs and taxes. The pro-Habsburg policies of the Obrenović dynasty prevented active collaboration between the Yugoslavists in

Croatia and Slavonia with the Serbian government in Belgrade. However, this changed with the assassination of King Alexander in 1903 and the placement of King Peter of the Karadjordjević dynasty upon the Serbian throne. Despite such a controversial beginning to his reign, many Serbs and Croats looked favorably upon Peter's ascent and Serbia saw a period in which democratization and modernization flourished.[16]

Despite all the difficulties in the relationships between Belgrade and Vienna, it was the 1908 annexation of Bosnia-Herzegovina by Austria-Hungary that radicalized political and nationalist circles. Reaction to the annexation was mixed throughout the region. The annexation was generally welcomed by those in Slovenia and Croatia who argued it would strengthen numerically South Slavs in Austria-Hungary which, in turn, could either increase the likelihood of trialism as a political solution or serve as a first step in forming an independent South Slav state by the unification of Bosnia-Herzegovina with Croatia-Slavonia. Instead, criticism was directed against the fact that Bosnia-Herzegovina remained a separate unit ruled directly by Vienna rather than attaching it to Croatia. However, the annexation was seen as a direct affront to Serbian nationalists who desired to incorporate Bosnia-Herzegovina into the Kingdom of Serbia. For all, the annexation signaled the hardball politics of Austria-Hungary and galvanized the South Slavs, both in Serbia and Austria-Hungary, against Vienna. The Balkan Wars of 1912–13 postponed the clash between Serbia and Austria-Hungary. It was the assassination of Archduke Franz Ferdinand by Gavrilo Princip, a teenage associate of the Black Hand movement, that led to the outbreak of the First World War and allowed Yugoslavism to move from a national movement focused on political reform within the existing imperial structure to a national movement focused on establishing a new state.

The Yugoslav Committee

The unification of all South Slavs into an independent and sovereign state presupposed the dissolution or at least partial fragmentation of Austria-Hungary.[17] However, the dissolution of Austria-Hungary was not a war aim of the Allies and for most of the war, the Allies did what they could to preserve, even if in diminished form, Austria-Hungary, seeing it as a stabilizing factor in Central and South Eastern Europe. Further, in order to fight the war effectively and protect their own interests, the Allies were willing to make promises that would assure that other states would remain neutral or join the war on their side. Such promises were made to Italy, Bulgaria, and Romania. The mission of the Yugoslav Committee was to convince the Allies to declare the unification of all South Slavs into a single state as a war aim and to gain international recognition for the Yugoslav nation and state. Through demarches, communiqués, and meetings, members of the Committee met with representatives of the British, French, Russian, and American governments to push their cause. Recognizing that the practicalities of warfare may prevent the governments themselves from willingly adopting their platform, the Yugoslav Committee adopted a strategy of action directed towards the educated and politically active public in the United Kingdom, France, Russia, and the United States in hope of convincing their governments to support the Yugoslav cause. To this end, the Yugoslav Committee used its publications such as the *Southern Slav Bulletin* to educate the reading publics on what was happening in the territories inhabited by South Slavs with the aim of getting British, American, Russian, and French civil societies to pressure their government to support the idea of South Slav unification.[18]

The Yugoslav Committee's ability to conduct high profile advocacy was due in large part to their network of international friends, scholars, journalists, and humanitarian workers who had traveled extensively through the Balkans or had worked in Vienna and/or Budapest and knew the main political figures in pre-war Austria, Hungary, Croatia, Slovenia, and to a lesser degree, Serbia. In particular, R.W. Seton-Watson and Henry Wickham Steed worked extensively with the Yugoslav Committee. Due to their travels and work, both Seton-Watson as an independent scholar and Wickham Steed as a journalist had extensive knowledge of the political conditions in Austria-Hungary.[19]

Seton-Watson and Wickham Steed, through their writings and contacts, raised the profile of the Yugoslav Committee by organizing exhibitions of Ivan Meštrović's work, giving lectures, publishing articles, writing editorials, facilitating introductions to governmental officials, maintaining links with other humanitarian agencies such as the Serbian Red Cross, and even founding a relief agency called the 'Serbian Relief Fund'. In addition, Seton-Watson and Wickham Steed were often called upon by the British Foreign Office to provide intelligence and advice about the South Slavs. Seton-Watson even worked in the Foreign Office for a short time and his responsibilities included providing reports on the situation in the future Yugoslavia. These connections provided the Yugoslav Committee with a backdoor to the British government that allowed their perspectives to be brought to the attention of the appropriate officials and allowed them to hold meetings with the decision-makers. At the Paris Peace Conference at the end of the war, both Seton-Watson and Wickham Steed had almost universal access to all members of the Allied delegations and actively lobbied on behalf of the Yugoslavs and served as conduits for intelligence between the various delegations.[20] Seton-Watson and Wickham Steed also were actively involved in the day-to-day affairs of the Yugoslav Committee. They helped draft documents, served as advisers on policy questions, and mediated conflicts that arose both within the Yugoslav Committee and between the Committee and the Serbian government.

The Yugoslav Committee focused on two primary issues: firstly, the recognition of the South Slavs as a separate nation with the accompanying right to self-determination; and, secondly, the territorial concessions promised to Italy by London, Paris and Petrograd in the secret Treaty of London of April 1915 (the terms of the Treaty, kept secret from enemies as well as Serbia and Montenegro, offered Italy most of eastern Adriatic in exchange for joining the

Allies). For themselves, the Yugoslav Committee wanted the same recognition that had been obtained by the émigré organizations of Czechoslovaks and Poles who also were actively lobbying for international support for the new Czechoslovak and Polish states and were seen as *de facto* governments for the new states.[21] The recognition of the Yugoslav Committee coupled with the recognition of the Yugoslav nation as an allied nation with the right to national self-determination would hopefully prevent the Allies from treating Yugoslav territory as enemy territory and thus allowing Italy to occupy it.

The Yugoslav Committee also sought to convince the Allies to nullify the Treaty of London and/or convince Italy to give up those claims. The Committee's first public statement, 'To the British Nation and Parliament', was issued in response to the news of the Treaty of London but tactically focused attention on the war itself. It named Austria and Germany as the primary aggressors, placed the South Slavs in alliance with the Triple Entente, and defined the war as instrumental to realizing the dreams of the South Slavs to be united into one independent and sovereign state. It needed support from the British Nation and Parliament to realize this dream. Italy was not directly mentioned in this statement but instead the Yugoslav Committee asserted that granting any portion of its territory to another state would violate its national unity. The *Southern Slav Programme* published shortly thereafter explicitly drew attention to the concessions made to Italy and sought to reassure Italy and the Allies that the creation of a Yugoslav state would not be a threat to Italy.[22]

The obligations of the Allies to fulfil the Treaty's provisions at the conclusion of the war created a complicated situation for the Yugoslav Committee. Even if the Treaty had not been signed, the South Slav provinces of Austria-Hungary still would be considered 'enemy' territory because they were part of Austria-Hungary and thus eligible for transfer to the authority of one of the Allies if they won. The Yugoslav Committee targeted the Allies in their advocacy efforts and relied on their governments for political support and their civil societies for political and/or financial support. Further, the Serbian army and government needed military and humanitarian assistance from the Allies. Consequently, the Yugoslav Committee and the Serbian government had to walk a fine line in maintaining a good relationship with the Allied governments while lobbying them to set aside their promises to another ally and follow the principle of national self-determination in the post-war settlements.

For the Yugoslav Committee, it was imperative for the Allies to support the unification of the South Slav provinces of Austria-Hungary with Serbia because by joining Serbia, the South Slavs of Austria-Hungary would no longer be part of an enemy state but instead would be considered 'allies' in the war against Austria-Hungary. If the South Slavs were considered allies then the land they occupy would be considered allied territory rather than enemy territory. Accordingly, the South Slav portions would not be transferred to Italy but would be retained by Serbia, also an ally.[23]

Through its publications, the Yugoslav Committee created a national discourse that would be recognizable and legitimate to members of the new Yugoslav nation and at the same time would allow its international audiences to recognize them as an 'allied nation.' Assuming that the need for national unity during a time of war would supersede any need to justify national unity among the Yugoslavs themselves, the Yugoslav Committee proclaimed that Serbs, Croats, and Slovenes were one people with three names, and assertions to the contrary should be ignored since they reflected biases forced upon them by foreign oppressors. Instead, confident of South Slav unity, they drew upon cultural repertoires provided by both Croatian and Serbian historical narratives, epic poetry, and literature to show that since the early Middle Ages, the South Slavs had served as defenders of Europe, Christianity, and Western Civilization against encroachments from the East, namely the Ottoman Empire. It was now time for the South Slavs to receive their reward for defending Europe – their reward would be the unification of all South Slavs within one independent and sovereign political unit, Yugoslavia. Blame should be placed on Austria and Germany for allowing the corruption of Western civilization for which the South Slavs have vigorously defended and sacrificed for over five centuries and dividing the South Slav lands according to political ideals incompatible with liberty and democracy.

Common to both Croatian and Serbian national discourses, the Antemurale Christianitatis metaphor symbolically placed the Croats and Serbs as the defenders of Europe and Christianity against external and internal enemies. The image of Croatia as the 'bulwark of Christendom' was in play since at least the fourteenth century when, according to the historical narratives, Croatia and the Croats were given a special mission by the papacy and the Christian monarchs of the time to defend Europe and Christianity. Accordingly, the rise and fall of the Croatian kingdom was firmly linked to the existential and spiritual battle between Europe and Asia, Christianity and Islam, East and West, civilization and barbarism, good and evil.[24] The Serbs also saw themselves as the defenders of Christendom and described their defeat at the 1389 Battle of Kosovo as a necessary sacrifice to prevent the Ottomans from making further advances into Christian Europe. If the Serbs had not been defeated, Europe would have been overrun by the infidel. At Kosovo, as described in Serbian epic poetry, ' … Serbian warriors defended the superior European civilization with the admirable, suicidal and immeasurable courage of the righteous, of those who embraced Good and rejected Evil'.[25] Nineteenth and early twentieth century Serbian political thought continued to describe Serbia as the defender of Christianity – not necessarily against non-Europeans such as the Ottomans but against 'corrupt' Christian nations such as Germany and Austria. The Serbs' legacy of sacrifice on behalf of Christianity gave them authority to root out corruption within Christianity.[26]

The Yugoslav Committee extensively used the bulwark metaphor and the Kosovo myth in their publications and advocacy events. Through their use, the Committee situated the new Yugoslav nation in a geopolitical position that renews its role as the defender of Europe; explicitly reminded its audience of the debt Europe owes to the future Yugoslavs; and for their British audiences, argued that only a strong Yugoslav state can protect British interests. For example, in its November 1915 Manifesto, the Yugoslav Committee asserted that the invasion of Serbia by the Central Powers was the manifestation of German imperialism as Germany pushed eastward. ' ... Freed, and linked with Serbia in the interest of her very existence as sentinel on the cross-roads of world politics, these millions [South Slavs in Austria-Hungary] would to-morrow form a sure and strong bulwark against German invasion ... the destruction of Serbia would open to the fore a broad and easy path in the heart of the British Empire'.[27] Rather than defending Europe from the advances of the Ottoman Empire and others coming from the east, the future Yugoslavia would defend the east from German imperialism, or rather the interests of the British Empire in the east. British support is needed to help Serbia in her defense against the German and Austrian onslaught.

In *The Southern Slav Programme*, the Yugoslav Committee names Austria-Hungary as responsible for preventing the unification of the South Slavs and doing everything possible against the Yugoslav idea:

> By every means in her power [Austria-Hungary] has tried to compromise, to defame, and to crush it [the Yugoslav Idea]. ... she encouraged mutual jealousies and conflicts between the Slav states in the Balkans, and finally, by threatening the sovereign rights of Serbia, Austria unchained the present war. For, in her subservience to German Imperialism, Austria thought by this war to crush Jugoslavdom, the great obstacle in the path of Germany and herself towards the East. ... But when Austria, as Germany's vassal state and pioneer, encountered the national resistance of Serbia, the Powers of the Triple Entente rose on behalf of the smaller nation. In this way the Jugoslav question became a European problem, and it is of paramount importance to Europe that it should be fully and finally solved; only a complete solution will ensure the results for which the Triple Entente has gone to war.[28]

While Austria-Hungary is to blame for starting the war and attempting to 'crush Jugoslavdom', German Imperialism is the ultimate culprit as Germany pursues its *Drang nach-Osten* policy that directly challenges the interests of the British Empire. In a separate pamphlet, Srdjan Tucić, one of the editors of the *Southern Slav Bulletin*, stressed the threat posed by Austrian and German imperialism.[29] In some very interesting comments, at least for the modern reader, considering the usual negative discourse directed at the Ottoman Empire and its long-term presence in the Balkans, Tucić stated:

> Here [South Slav lands in Austria-Hungary] as elsewhere throughout all her dominions Austria has applied her principle of dividing and

dismembering, and the Southern Slavs provinces were shared between two spheres of power. ...

The one thing Turkey has left untouched in the Serbs and Bulgars – *the heart of the people* – is the very thing that Austria has sought to destroy in her Southern Slav subjects. Turkish captivity has steeled the hearts of the Slavs she oppressed, but Austrian captivity has cankered them and made them effete.

Austria and Prussia are the natural heirs of Ottoman Islam, and the Southern Slavs have made a heroic stand against this latter-day *Prussian Islam.* Civilization owes them a debt of honour, and it is only their due that Europe should give them justice.[30]

This reveals a distinctive shift in the Serbian, Croatian, and Yugoslav national discourse that emphasised the defence of Europe (including Austria and Germany) and Christendom against the threat of Islam and the Ottoman Empire to naming Austria as 'natural heirs of Ottoman Islam' and defining the new threat as 'Prussian Islam.' Not only were Serbia and the other South Slavs defending the interests of the British Empire against German imperialism but it also was defending Europe from an Austria that had strayed away from its European and Christian heritage. To fulfil their destiny as the bulwark and guarantor of peace within Europe, the unification of the South Slavs into an independent state must be realized upon the conclusion of the war.

The Yugoslav Committee used Kosovo Day 1916 (28 June 1916) as an opportunity to educate the British public on the situation facing the Yugoslavs. Members of the Committee and their British supporters organized a series of rallies, lectures, concerts, and school assemblies and published leaflets and placed editorials, letters to the editors, and articles in the leading English-language newspapers. In a special issue of the *Bulletin*, the opening article describes the significance of Kosovo. Serbia's defeat at the hands of the Ottomans 527 years prior laid the 'fresh foundation for a new empire, joining stone to stone for the great temple of freedom and independence ... and accomplished the salvation of the whole Serbian race'.[31]

The current war led Kosovo, just recently regained in the Balkan Wars of 1912–13, to fall again into the hands of Serbia's foes:

But, unlike in 1389, the Serbian army was not defeated and – thanks solely to Great Britain and France – it is again at its post, ... [the anxiety of the unredeemed Jugoslavs] is relieved by the firm belief in the victory of the cause of the Allies, and yet more by the firm belief that Great Britain, France, and Russia, the apostles of world freedom, the protectors of small nations, will no longer permit that ten million Croats, Serbs, and Slovenes shall remain under an alien and hostile yoke, but will insist upon their entire liberation and unification with Serbia and Montenegro in one single Jugoslav state.[32]

The *Bulletin*'s next issue, published on 1 August 1916, describes the success of the Kosovo Day celebrations throughout Great Britain. The editors comment that the sympathy of the British nation far surpassed expectations and showed 'its determination not to sheathe the sword until all wrongs this war had brought upon mankind are righted, and the small nations given their freedom and independence'.[33] They continue by stating that:

> For more than five centuries Kossovo was the banner of our national pride, the sum and substance of our national unity, and as it was, thus it is and will remain – the watchword of every Jugoslav wherever he dwells, the watchword of a race which longs, aspires, and demands its proper place, and the right of governing its own destiny among other cultured nations. The celebration in Great Britain of this day of tragedy, pride and hope is not merely an accident, it is a document, a warrant of that great understanding which in this terrible war of liberation has drawn nations closer together, has made them join, not only for the sake of destroying barbarian and imperialist greed, but far more for the sake of love and peace among the good and worthy.[34]

As part of the Kosovo Day celebrations, Dr Bogumil Vošnjak, a member of the Yugoslav Committee, gave a lecture entitled 'Kossovo [sic] and the Unity of the Nation' at Leeds University. Dr Vošnjak opened his lecture by invoking the significance of Kosovo and what it represents. He stated, 'Kossovo is the past, the present, and the future of the nation. It is the dream of the shepherd, the political ideal of the unquiet student and the intellectual, the action of the man. Kossovo is more than a battle – it is a programme, a political ideal; it is the state of the morrow; it speaks of resurrection and national happiness'.[35] Using Serbian epic poetry, he described the moral dilemma that Tsar Lazar (who in reality was a Prince) faced – to choose the empire of heaven or the empire of earth. Dr Vošnjak then compares the choice made by Tsar Lazar to the 'Car [sic] Lazar of our times' implying Prince Alexander of Serbia and the choice that he made in retreating across Albania to the Adriatic in the winter of 1915–16. 'But the rulers chose the destruction of a country, the road to Albania and the Adriatic, through wild, snowy mountains, and in the midst of a cold winter; they chose exile, poverty, and death. In faithful loyalty and fidelity they chose the Empire of Heaven. That is national resurrection – national unity'.[36]

As Tucić did above, in a confusing blend of historical narratives, Vošnjak also shifted the blame away from the Ottoman Empire and argued that Kosovo would not have happened if it were not for the Germans.

> Serbia, allied with her Bosnian and Croatian brethren, alone stood the test … From the West came no help … The German Empire, in its monstrous turpitude, in its political stiffness, paid attention only to the internal quarrels between the numberless German states, [. …] What

calamities, what sufferings of entire nations had been avoided, if Germany had arrested the impetus of the Turkish armies in those days![37]

Instead of European assistance, Tsar Lazar had his 'faithful allies' King Stephen Tvrtko of Bosnia and John Horvat, Ban of Croatia, who were both fighting against German domination within their own territories. Instead of fighting the Turks, the German Emperor Sigismund was determined to conquer Croatia, Bosnia, and parts of Serbia, thus distracting the Croats, Bosnians, and Serbs and allowing the Turks to advance towards Europe. 'The German Empire was victorious. The German Empire was able to kill Southern Slav independence, but not to defend these countries against the Turk'.[38] Ultimately Lazar and the Serbian armies mustered the strength to fight the Turks at Kosovo and defend Christianity even while sacrificing their own empire.

In his conclusion, Vošnjak raised the moral bar for the Allies, and in particular his British audience. The South Slavs have remained loyal to Christianity and the defence of Europe and it is now time for them to be compensated for all that has happened as they served as the defender of Europe.

> To back Serbia after her reverse is a great question of international morals. We are deeply convinced that the Allies will show us in the foundation of a strong Southern Slav state an example of gratitude for loyalty so needed in the Balkans [. ...] What we people without home wish to see is the stern, imperturbable will of English public opinion to destroy this despair of an Empire. Success in private and public life is only dependent upon the tenacious will to realize our aim. The destruction of Austria is more difficult than the defeat of Germany. With her will fall a world of prejudices, rotten traditions, extinct political theories. Without the disruption of Austria no peace in Europe, no better European commonwealth of the future.[39]

In the 'Manifesto', Britain, and by extension Europe, is further reminded of the sacrifices that Serbia made on its behalf at Kosovo:

> When five centuries since, on the field of Kossovo, the Turk annihilated the Serbian State, Europe admired Serbian valour, as she admires it to-day, well knowing that at Kossovo the Serbs, in defending themselves, were fighting the battle of civilization against Ottoman barbarism. But Europe gave no help, and Serbia succumbed. Her downfall cost Europe five centuries of bloody war and sufferings untold. The triumph of the Turco-German cause on the soil of conquered Serbia would to-day renew these evils on a vaster scale.[40]

By May 1916, the campaign directed towards the British audience is almost desperate in its intensity. In describing a visit to London by Crown Prince Alexander of Serbia, the Yugoslav Committee thanked the British public for the warm and friendly welcome extended to the Prince in private and public receptions and events, and in the London press. However, they then stated:

> Although we are full of hope and have every confidence in the love of righteousness and justice inherent in the British nation throughout the Empire, we feel it our duty to point out again and again the importance and extreme gravity of the Southern Slav question. *It is a question of paramount importance, not only to the Southern Slavs themselves, but, in an equal degree, to the interests of all the Allies, first and foremost those of Great Britain.* For centuries the Jugoslavs have guarded the gate of the East against German pressure, and thus the security of British interests in Persia, Mesopotamia, and consequently in India and Egypt, was, to a great extent, due to Jugoslav zeal, endurance, and tenacity. But the Jugoslavs, politically divided and subject to foreign rule, weakened by German oppression and Magyar corruption, cannot be expected for ever to hold up the German menace to the East.[41]

It was imperative for the British nation to help the Serbian government and people withstand the Germans and Austrians; failure to do so would not only affect Serbia but it would impinge on British imperial interests in the East. The Yugoslav Committee alerted its British audience not only to the sacrifices that the South Slavs have made on behalf of Western civilization and Christianity and the failure of the Christian nations to assist them but also showed common cause in that the South Slavs are allies in the British struggle against German imperialism. The South Slavs and the British nation were 'allied nations' in their fight against Germany and Austria and more specifically in their spiritual battle against evil power and the corruption of Western civilization. Kosovo became an important metaphor not just for the Serbs or the South Slavs, but for all of Christian Europe.

The Yugoslav Committee not only sought to ally the Yugoslav nation with the British nation, but also to reassure another allied nation, the Italian nation, that the Yugoslavs and specifically, the formation of a new Yugoslav state would not threaten it and in fact, the Yugoslav nation would help Italy fulfil its national destiny. The Yugoslav Committee needed to avoid antagonizing Italy in the hopes of getting Italy to voluntarily give up its demands. However, it also saw the possibility of Dalmatia and Istria going to another foreign power as completely injurious to the very idea of national oneness of the Yugoslavs. While they were fighting the war against Austria-Hungary and Germany, the real threat to national unity came from the Italian demands. Consequently, the Yugoslav Committee repeatedly sought to reassure the Italians that by acting as a barrier against German imperialism, the proposed Yugoslavia would protect Italy and Italian interests:

> In the accomplishment of Southern Slav union, Italy is, indeed, as vitally interested as are England, France, and Russia; for only in close agreement

with a united Jugoslav State – which cannot menace her justified supremacy in the Adriatic – can Italy securely withstand the pressure of the Austro-German group. Only so can she be sure that her eastern blank and the path to the Balkans will be guarded by a race whose devotion to the cause of European and Balkan freedom is no longer open to any shadow of doubt.[42]

The Yugoslav Committee needed to avoid antagonizing the Italian government so it refrained from directly criticizing it. The only times Italy is directly mentioned is in comments, such as those above, that positively state the contributions and benefits that a strong Yugoslav state could provide to Italy. However, Italy (and the Allies for agreeing to the Treaty of London) indirectly are at times gently admonished and other times desperately reminded of the right to national self-determination and the principle of nationality in defining territorial boundaries, determining forms of governance, and setting international treaty obligations.

Conclusion

The outbreak of the First World War provided the political opportunity for Yugoslavism and the Yugoslav movement to actually move beyond being 'daydreamers' and begin working towards the unification of all South Slavs into one political unit.[43] The Yugoslav Committee utilized myths, symbols and other markers considered legitimate to the Serbian, Croatian, and Slovenian national movements and adapted them to the new political, military, and security context provided by the war and its potential threat to the stability of Austria-Hungary. By doing so, the Yugoslav Committee symbolically aligned the Yugoslav nation with other nations to gain international support for their efforts.

The Yugoslav Committee, in their self-assigned role and in agreement with the Serbian government, was tasked with gaining and solidifying international support for the future Yugoslavia. Due to their émigré status they could talk directly with diplomats and government officials of the Great Powers and lobby for their support of Yugoslavia. In addition, they used the *Southern Slav Bulletin* and their other publications to reach not just the governments but the civil societies of each of the Great Powers in the hope that civil society members could change the direction of the foreign policies of their respective governments. The Yugoslav Committee sought to not only create diplomatic and military alliances between the Allied states but also to create symbolic alliances between the nations in order to counter the threat of Austria-Hungary and Germany and to gain international support for and recognition of the proposed Yugoslav state. The Yugoslav Committee used images and symbols that would resonate within its target audiences and made connections between the experiences of the other nation and its own. For instance, the Committee symbolically joined the Yugoslav nation with other 'freedom-loving' nations in their struggle against German imperialism. It is important to note that the Yugoslav Committee did not bring the other nation into their own, making them one of 'us,' but rather saw the other nation as a distinct nation with their own traditions, cultures, and experiences. The goal was for the other nation to recognize the Yugoslav nation as an allied nation so it can push its government to recognize the new state. This construction of alliances between nations reflected a pragmatic assessment of the political opportunities and the realities of the international context dictated by war.

To be successful, the Yugoslav movement or more generally any national movement in the late 1800s and early 1900s had to negotiate a complex network of international state and non-state actors and a web of military and non-military alliances institutionalized by Great Power diplomacy and treaty-making. Local and national political movements operated within imperial political structures localized to particular conditions. So even movements that targeted reform at a local level needed to keep the interests of the imperial center in mind and create a balance between the goals they hoped to achieve and what the imperial authorities would accept. Appeals to outside powers for support and the gaining of that support could tilt things in favor of the movement at the expense of the imperial center. As Wachtel notes, 'Russia, the Habsburgs, Britain and France were only too happy to interfere ... [rarely] were these interventions for the good of the Balkan peoples'.[44] Each power was attempting to gain or preserve its control in the Balkans without disturbing the balance of power within Europe. Consequently, any movement that managed to forge an alliance, however brief and transitional, with a great power could achieve some measurable success although that success could be lost as the balance of powers reshifted, as was aptly demonstrated when the Congress of Berlin basically rewrote the Treaty of San Stefano in 1878.[45]

The likelihood of success or failure of a national movement and the creation of a new state in the pre-1914 era was less dependent upon the desires, actions, or decisions of national political actors but instead was more depen dent on what the international actors will accept and what can be negotiated through diplomacy and treaty-making with governments far removed from the local and/or national context. The Yugoslav Committee learned this lesson well. The Committee recognized that the creation of Yugoslavia would depend upon what the Allied powers would accept, the outcome of the war, and importantly the outcome of the peace treaty negotiations. Consequently, they used its national discourse to symbolically place the Yugoslav nation within the community of nations in order to elicit international support for the creation of Yugoslavia. However, as they soon discovered at Versailles in the negotiations to finalize territorial borders and other issues leading to the conclusion of the peace treaties and formal recognition of the Yugoslav state, the principle of national self-determination only goes so far when challenging the interests and goals of more powerful states.

Notes

1 I presented an earlier version of this chapter at the April 2007 meeting of the Association for the Study of Nationalities at Columbia University. I thank Dejan Djokić, Nadine Akhund, and my co-panelists for their useful comments.

2 C. Calhoun, *Nations Matter: Culture, History, and the Cosmopolitan Dream* (London and New York: Routledge, 2007), pp. 27, 30; C. Calhoun, *Nationalism* (Minneapolis, MN: University of Minnesota Press, 1997); A. Thompson, 'Nations, National Identities and Human Agency: Putting People back into Nations,' *The Sociological Review*, vol. 49, no.1 (February 2001), pp. 18–32; M. Billig, *Banal Nationalism* (London: Sage Publications, 1995).

3 E. Despalatović, 'The Illyrian Solution to the Problem of a National Identity for the Croats,' *Balkanistica*, 1, 1974, pp. 79–84; J. Lampe, *Yugoslavia as History: Twice There Was a Country* (Cambridge: Cambridge University Press, 2000), pp. 45–46; M. Biondich, *Stjepan Radić, the Croat Peasant Party, and the Politics of Mass Mobilization, 1904–1928* (Toronto: University of Toronto Press, 2000), p. 6.

4 T. Cipek, 'The Croats and Yugoslavism,' in D. Djokić (ed.) *Yugoslavism: Histories of a Failed Idea 1918–1992* (Madison, WI: University of Wisconsin Press, 2003), p. 73.

5 F. Singleton, *A Short History of the Yugoslav Peoples* (Cambridge: Cambridge University Press, 1985), p. 107.

6 A. Pavković, *The Fragmentation of Yugoslavia: Nationalism in a Multinational State* (New York: St. Martin's Press, 1997), p. 12; I. Banac, *The National Question in Yugoslavia: Origins, History, Politics* (Ithaca, NY: Cornell University Press, 1984), p. 89.

7 A. Djilas, *The Contested Country: Yugoslav Unity and Communist Revolution 1919–1953* (Cambridge, MA: Harvard University Press, 1991), p. 27.

8 D. Djordjević, 'The Idea of Yugoslav Unity in the Nineteenth Century,' in D. Djordjević (ed.) *The Creation of Yugoslavia 1914–1918* (Oxford: Clio Press, 1980), p. 8; St. K. Pavlowitch, *Serbia: The History of an Idea* (New York: New York University Press, 2002).

9 D. Rusinow, 'The Yugoslav Idea Before Yugoslavia', in Djokić (ed.) *Yugoslavism*, pp. 11–26.

10 Singleton, *A Short History of the Yugoslav Peoples*, p.108; Djilas, *The Contested Country*, p. 37–48.

11 N. Miller, *Between Nation and State: Serbian Politics in Croatia Before the First World War* (Pittsburgh, PA: University of Pittsburgh Press, 1997).

12 Miller, *Between Nation and State*, pp. 88–89.

13 Ibid, p. 68.

14 Pavković, *The Fragmentation of Yugoslavia*, p. 13.

15 Ibid; D. Djokić, *Elusive Compromise: A History of Interwar Yugoslavia* (New York: Columbia University Press, 2007).

16 W. Vucinich, *Serbia Between East and West: The Events of 1903–08* (Stanford, CA: Stanford University Press, 1954). For a recent re-assesmet of this period see D. Stojanović, *Srbi i demokratija* (Belgrade: UDI, 2003).

17 I. Lederer, 'Nationalism and the Yugoslavs,' in P. Sugar and I. Lederer (eds.) *Nationalism in Eastern Europe*, Seattle: University of Washington Press; D. Rusinow, 'The Yugoslav Idea Before Yugoslavia,' p. 23.

18 Here I only cover some of the English-language publications.

19 A. May, 'R.W. Seton-Watson and British Anti-Hapsburg Sentiment,' *American Slavic and East European Review*, Volume 20, Number 1, 1961, pp. 40–54; H. Seton-Watson and C. Seton-Watson, *The Making of a New Europe, R.W. Seton-Watson and the last years of Austria-Hungary* (Seattle, WA: University of Washington Press, 1981); N. Miller, 'R.W. Seton-Watson and Serbia During the Reemergence of Yugoslavism, 1903–14,' *Canadian Review of Studies in Nationalism*, vol. XV, no. 1–2, 1988, pp. 59–69.

20 I. Lederer, *Yugoslavia at the Paris Peace Conference: A Study in Frontiermaking* (New Haven and London: Yale University Press, 1963); H. Seton-Watson and C. Seton-Watson, *The Making of a New Europe*, op. cit.

21 D. Šepić, 'The Question of Yugoslav Union in 1918,' *Journal of Contemporary History*, vol. 3, no. 4, 1968, p. 36.
22 Yugoslav Committee, *Southern Slav Programme*, hereafter 'SSP', 1915, pp.16, 20.
23 K. St. Pavlowitch, 'The First World War and the Unification of Yugoslavia,' in Djokić (ed.) *Yugoslavism*, p. 30.
24 I. Žanić, 'The Symbolic Identity of Croatia in the Triangle *Crossroads-Bulwark-Bridge*', in P. Kolstø (ed.), *Myths and Boundaries in South-Eastern Europe* (London: Hurst, 2005), pp. 37–40.
25 A. Antić, 'The Evolution of Boundary: Defining Historical Myths in Serbian Academic and Public Opinion in the 1990s', in Kolstø (ed.), *Myths and Boundaries in South-Eastern Europe*, p. 192.
26 Ibid; I. Čolović, *Politics of Identity in Serbia* (New York: New York University Press, 2002), p. 8.
27 Yugoslav Committee, 'Manifesto,' *Southern Slav Bulletin* (hereafter SSB, 3) 13 November 1915.
28 SSP, pp. 12–13.
29 S. Tucić, *The Slav Nations*, The Daily Telegraph War Books, 19, English translation by Fanny S. Copeland (London: Hodder and Stoughton, 1915), p. 13.
30 Ibid, pp. 139–40, 144, 177; italics in original.
31 SSB, nos 16 and 17, p. 1.
32 Ibid.
33 SSB, no. 18, p. 1.
34 Ibid.
35 B. Vošnjak, *Jugoslav Nationalism: Three Lectures* (London: Polsue Limited, 1916), p. 7.
36 Ibid, p. 9.
37 Ibid, p. 13.
38 Ibid, p. 16.
39 Ibid, pp. 21, 23.
40 SSB, no. 3, p. 1.
41 SSB, no. 12, p. 1, italics in original.
42 Ibid, p. 2.
43 Djordjević, op. cit., p. 3.
44 A. B. Wachtel, *The Balkans in World History* (New York: Oxford University Press, 2008), p. 76.
45 St. K. Pavlowitch, *A History of the Balkans 1804–1945* (London and New York: Longman, 1999), chapters 5–7.

2 The Great War and the Yugoslav Grassroots

Popular mobilization in the Habsburg Monarchy, 1914–18

Mark Cornwall

On 3 December 1917 in Vienna, some ferocious language was employed in a debate in the Austrian parliament (the *Reichsrat*). On behalf of the club of South Slav deputies, Vjekoslav Spinčić, a Croat from Istria, lambasted the monarchy's wartime regime: 'How we have been treated during the war exceeds anything that has occurred in the history of humanity. Never, nowhere, have governments dealt so badly, so terribly, so cruelly, so criminally with their own citizens, as our governments with us Croats, Serbs and Slovenes during this ever lasting war'. In short, it had been a veritable 'reign of terror'. It was a genocidal image, conjured up again a few months later when a Serb deputy described the wartime 'reign of terror' as comparable only to the Spanish Inquisition or the atrocity of St Bartholomew's Night. Yet out of this nightmare, he claimed, the final victor would be the idea of freedom for all peoples and, in particular, an independent southern Slav state.[1]

This exaggerated rhetoric fell at a time when the so-called 'declaration movement' was in full swing in the southern regions of the Austro-Hungarian empire, a Yugoslav agitation that challenged individuals to question the monarchy's legitimacy in its then form. Historians of the Yugoslav space have been very slow to examine critically this grassroots phenomenon, usually paying more attention to Serbia's wartime mission or the broader international context for creating Yugoslavia in 1918.[2] Yet adopting a cultural approach, notably probing mentalities in the South Slav regions of Austria-Hungary, is crucial if we are to understand why the new state could emerge and, most importantly, why Slovene and Croatian expectations might chafe so roughly against the stance of the victorious Serbian leadership. In the scope of recent Habsburg historiography on the war, Czech scholars have begun to question stereotypes about Czech wartime loyalties. For Vienna, too, Maureen Healy has set out an imaginative framework for studying how inhabitants in the imperial capital might interpret the concepts of sacrifice and allegiance.[3] In the same way, we now require an integrated study of the monarchy's wartime 'South', particularly exploring the diversity of public opinion as well as the meshing of mentalities, even if the sources for this are not easy to access.[4] Not only will it illuminate the fluidity and complexity of 'Yugoslav' loyalties (where they existed at all), it will probably underline persistent levels of Habsburg allegiance that defied the stark rhetoric emitted by many South Slav politicians.

The launch-pad for domestic Yugoslav agitation in the final phase of the war was the 'May declaration' of 30 May 1917 by the 33 South Slav politicians who composed the Yugoslav club in the *Reichsrat*. Since parliament in Austria (Cisleithania) had not met since March 1914, and wartime censorship was tight, there had been few outlets for political expression. Exploiting the new emperor Karl's desire for constitutional government and his reconvening of the *Reichsrat*, the non-German deputies proceeded to coordinate their attacks on the 'pernicious' Austro-Hungarian structure of the empire. In its statement of 30 May, the Yugoslav club (following soundings since late 1916 with religious and political leaders in Croatia) demanded unification of Slovenes, Croats and Serbs in a special democratic state entity under the Habsburg dynasty. The claim was made on the basis of the 'national principle' but also of 'Croatian state right'. Despite this clear nod to Croatian historical arguments, the movement that took off from the summer, permeating southwards into Dalmatia, Croatia and Bosnia, received its dynamism especially from Slovene initiatives in the hands of the clerical leader Anton Korošec. On that basis, some observers quickly surmised that radical Slovenes ('the culturally most advanced nation of the South Slavs') would take the lead in any future Yugoslav state.[5] Certainly, it was the case that the 'declaration' agitation was most vibrant in the Slovene lands. Characterized by a mass-signing of petitions and enormous rallies, it was there especially that a campaign of popular participation seemed to be taking place, reinforcing the idea that many Slovenes consciously desired to enter some Yugoslav unit.

Yet if there were loud echoes in both Istria and Dalmatia (Austrian provinces), the reception in Croatia or in Bosnia was more equivocal. As we will see, the political stance in Croatia was complicated by conflicting interpretations of Croatia's own national mission and what meaning was ascribed to the May declaration; in Bosnia, the chance for any popular mobilization was restricted by the military regime of General Stjepan Sarkotić. In contrast, for the Southern Slavs of Cisleithania there was not only greater freedom of association permitted, but their leaders in the Slovene and coastal lands were increasingly alarmed from 1917 by a two-fold nationalist threat: a perceived German nationalist course at home, and an Italian imperialist menace from abroad. In the face of these it was easy to exploit local national insecurities, especially if they were matched by acute economic insecurities which the Habsburg regime seemed powerless to resolve. Some form of Yugoslav unity, however conceived (and there were numerous interpretations), could offer many a panacea for basic threats to their everyday existence.

The economic insecurities

Indeed, the monarchy's economic catastrophe after 1916 was fundamental in exacerbating national or regional grievances which, for some, had manifested themselves early in the war due to the heavy-handed tactics of the political and military authorities. Here we should note immediately the diversity of wartime economic experience across the southern Slav region. While the Austrian half of the empire suffered a major calamity (especially as the 'bread-basket' in Galicia was under Russian occupation until August 1917), the Hungarian half – which included Croatia-Slavonia – remained largely self-sufficient and always looked to its own needs first. With no empire-wide systemization of rationing and no attempts made to equalize prices until mid-1918, the monarchy from early in the war had ceased to act as an economic unit.[6]

Of the South Slav lands, only Croatia really held its head above water. In May 1917, General Ottokar Landwehr, newly appointed as coordinator of the empire's food supplies, travelled by train to Zagreb. He passed only women and children working in the fields, but noted good bread at the stations. He found the Croatian governor (*ban*) unwilling to tighten regional rationing, let alone send food reserves to starving Bosnia.[7] A year later when Landwehr returned to Zagreb he could still observe that 'everything swims in fat and the black-market blossoms'; it might be forbidden now to sell bread in public places, but much of Croatia was still suffering less than elsewhere, as evidenced by the migrant beggars from Istria or Bosnia who loitered around the railway stations. By this time the new *ban*, Antun Mihalovich, was more receptive to Landwehr's request for sharp requisitioning, promising to supply 40 wagons of macaroni, potatoes and fat in order to alleviate famine in Istria, Dalmatia and Bosnia.[8] Indeed, Mihalovich's concern for these 'Croat lands' reflected his own 'Yugoslav sympathies'. When appointed as *ban* in June 1917 he had assured the *Sabor* (assembly) in a stirring speech that his regime would be 'democratic and Croat', defending the interests of all Croats. By early summer, Landwehr for one felt there was a fast-accelerating Yugoslav band-wagon in Croatia, onto which the *ban* himself had already climbed with a largely pan-Croatian agenda.[9]

In contrast, the inhabitants of the southern Austria crownlands and Bosnia-Herzegovina had been living from hand to mouth for years, their poverty exacerbated by the Habsburg regime's inefficiencies in transport and coordination. Thus in June 1917, maps produced by the Viennese postal censors revealed famine in most towns in southern Styria, Istria, Herzegovina, Dalmatia and the Adriatic islands. The maps also correctly predicted bad harvests in these regions for the summer.[10] A few months later, in detailing a drop in the harvest for some crops by up to 60 per cent from the previous year, Korošec predicted for Austria a food catastrophe.[11] In stormy *Reichsrat* debates the Yugoslav club was regularly protesting about the chronic lack of food supplies to the south. On the one hand they blamed Hungary's selfish attitude. According to a Slovene deputy, Karel Verstovšek, 'our Slovene nation has always had only the feeblest impression of the Magyars. We have long wished for all Slavs to be separated from those hunnish people'. Irrespective of nationality, all Austrians, he claimed, now hated the Magyars most because of their economic exploitation of others: at the grassroots there was a bitterness worse than any hatred of the enemy.[12]

On the other hand, in the deputies' views the regional economic crisis was compounded by inefficiency or corruption on the spot. Korošec, after visiting Bosnia on a fact-finding mission in the summer of 1917, made repeated attacks on the regime there, including Sarkotić's own ignorance of economics. Certainly, Bosnia could not survive on its own resources even in peacetime and now needed a constant bail-out by Hungary; its economy suffered from a feeble workforce, a series of bad harvests, and villagers who vehemently opposed requisitioning to aid cities like Sarajevo or Mostar.[13] It was a situation very similar to Austria where, through strict requisitioning, the countryside of Carinthia or Istria was constantly exploited to feed the urban conglomerations of Ljubljana or Trieste; for Istria and Dalmatia, many rural supply centres or supply routes (served by steamers in the Adriatic for instance) had ceased to function. On top of this was an inequality of prices which stimulated smuggling and the black market. Stories were rife of intrepid Istrian women who walked miles to Trieste to barter their local produce in return for bread, or tried to smuggle more attractive goods back across the border from Croatia.[14]

This Austrian crisis slowly worsened in the final year of the war. If in 1917 economic issues were certainly to the fore in censored material from the South Slav regions, by mid-1918, 90 per cent of letters handled by the central Austrian censor offices complained about food.[15] The grassroots misery is clear in correspondence from Pazin, high up in the centre of Istria. In late May 1918 the Pazin censor told of 47 deaths from starvation: 'the plight is so great that people are forced to live on wild plants, water and some milk without bread; this, coupled with terribly high prices for even the most basic foodstuffs, steadily increases the population's exasperation'. A month later the same source noted that food provisioning in central Istria has broken down completely, producing famine and some suicides; local inhabitants while placing all hope on the next harvest were cutting even half-ripe grain to make flour and 'preparing for their meals not only nettles but all kinds of edible and inedible grasses'.[16] According to one letter-writer, a chemist's wife from coastal Rovinj, 'the land looks as if the enemy had destroyed everything, dried up and contaminated ... People wander around like ghosts, dead from hunger ... [but] one minister has said "the people down there should get used to starving and dying"'.[17] Not surprisingly, the Istrian peninsula by this time was one of the most fertile areas where popular Yugoslav agitation could take root; it seems to have flourished wherever civilians felt most insecure about the war and the future.

Allegiances to empire and homeland, 1914–16

This underlying socio-economic insecurity from 1916 was intertwined, at least for many, with uncertainty about the fate of their region or nation if it stayed part of the Habsburg empire. In analyzing the slippery concept of allegiance to the wartime regime, we must be cautious in accepting at face value the nationalist rhetoric about Austro-Hungarian repression. According to one post-war Western account, 'in practice there was brutal and savage repression in all Yugo-slav areas both within and without Austria-Hungary by Austrian and Hungarian officials and military commanders'.[18] In fact, as in the Czech lands, and notwithstanding the severe disruption to civilian life-styles, the early years of hostilities seem to have witnessed sustained loyalty to the Habsburg war from large sections of the South Slav population. In the Slovene regions a lead was given by the prominent Catholic conservative politician, Ivan Šušteršič, who pledged full support to the emperor. Recent research has shown how this was matched generally by the Slovene clergy's loyal stance and the degree of influence that they wielded in local communities. Essentially, the Slovene Catholic establishment propagated the notion of a just Habsburg war (Catholic and anti-Orthodox), out of which sacrifice the empire would emerge rejuvenated. This combined spiritual-imperial mission could gain added national bite when in May 1915 Italy entered the war; for not only could the new enemy be portrayed as a liberal menace but it was one threatening to invade and destroy the Slovene national homeland.[19] The call for allegiance to both a Slovene and Austrian fatherland, backed by a powerful redemptive message, probably resonated with thousands of Slovene soldiers and civilians. But a shift would occur when war-weariness set in and the clergy themselves began to outline a new priority for Slovene allegiances.

In Croatia similarly, despite the years of Habsburg absolutist rule, the war from the start had some very vociferous adherents (evident in the anti-Serb riots in Zagreb after Archduke Franz Ferdinand's murder, and in celebrations in the streets when Habsburg troops captured Belgrade in December 1914). In early 1915 the military commander of Zagreb still felt that 'the present generation of Croats may be described as unconditionally loyal and faithful to the dynasty'.[20] This was deceptive. For all the thousands who followed military orders, many were fluid in their allegiance depending on how they interpreted the framework for the Croatian national mission. Some, like bishop Antun Mahnić and the activist Catholic Movement, saw the defeat of liberalism as one essential crusade, but also advocated Slovene-Croatian unity in their Rijeka memorandum of March 1915; it was an ideological precursor of the May declaration.[21] For supporters of Josip Frank's party (Pure Party of Right) or Stjepan Radić's small Peasant Party, creating a greater Croatia within the monarchy was the priority. For the Croat-Serb Coalition, which had a majority in the *Sabor*, the future choices for any Yugoslav unity depended on how the Habsburg regime behaved. However, when the *Sabor* reopened in June 1915, the conditional stance was clear: the majority asserted their dynastic loyalty but also demanded greater Croatian unity (with Dalmatia and Bosnia) in a post-war restructured monarchy.[22]

For all those who professed allegiance and backed the war, the repercussions of disloyalty against the 'Habsburg establishment' (whether in Austria or Hungary) were clear. From the start of hostilities against Serbia, the military's paranoia about 'Yugoslav' or pro-Serb sympathies had led to mass arrests; radical German or Hungarian language was aimed not just at Serbs but at Slovenes and Croats who seemed insufficiently patriotic. By 1915, hundreds of community leaders in Dalmatia and the Slovene lands had been interned, including politicians like the Croat Ante Tresić-Pavičić. In Croatia, while many politicians survived by toeing ostensibly a pro-Hungarian line, Yugoslav papers like the Catholic Movement's *Riječke novine* (*Rijeka Newspapers*) were simply closed down. The tightest grip however was maintained in Bosnia-Herzegovina. There in the heart-land of 'Serb treachery' and next to the war zone, it was not surprising that the Croat Sarkotić maintained strict vigilance. Far from being lulled by the semblance of calm in 1915, he scribbled in his diary that he was 'sitting on a volcano' and hoped 'with God's help to prevent any outbreak of lava'. His solution was to ban all political activity, closing the Bosnian *Sabor* and the Sarajevo city council and targeting the Bosnian Serb population. National or confessional equality, he argued, could not apply to Serbs because of the war; their professed loyalty was simply a mask. Their confessional schools were put under state control, their cultural societies closed down and even the cyrillic alphabet was banned. The climax came in early 1916, in the wake of Austria's conquest of Serbia, when 156 Serbs were put on trial in Banja Luka for connivance with the enemy and 16 were given the death penalty.[23]

The declaration movement and the Slovenes

The regime's vigilance on the home-front, however understandable, would begin to back-fire by 1917 when, under emperor Karl's 'constitutional' regime, the military-political shackles began to be loosened in some regions of the empire. Expressing discontent was most likely and possible in Austria's South Slav regions where the economic crisis was worst and the re-convened *Reichsrat* suddenly offered a political forum for grievances. In the wake of its May declaration, the Yugoslav club had at first been optimistic, especially when an imperial amnesty freed some of their number like Tresić-Pavičić. But any goodwill from the emperor was offset by the backing he gave to Ernst von Seidler's Germanophile Austrian government. Veering increasingly upon a 'German course' for Austria, Seidler's only concession was to suggest some extra autonomy for the Slovenes but certainly no restructuring of the dualist system to allow fuller Slovene-Croat unity. By August 1917 while the club went into opposition in parliament, the public, war-weary and famished, seemed also to be inclining in private towards the panacea of the southern Slav message.[24]

The real impetus to a mass-movement however came only with the open statement of support from bishop Anton Jeglič of Ljubljana. In the face of a German radical agenda, Jeglič in the course of 1917 had come to question Šušteršič's persistent German-Austrian allegiance and moved slowly towards the alternative clerical position, a 'Yugoslav' agenda as espoused by Janez

Krek and Anton Korošec. His statement in the radical Slovene press on 15 September expressed solidarity with the Pope's peace initiative but also with the Yugoslav club's stance. It is clear that Jeglič, like Korošec and most club members, interpreted the May declaration as prioritizing Slovene-Croat unity within the empire, less so any unification with Serbia, and even less the prospect of an independent South Slav state. Looking back in July 1920, Jeglič insisted that he had always been a 'loyal Austrian', disgusted at those working against the monarchy, but equally he had always hoped for some kind of Yugoslav unity. He therefore perceived the declaration as an opportunity that had to be seized both to protect his flock internally (against German domestic dominance) and strengthen the monarchy's strategic position in the south against Italy:

> I felt that all would be lost and we would be powerless if at this propi-tious moment we did not rise up. I acted so that all parties would sign. My signature was authoritative and started the movement that made Yugoslavia possible. Thank God that He guided everything in such a way that my steps at the end of the war were completely legalised.[25]

Korošec too would later marvel at the push that Jeglič's backing gave towards South Slav unity. From October 1917, parish councils in Carniola, the only pure Slovene crownland, began to announce adherence to the May declaration and a machinery of mass signature-gathering ground into action. The climax of this was to be the winter of 1917–18, for from March the movement changed tactics, developing into a series of mass rallies.

Some historians have viewed the declaration as increasingly a legal cloak beneath which a more radical agitation was fermenting in 1918. In other words, much of the movement was paying lip-service to a statement loyal to the dynasty while actually working towards an independent Yugoslav state outside the Empire.[26] A more recent analysis by Vlasta Stavbar suggests however a complex series of motives inspiring those who signed or supported petitions for the declaration.[27] She concludes, on the basis of hundreds of statements in the Maribor archives, that many Slovenes signatories continued to feel strong allegiance to the Habsburg dynasty as well as to some concept of Yugoslav unity. Some signed with a more radical political design in mind, some were certainly jumping on a band-wagon whose wheels were greased by war-weariness, social hardship and food grievances. Others may well have experienced Jeglič's crisis of conscience – torn between loyalty to Catholic Austria and the security of a South Slav entity.

On Stavbar's evidence, the main grassroots movement started first in Carniola, stimulated directly by the local bishop's adherence. In one village the inhabitants added a personal postscript to the basic declaration: 'we love the Habsburg monarchy, and for that reason we demand for her peoples their own statehood and for us Yugoslavs our own independent state within her, for only thus can the monarchy continue'. Most Carniolan petitions, encompassing 30,500 signatures, were sent to the Yugoslav club primarily by parish councils; over half the councils of Carniola finally backed the declaration. Their number seems to have been weakened firstly because parts of the crownland were in the war zone and subject to military vigilance. But secondly, Šušteršič's continued influence may have played a role; although he had supported the initial May declaration, he saw its framework as confined to Cisleithania (excluding Croatia) and by late 1917 had broken with the rest of the radical Yugoslav club.[28] In doing so he increasingly identified himself with the sinking Habsburg ship.

In southern Styria, Korošec's home base, the movement was livelier than in Carniola but also cautious since the German language border was close. The declaration was backed by 70 per cent of parish councils as well as some societies and banks, and over 70,000 signatures were collected, mostly women and children. While some petitions emerged after political meetings, many hint at a strong degree of local initiative since (compared to Carniola) they were handwritten rather than duplicated texts. Many contained a special Habsburg clause such as 'Long live Yugoslavia, Long live our Emperor Karl!', or 'Long live the beloved Habsburg dynasty and lucky Yugoslavia under its glorious sceptre!' Mass meetings from spring 1918 also seemed at first to be spontaneously loyal. At one in March, when Korošec spoke about the wonderful Yugoslav future, the mass cry went up, 'We want to be free in a great Habsburg Yugoslavia'. At another on 21 April the resolution mentioned for the last time an allegiance to the Habsburg dynasty. These rallies and petitions were also permeated by the sense of a growing German threat; indeed Slovene signatories in the Ptuj district seem to have suffered ethnic intimidation. On the face of it there is interesting evidence of grassroots defence. One petition dispatched in January to Korošec by 558 women from near Maribor was strident:

> Concerning the audacious plan of our religious and national opponents who wish, with the help of the German School Association (*Südmark*) to seize by force our beautiful Slovene lands, owned by the Slovene people for centuries, we are inspired by the idea of unification of all the Yugoslav regions of Austria-Hungary [under the Habsburg sceptre].[29]

It was in Carinthia however that a German menace to Slovene existence was portrayed as especially dangerous. Janko Pleterski has suggested that there in particular a German-Austrian persecution from early in the war was turned into a 'crucial mass political experience', making numerous Slovenes alert to some peril to their national existence should Austria win the war and implement a 'German course'.[30] Even if we should be cautious about generalizing an image of Slovene national suffering, it was the case that even after May 1917 the regional governor of Carinthia, Count Lodron (a German nationalist speaking no Slovene), was determined to suppress the declaration movement; already in 1916 he had clamped down hard on any Slovene dissent, arresting the only Slovene MP while the only newspaper was very strictly censored. In 1917–18 he banned almost all Slovene national rallies and only ten parish councils ventured to announce support for the May declaration. Yet over 19,000 signatures were collected, representing over 20 per cent of the Slovene population. Lodron dismissed these, claiming that most Slovenes had little idea about what they were signing. Certainly, there may well have been some abuses, with villagers simply signing what their local priest advised. Against this must be set Pleterski's own analysis of the Carinthian petitions preserved in the Ljubljana archives, for they suggest that individual grievances against German aggressiveness and the war were now widespread among Slovene-speakers.[31]

The declaration movement therefore had snowballed in the particular circumstances of winter 1917–18. While it was stimulated from above by the clerical lead and by Yugoslav club rhetoric about self-determination, it was nourished at the grassroots by hopes of peace in the East, as the monarchy started talks with Russia's Bolshevik regime, and by a gathering belief that it was publicly acceptable to challenge the miserable war conditions (exemplified by the empire-wide food and labour protests of January 1918). In the south, agitation for the declaration provided a positive focal point for negative frustrations. Thus, one postal censor report in April noted how ordinary people who 'normally ignored such things' had been indoctrinated; it was obvious from letters sent by the lower classes and even working women who were 'not tired of asserting that everyone fights for "Yugoslavia", admonishing their relatives and friends in neutral countries to remain true to the Slovene cause in heart and mind'.[32] The gendarmerie commander in Celje concurred that the movement was unstoppable: 'it includes all people without distinction of party bias … the agitation has been skilfully organized and skilfully executed. People who lived in peace up to now have been shaken to the core'. In the face of this the Habsburg authorities in most areas remained relatively powerless. Already in February 1918 the regional governor of Carniola, Count Attems, warned the ministry of interior about a phenomenon that seemed to be spreading into all South Slav regions and all layers of the population. Yet not only was the Yugoslav club protected by parliamentary immunity. A legal ruling of February announced that the agitation because of the 'Habsburg clause' was still within the law. Lodron's arbitrary behaviour was therefore exceptional, pre-empting the minister of interior who only on 12 May forbade further declaration rallies or propaganda.[33]

The ban was prompted by events in Ljubljana where the agitation was beginning to infect the armed forces. On 22–24 April spontaneous food demonstrations had occurred in the city. Many displayed their Yugoslav sympathies, directing their frustration against Šušteršič and against German property. According to Attems whose office was invaded by 200 Slovene women:

> Through systematic agitation in the press and in meetings dealing with the Yugoslav question, a great mass of inflammable material has been

gathered together. It has now blazed up, on the one hand targeting the head of the provincial diet [Šušteršič], on the other against Germans.[34]

More alarming was the fact that Slovene troops had refused to move against the rioters, 'clear evidence' that Yugoslav propaganda was starting to infect the army. A military investigation revealed that, a few evenings before the disturbances, two officers of the local regiment had been heard shouting Yugoslav and treasonable slogans in the streets. The local military commanders were clear that the 'Korošec party' was to blame:

> Many men, even the companies who departed in April, wore national (tricolour) ribbons and cockades on their march to the railway station … Everybody agrees on one point: that the agitation originates with a section of the Slovene clergy, incited and backed by the bishop [Jeglič]. Whereas those in the countryside are roused only with difficulty and reluctance, the urban population, especially sections of the educated classes and the younger generation, follows more willingly.[35]

Reports such as this led the Austrian defence minister to warn the government on 1 May about the 'unbridled agitation of the Korošec party' and its impact on army morale. The military authorities were usually inclined to make mountains out of any nationalist mole-hills. Nevertheless, when six military revolts occurred in the hinterland a few weeks later, while the core grievances were war-weariness and inadequate food as well as some Bolshevik 'infection', a nationalist ingredient was also present. The three rebellions in Styria involving Slovene soldiers all seemed to have some links to the agitation at home (not least through the local radical press), and were a hint that morale in the hinterland and at the front could be closely connected.[36]

That of course was the military's real fear. As yet, the cases of open Slovene or Croat insubordination in the front-line seem to have been small, especially on the Italian front where Habsburg officers could tell their troops that Italy had rapacious designs on the Slovene-Croatian homelands. There had however already been some notorious cases of 'treachery', most notably that of Ljudevit Pivko, a remarkable Slovene officer who in September 1917 had deserted to Italy and tried to organize propaganda troops there to subvert the empire (he found that recruiting Slovenes or Croats for his cause was very difficult). In May 1918 the desertion to Italy of a handful of Croat officers from the 42nd *honvéd* division was further evidence that a minority of soldiers, depressed by the material catastrophe, were listening to the Yugoslav message emanating from Zagreb. They, like the Slovene military rebels in the hinterland, were finally prepared to make a clear leap away from their Habsburg allegiance.[37]

The military duly used these incidents to put pressure on what they saw as lax rule at home, and in part the government responded. On 12 May the declaration movement was officially banned, and at the same time both the emperor and prime minister Seidler publicly refuted the idea that Slovene regions would be allowed to join in any South Slav union or even to form a Slovene entity within Austria. Yet these pronouncements were no longer enforceable. Seidler's stance in particular confirmed for Slovene politicians and their constituencies that, with momentum for a 'German course' picking up, they could expect no help from Vienna for their national security. As the empire's fate in the war looked ever more precarious and the prospect of an Italian invasion loomed, they were pushed to think of more radical Yugoslav options.

In the Slovene lands ordinary people encountered these ideas through the press or through continuing mass rallies. On 2 July for instance, at a huge, officially-prohibited gathering in Vrhinka, Korošec was able to address the crowds from a hotel balcony while the masses handicapped the local gendarmes. Later Korošec attributed the rally's triumph to the government's wisdom in banning it, for that had simply increased curiosity as well as confirming the need for a constitutional state.[38] Although the authorities were suitably alarmed, Korošec himself was quite free to operate in Austria or further afield, inspiring many Slovene women to wear his portrait in a locket upon their breast; at the same time, most Catholic clergy since a meeting in February were backing 'reform' and preaching it from their pulpits.[39] The agitation in the Slovene lands was to climax in mid-August in the 'Slav days' in Ljubljana where, in defiance of the authorities, a National Council of Austria's South Slavs was proclaimed as part of a future national council working towards 'Yugoslav unity'. Korošec read out a letter from Jeglič urging his flock to continue fighting for the May declaration. But one police report stressed how the concept of 'unity' was now interpreted. The monarchy was not mentioned, nor the birthday of the emperor; it appeared that 17 August had deliberately been chosen to highlight a shift of allegiance.[40]

Dissemination in Dalmatia and Croatia

That the declaration movement could spread so successfully in Slovene regions from late 1917 owed much to a mesh of circumstances. In the face of Vienna's obstinate 'German course' (both domestically in Austria and in a tighter alliance with Germany) the Slovene clerical leadership had launched a campaign that fed off war-weariness and abundant misery in local communities: a growing sense that the Habsburg regime would not provide national security while some South Slav entity could. Not surprisingly, in the starving crownlands further south, *Reichsrat* deputies could stir a similarly explosive concoction with the same arguments. Croat politicians and community leaders there took note not only of the Yugoslav club's tactics but also the signs across the border in Croatia, particularly the support that the Starčević party had given to the May declaration. In Istria, Croat deputies like Spinčić and Matko Laginja (both Starčević party members) took the lead with propaganda. In May, the provincial gendarmerie commander suggested that their campaign had failed to win over the locals, but this was just one perspective. In fact, at least 15,000 people (perhaps 10 per cent of the Slavs of Istria) signed up with petitions in early 1918.[41] Open support was also suggested in censored correspondence. On northern islands like Krk where the pro-Yugoslav bishop Mahnić held sway, 2,000 signatures were collected. And among the starving inhabitants of Pazin, the censor concluded in June:

> There is very lively interest in the South Slav declaration. In the correspondence of intelligent people there are more detailed statements about it, while in that of the less educated one can read short allusions like the greeting 'Long Live Yugoslavia'.[42]

By September the censor was noting an ever stronger fervour in central Istria, and joy at news of the National Council founded in Ljubljana:

> The people are convinced that [the declaration] will be realized and therefore expect a better future. They have full confidence in the *Reichsrat* deputies and are pleased that they have finally chosen the radical path. ... The national struggle between Croats, Slovenes and Italians has ceased – all hatred is directed against the Germans and Magyars.[43]

In Dalmatia in 1918 the declaration echoes were perhaps even stronger. According to the regional governor in Zadar, already in the spring the Slovene leadership enjoyed such a reputation in Dalmatia that educated people had decided for Yugoslav unity within the empire. The number of signatures gathered was over 16,000 with petitions dispatched, for instance, from the Catholic women's movement in Zadar and the Croat reading-room in the Serb bastion of Knin.[44] In April Korošec himself visited Split, having received a petition and invitation from 7,000 of its inhabitants. A few days later the amnestied deputy Tresić-Pavičić, who had been publicly scathing about Habsburg 'atrocities', arrived and was given a tumultuous welcome; a crowd of several thousand cried 'Long live Croatia in a united Yugoslav state' while students unfurled the Yugoslav tricolour. Such open propaganda regularly irked Sarkotić in Sarajevo but he could do little to curb the freedom of assembly allowed in Dalmatia or the rather lax censorship law.[45] Thus on 2 July, Croat and Serb delegates from all parts of Dalmatia were able to assemble in Split, announce their goal of a completely independent Yugoslav state and form a committee to agitate in that direction.

It might be assumed that Croatia-Slavonia too would be at the forefront of south Slav mobilization after 1916 in view of its pre-war history and a majority in the *Sabor* that had expressly rejected the Austro-Hungarian state structure. In fact, while some concept of Yugoslav unity was probably more entrenched than in neighbouring 'Slovenia', a similar public agitation did not develop or at least its percolation into the communities was more subtle. There were a number of reasons. Firstly, the politicians were both opportunistic and mindful of Croatia's own historic priorities. The Croat-Serb Coalition until the end of the war waited on events and declined to embrace the May declaration; the Frank and Radić parties gave priority to Croatian state right, a 'Yugoslav' unity that focused on the Croats of Bosnia and Dalmatia. Instead therefore it was the small Starčević party that picked up the *Reichsrat*'s torch, its leader Ante Pavelić welcoming the declaration and announcing in June 1917 that it would mobilize national forces.[46] This then was a key axis for interaction with Korošec and the agitators in Dalmatia or Istria, while the main political force, the Coalition, gave no lead.[47] When the Starčević party met Yugoslav club deputies in Zagreb in early March 1918, the Slovene leaders saw little point in proclaiming 'unity' because it was self-evidently absent in Croatia. By the summer there had been some shifts. Not only were some Coalition deputies defecting to the Starčević grouping, but Radić in April had 'crossed the Rubicon of his political career', abandoning the Frankists and adhering to the declaration. Nevertheless, it was the Slovenes who felt most urgency. Korošec in the summer did not wait for a joint initiative with Zagreb before announcing a National Council. As one radical Zagreb journal noted, the Slovenes 'who have the longest and most threatened national border cannot wait for conditions in the *banovina* [Croatia-Slavonia] to clear up completely'.[48]

At the Croatian grassroots a Yugoslav message seems particularly to have spread via a radical press and, as in Austria, via the clergy's direction. New papers were appearing from early 1918 such as *Jug* (*South*) in Osijek and *Glas Slovenaca Hrvata i Srba* (*The Voice of Slovenes, Croats, and Serbs*) in Zagreb. Others like the Catholic non-party organ *Novine* (*Newspaper*) of Archbishop Bauer of Zagreb, which since 1914 had been a new base for the pro-Yugoslav Catholic Movement, began to be more strident. In late 1917, 52 clerics in Zagreb supported a *Novine* statement advocating a Croat-Serb-Slovene nation. In January the paper commented that the Yugoslav problem was a 'Gordian knot' that awaited its own Alexander (a clear reference to Regent Alexander of Serbia).[49] This was a stance by the Catholic Movement and its hierarchy, notably bishops Mahnić and Bauer, that seemed to exceed the May declaration and undoubtedly it had a major impact, not least among Catholic students. Yet, as in the Austrian crownlands, the Croat Catholic position was by no means clear-cut. Its reference points were not only the declaration movement, but also those clergy in Slavonia (the 'Djakovo circle') who still wished to prioritize spiritual matters, and Archbishop Stadler of Sarajevo who on 16 November had publicly opposed the declaration and insisted on Croatian state interests. While Stadler remained adamant, the hierarchy in Croatia-Slavonia went their own way in league with their Slovene neighbours. Bishop Mahnić for example was converted to a fully independent Yugoslav state by May 1918. He could still interpret this chiefly as Croatia's Catholic mission by which Slovenes but also Serbs would be protected from the evils of German Protestantism; in other words, the spiritual and national crusade were intertwined.[50]

Where and how far this message penetrated into local communities requires far more research. In Croatia-Slavonia there seem to have been no mass petitions for the May declaration, although some signature-gathering spilled over from Austria (for example in the western-most Modrus-Rijeka komitat where the authorities observed 'only Yugoslavs left').[51] What is striking is also the gulf between the educated urban sector, receptive to the South Slav message, and a rural peasantry antagonized by requisitioning of their food supplies. The dangers were summed up by one politician, Živko Bertić, who addressed the *Sabor* in July 1918. Although he felt from his own experience that many Croat soldiers were inclining towards the idea of Yugoslav unity, he warned his colleagues that the movement in Croatia was 'young and green': 'great swathes of our people still act more according to their dark instincts than under the influence of this great idea'.[52] These 'dark instincts', reacting to social and material grievances, would come to the fore at the war's end. While the educated sectors were busy discussing Yugoslav unity or cheering the collapse of the monarchy, many peasants in league with thousands of deserters (the so-called 'green cadres' hiding in the countryside) vented their anger upon the symbols of authority, pillaging towns and estates.[53] The social explosion mirrored that in Hungary proper. It was also a contrast to the relative stability in Slovene society where over the previous two years the shifts in allegiance had been managed quite successfully.

The view from Bosnia-Herzegovina

Late in the war, the Habsburg elite's general perception was that the main sources for the Yugoslav poison were either the 'Korošec movement' or unspecified enemy centres abroad. In the same way, Sarkotić in Bosnia always portrayed the agitation as largely external to his domain.[54] Nevertheless, as in Croatia, there was much fertile soil in Bosnia. In the wake of the May declaration, Sarajevo's Serb and Croat politicians were in contact with the Yugoslav club, and in September 1917 Korošec made a well-publicized visit to drum up support. From Vienna, Count Burián, the minister with special responsibility for Bosnia, observed that Korošec could indeed do great damage, that the authorities were trying to confine his peregrinations, but that the journey to Bosnia was legal and could not be prevented.[55] The visit indeed seems to have moved most Bosnian parties in a Yugoslav direction. Although the privileged Moslem leaders were largely hostile to the declaration until the end of the war, fearing submersion in a Yugoslav entity, Korošec found some sympathizers, and by 1918 an alarming number of Moslem women were backing the pro-Yugoslav Social Democratic party. Many Croats were divided between Stadler and his supporters who advocated 'Greater Croatia' and those like Jozo Sunarić and the Franciscan clergy who backed Korošec; but in both camps this was still a message for some kind of South Slav unity that challenged the existing state structure. As for the Bosnian Serbs, their 'Yugoslav' credentials were taken as read by Sarkotić, but their leaders like their supporters naturally had special reason to remain cautious. Vojislav Šola and Danilo Dimović were quietly developing their links to Vienna and Zagreb but they had to keep their grassroots base even more secret.

In the early summer of 1918, Sarkotić read the report of a lawyer, Milan Katičić, who had travelled across the South Slav region and who painted a dismal picture. Everywhere he felt the Habsburg idea was losing ground; even in Bosnia most politicians were in the enemy camp and the climate was ripe for revolution. Sarkotić did not agree. He continued to view Dalmatia, Carniola and Croatia as the chief sources for Yugoslav propaganda.[56] The lack of security in Dalmatia (where there was no state police) was particularly alarming as it undermined military discipline and allowed deserters to roam free. The dangers from elsewhere had been vividly brought home to him, personified in bishops Jeglič and Bauer who in June had visited Sarajevo to celebrate the 50th anniversary of Stadler's consecration; it was an encounter with clergy whom he felt were 'swimming in the South Slav declaration'. It made Sarkotić question how far the national calm in Bosnia was skin deep and only ensured by his strict regime. As he warned Burián:

> Foreign and domestic propaganda is working in a Yugoslav – in other words a Serbian – direction, and the danger exists that this propaganda will overwhelm not only the [Bosnian] Serbs but also the Moslems. For it is clear that those who have a positive goal like the Yugoslavs, who steer unswervingly towards that goal and spare neither toil or effort, have a real chance of success. To view this propaganda with folded arms, in other words not to pursue our own goals with the same determination can really only bring disappointments upon us.[57]

In fact, the Habsburg leaders in Vienna and Budapest could never agree on a solution for the South Slav problem and were still bickering over it as the empire disintegrated around them.

Conclusion

The 'secondary mobilization' that took off in the south of the Habsburg monarchy after 1916 was, unlike the patriotic mobilization of 1914, out of the hands of the authorities and largely at a tangent to Habsburg interests.[58] As we have seen, it was not uniform across the southern Slav region, but where it succeeded it acted as something of a plebiscite for the Yugoslav future. Its main fulcrum was in the western Balkans, in Slovene communities and in the southern Austrian crownlands, where a short-term convergence of material hardships, war-weariness and mounting anxiety about German or Italian encroachment gave the Yugoslav Club ample scope to pursue a crusade for Slovene-Croat solidarity. The degree to which this cause penetrated to the grassroots does much to explain the fresh legitimacy accorded to Cisleithanian Slovene and Croat politicians and the simultaneous shift in popular loyalties, away from an empire that seemed unable to satisfy basic concerns about security. The leadership of these territories could enter the new Yugoslav state with some kind of popular mandate.

In contrast, the much more confused picture in Croatia and Bosnia in 1917–18, in terms of competing concepts of South Slav unity and social-ethnic diversity, helps us understand the future traumas in interwar Yugoslavia. Despite the radical lead of the Catholic church in Croatia from late 1917, and the interaction of Croat-Serb leaders in Croatia and Bosnia with the declaration initiative, there remained a host of competing Yugoslav agendas in both regions and both entered the new Yugoslavia with the myriad allegiances unresolved. Most notably, for a large educated strata of Croats the 'Yugoslav' idea meant a Greater Croatia, while for many Bosnian Muslims the priority was to shore up Muslim autonomy and preserve their influence; both groupings, even in 1918, felt their goals might still be achieved within the Habsburg monarchy rather than in any new state entity. At the same time, the peasantry in Croatia was largely divorced from the national discourse, or the latter was hooked up too late to peasant material anxieties. In short, most Croatian and Bosnian politicians could not claim popular mandates except in the towns, while the countryside remained a force to be harnessed in the future (for instance by populist leaders like Stjepan Radić).

Across the South Slav region any imperial legitimacy had substantially weakened as the empire suffered an economic and then a military catastrophe. But if as a viable alternative many 'Habsburg' Serbs naturally welcomed the union with Serbia, and many Slovenes entered into it to secure their existence, it was the Croatian outlook that was most conditional and most equivocal. As a result, in terms of a Habsburg legacy to Yugoslavia, it was the thorny Croatian question that would most bedevil the new state's stability.

Notes

1 *Stenographische Protokolle über die Sitzungen des Hauses der Abgeordneten des Österreichischen Reichsrates*, XXII Session, vol. III, Vienna: Staatsdruckerei, 1918, 47th sitting, 3 December 1917, p. 2484, speech by Vjekoslav Spinčić; and 58th sitting, 6 February 1918, pp. 3058–59, speech by Vukotić.
2 The best general surveys remain (all from the Slovene perspective): J. Pleterski, *Prvo opredeljenje Slovenaca za Jugoslaviju* (Belgrade: Nolit, 1976); L. Ude, 'Declaracijsko gibanje na Slovenskem', in V. Čubrilović, F. Čulinović and M. Kostrenčić (eds), *Naučni skup u povodu 50-godišnjice raspada Austro-Ugarske Monarhije i stvaranje Jugoslavenske države* (Zagreb: Jugoslavenska akademija, 1969); Ude, 'Declaracijsko gibanje pri Slovencih', *Zgodovinski časopis*, Volume 24, 1970. In English there is little. The subject receives no mention in I. Banac, *The National Question in Yugoslavia. Origins, History, Politics* (Ithaca: Cornell University Press, 1984); and is weakly treated in J. Lampe, *Yugoslavia as History. Twice there was a Country* (Cambridge: Cambridge University Press, 1996). For a useful overview see Pleterski, 'The Southern Slav Question', in M. Cornwall (ed.), *The Last Years of Austria-Hungary: A Multi-National Experiment in Early Twentieth Century Europe* (Exeter: Exeter University Press, 2002), and for Serbia's role: A. Mitrović, *Serbia's Great War 1914–1918* (London: Hurst, 2008). The best political-diplomatic analysis remains D. Šepić, *Italija, saveznici i jugoslavensko pitanje 1914–1918* (Zagreb: Školska knjiga, 1970).

3 I. Šedivý, Češi, české země a velká válka 1914–1918 (Prague: Lidové noviny, 2001); M. Healy, Vienna and the Fall of the Habsburg Empire. Total War and Everyday Life in World War I (Cambridge: Cambridge University Press, 2004).

4 For some recent work see W. Lukan, 'Die politische Meinung der slowenischen Bevölkerung 1917/18 im Spiegel der Zensurberichte des Gemeinsamen Zentralnachweisbureaus für Kriegsgefangene in Wien', in J. Pokorny et al. (eds), Nacionalismus, společnost a kultura ve střední Evropě 19. a 20. století (Prague: Karolinum, 2007).

5 Österreichisches Staatsarchiv Vienna, Kriegsarchiv [KA], Evidenzbüro 1918 [EvB], nr 3442, Militäranwalt des Milkmdo in Vienna to EvB, 31 January 1918.

6 There is no thorough analysis of the Habsburg Empire's economy in wartime, but useful introductions are G. Gratz and R. Schüller, Die wirtschaftliche Zusammenbruch Österreich-Ungarns. Die Tragödie der Erschopfung (Vienna: Holder-Pichler-Tempsky, 1930); and E. März, Austrian Banking and Financial Policy. Creditanstalt at a Turning Point 1913–1923 (New York: St Martin's Press, 1984).

7 O. Landwehr, Hunger. Die Erschöpfungsjahre der Mittelmächte 1917/18 (Zurich, Leipzig and Vienna: Amalthea, 1931), p. 56.

8 KA, Militärkanzlei seiner Majestät [MKSM] 1918, 93–2/35, Landwehr to MKSM, 5 May 1918; J. Horvat, Politička povijest Hrvatske, 2 vols (Zagreb: August Cesarec, 1990), II, pp. 22, 42.

9 B. Krizman, Hrvatska u prvom svjetskom ratu. Hrvatsko-srpski politički odnosi (Zagreb: Globus, 1989), p. 113; Landwehr, Hunger, pp. 182, 235, 239.

10 KA, EvB 1917, nr 11609, Zensurstelle Vienna to EvB, 7 July 1917.

11 Stenographische Protokolle: 41st sitting, 21 November 1917, pp. 2184ff.

12 Ibid., 48th sitting, 4 December 1917, pp. 2558–60.

13 Ibid., p.2186. See also H. Kapidžić, Bosna i Hercegovina pod austro-ugarskom upravom (Sarajevo: Svjetlost, 1962), pp. 214–16; Landwehr, Hunger, pp. 58–59 for the Bosnian situation in mid-1917.

14 See Stenographische Protokolle: pp. 2186, 2809 (Korošec speeches), 2410–11 (Spadaro), 2857 (Jarc), 3010ff (Laginja).

15 KA, EvB 1918, nrs 23324, 23412.

16 KA, EvB 1918, Intelligence centre [NaStelle] Udine reports: EvB nr 15188, 21 May; nr 17812, 15 June; nr 21616, 16 July 1918.

17 KA, EvB 1918, nr 28731, Zensurstelle Udine to Feldmarschall von Boroević, 5 September 1918.

18 R.D. Laffan, 'The Liberation of the New Nationalities. Part I The Yugoslavs', in H.W.V. Temperley (ed.), A History of the Peace Conference in Paris, 6 volumes (London: Hodder and Stoughton, 1921), vol. IV, pp. 178–79.

19 See P. Bobič, War and Faith: The Catholic Church in Slovenia 1914–1918 (DPhil thesis, Oxford, 2009). Chapter 4 suggests the mediating role of the clergy between front and home-front. See also J. Pleterski, Dr Ivan Šušteršič 1863–1925. Pot prvaka slovenskega političnega katolicizma (Ljubljana: Založba, 1998); and, for a local perspective, E. Škulj (ed.), 'Jerebova kronika župnije Škocjan pri Turjaku', Acta Ecclesiastica Sloveniae, XXIX (Ljubljana, 2007).

20 F. Barac (ed.), Croats and Slovenes: Friends of the Entente in the World War (Paris: Lang, Blanchong, 1919), p. 36.

21 Z. Matijević, 'Croatian Catholic Movement and the Creation of the Yugoslav State (1912–18)', Review of Croatian History, Volume 1, Number 1, 2005, pp. 165–67. The bishop's name is usually spelled in Slovene sources as Anton Mahnič.

22 Horvat, Politička povijest Hrvatske, I, pp. 333–34; and M. Biondich, Stjepan Radić, the Croat Peasant Party, and the Politics of Mass Mobilization, 1904–1928 (Toronto: University of Toronto Press, 2000), p. 122.

23 Sarkotić diary, 1 January 1915: quoted in S. Klein, Freiherr Sarkotić von Lovćen. Die Zeit seiner Verwaltung in Bosnien-Herzegovina von 1914 bis 1919 (PhD thesis, Vienna, 1969), p. 38. Also Kapidžić, Bosna i Hercegovina, pp. 205–13.

24 KA, EvB 1917, nr 9336/III, Zensurstelle Feldkirch report on southern Slav movement (monthly report for August 1917); Lukan, 'Die politische Meinung', p. 233.

25 J. Pleterski, 'Zapis ob razpravi o izjavah za majniško deklaracijo', Zgodovinski časopis, vol. 47/4, 1993, p. 572. See also Pleterski, Prvo opredeljenje, pp.197ff; and Bobič, War and Faith, pp. 216–20.

26 Ude, 'Declaracijsko gibanje na Slovenskem', p. 144.

27 V. Stavbar, 'Izjave v podporo Majniško Deklaracije', Zgodovinski časopis, 1992–93, vols. 46/ 3, pp. 357–81; 46/4, pp. 497–507; 47/1, pp. 99–106.

28 Ibid., pp. 497–507. Three-quarters of the petitions from the Ljubljana judicial district mentioned the 'Habsburg clause'. For Šušteršič's behaviour: Pleterski, Dr Ivan Šušteršič, pp. 408–14.

29 Ibid., pp. 358–81. In view of this mass 'national defence', we might seriously question a recent claim that during the war 'nationalist feeling counted little when survival was at stake': P. Judson, Guardians of the Nation. Activists on the Language Frontiers of Imperial Austria (Cambridge, Mass.: Harvard University Press, 2006), p. 227.

30 J. Pleterski, 'Koroški Slovenci med prvo svetovno vojno', in J. Pleterski, L. Ude and T. Zorn (eds), Koroški plebiscit. Razprave in članki (Ljubljana: Slovenska matica, 1970), p. 85.

31 Ibid., pp.104ff. Stavbar in contrast found few Carinthian petitions in the Maribor archives.

32 KA, Zensurstelle Feldkirch files, Fasz.5952, monthly report (Beilage 29: South Slav movement), 29 April 1918.

33 Pleterski, Prvo opredeljenje, pp. 246–48, 255, 260 (Celje report).

34 Ibid., pp. 321–23.

35 Barac (ed.), Croats and Slovenes, pp. 68–69.

36 See the detailed study of military revolt on the home-front: R. Plaschka, H. Haselsteiner and A. Suppan, Innere Front. Militärassistenz, Widerstand und Umsturz in der Donaumonarchie 1918, 2 vols, (Vienna: Verlag für Geschichte und Politik, 1974), I, pp. 324ff.

37 For the cases of Pivko and the Croat desertions see M. Cornwall, The Undermining of Austria-Hungary. The Battle for Hearts and Minds (Basingstoke: Macmillan, 2000), pp. 131–49, 231–39, 287–99.

38 Ude, 'Declaracijsko gibanje pri Slovencih', pp. 201–2; and for a full review of the Slovene mass-rallies, pp. 198ff.

39 KA, Feindespropaganda-Abwehrstelle 1918, res.185, report to army high command, 19 June 1918. For the compromise that led to most clergy taking Jeglič's line: Bobič, War and Faith, pp. 239ff.

40 Ude, Declaracijsko gibanje na Slovenskem', p. 156. The event was also celebrated in Allied propaganda leaflets that were showered over the Italian front in September: Cornwall, Undermining, p. 352.

41 Stavbar, 'Izjave v podporo', pp. 102–4; Pleterski, Prvo opredeljenje, p. 262.

42 For Pazin: KA, EvB 1918, nr 17812, NaStelle Udine to EvB, 15 June. (Over 800 women and girls had signed a petition in January). For the islands: KA, EvB 1918, nr 11932, Zensurstelle Udine, 18 April 1918.

43 KA, EvB 1918, nr 28731, Zensurstelle Udine, 5 September 1918.

44 Stavbar, 'Izjave v podporo', p. 105.

45 KA, EvB 1918, nr 15181/18, Sarkotić report to army high command [AOK], 18 May; KA, AOK Op.Abteilung 1918, nr 110077, Sarkotić report, 26 July 1918.

46 Not to be confused with the ustaša leader of the same name.

47 Krizman, Hrvatska, pp. 109, 114; Horvat, Politička povijest Hrvatske, II, p.32. See also Z. Matijević, 'Reakcije frankovačkih pravaša na "Svibanjsku deklaraciju"', in F. Hoško (ed.), Prošlost obvezuje: povijesni korijeni Gospićko-senjske biskupije (Rijeka: Teologija u Rijeci, 2004), pp. 439–74.

48 Glas Slovenaca Hrvata i Srba, quoted in Pleterski, Prvo opredeljenje, p. 337. For Radić: Biondich, Stjepan Radić, pp. 131–33; Horvat, Politička povijest, II, p. 38 ('crossed the Rubicon').

49 Ibid., p. 34; and see the comments on pro-Serbian propaganda circulating in Osijek: Barac, Croats and Slovenes, pp. 60–61.

50 J. Krišto, *Hrvatski katolički pokret (1903–1945)* (Zagreb: Glas koncila, 2004), pp. 108–16; Matijević, 'Croatian Catholic Movement', pp. 172–73.
51 KA, EvB 1918, nr 13508, NaStelle Udine report, 5 May 1918.
52 Horvat, *Politička povijest*, II, pp. 56–58. See also Barac, *Croats and Slovenes*, p. 67: 'The Yugoslav movement … is the exclusive common property of the more educated, politically active classes'.
53 For the mass phenomenon of deserters in Croatia, see Plaschka, Haselsteiner, Suppan, *Innere Front*, II, pp. 70–89. In September 1918 it was estimated at 25,000 (p. 78).
54 Cornwall, *The Undermining*, pp. 264–65.
55 Kapidžić, *Bosna i Hercegovina*, pp. 221ff. Burián until the end felt that Korošec's agitation represented the South Slav danger in its 'most intensive form': Cornwall (ed.), *The Last Years*, p. 198.
56 Klein, *Freiherr Sarkotić von Lovćen*, pp. 190–91.
57 Hrvatski državni arhiv (Croatian State Archives), Zagreb, Sarkotić MSS, Sarkotić to Burián, 16 June 1918; and ibid., the entries in Sarkotić's diary for this period.
58 For more general analysis of this theme see the essays in J. Horne (ed.), *State, Society and Mobilization in Europe during the First World War* (Cambridge: Cambridge University Press, 1997).

3   Forging a United Kingdom of Serbs, Croats, and Slovenes

The legacy of the First World War and the 'invalid question'

John Paul Newman

In Miroslav Krleža's short story *Barracks Five B*, a conscripted soldier, Vidović, is mortally wounded whilst serving in the Habsburg army during the First World War. In the story, from the collection *The Croatian God Mars*, Krleža told of the suffering and slow death of his ill-fated protagonist in a ramshackle military hospital, situated near the front line. Barracks humour turns to gallows humour as Vidović's companions take bets on whether the injured soldier will make it through the night (the odds are long). The hospital/ barracks is expected to be captured at any moment in a Russian assault, and an atmosphere of hedonistic reverie takes hold amongst the soldiers, depriving Vidović of a few last moments of tranquillity before he dies.[1]

Krleža knew about the squalor of barrack life and about wounded soldiers: he had served with the Habsburg army in Galicia, and towards the end of the war he worked with injured soldiers and war orphans in Zagreb. His fictional soldier Vidović did not survive, but in reality tens of thousands of disabled veterans were an important part of the legacy left by the war on the Kingdom of Serbs, Croats, and Slovenes (hereafter Yugoslavia). This chapter will chart the various attempts to provide welfare and to reintegrate these disabled veterans into post-war society, a concern known in Yugoslavia as the 'invalid question'. The evolution of this question was closely connected with the transition of society from war to peace, as well as with the unification of the South Slav lands and the separate wartime histories of South Slav soldiers. In attempting to formulate social policy in the wake of the devastation left by war, initial optimism about what could be done for disabled veterans proved premature. At the end of the 1920s, financial hardship compelled the state to withdraw most material support for disabled veterans, many of whom became despondent about their post-war fate. In the Yugoslav kingdom, problems caused by budgetary restrictions were compounded by the heterogeneous nature of the South Slav 'war experience'. South Slav disabled veterans had fought on different fronts and – importantly – in different, opposing armies. Traces of official hostility towards soldiers who had fought in the Habsburg army lingered on in the new state. Those prejudices were a reflection of a post-war society whose culture emphasized the sacrifices and triumphs of the Serbian army during the war. In addition to this, South Slav disabled veterans themselves were not in agreement over what had been won or lost during the war, what they had fought for, and how best to make their appeal to the government and the civilian public in the new state. Their history in the 1920s shows how many disabled veterans were ambivalent about their identity as ex-soldiers in the new state, simultaneously bound to one another as *ratni invaldi* ('war invalids') and yet divided by their divergent wartime experiences. At the beginning of the 1930s, as Yugoslavia faced greater domestic and international challenges, most disabled veterans and officials agreed that the 'invalid question' had still not received a satisfactory answer.

The cost of war

The failure was not considered inevitable in 1918, although at the end of the war few people in the newly-unified Yugoslav kingdom had illusions about the challenges they faced in the wake of the war. In terms of casualties, both civilian and military, no belligerent state had suffered as greatly as Serbia. When the Serbian army broke through the Salonica front and returned home in September 1918, it had been under arms for over six years.[2] Including the losses of Serbia's allies in the Montenegrin army, the First World War had claimed the lives of over 300,000 soldiers, about 40 per cent of mobilized men. Added to civilian casualties, total war losses for Serbia and Montenegro were between 750,000–800,000, from a population of around 4.5 million.[3] The efforts of 'gallant little Serbia' against the Central Powers were recognized throughout the Allied nations, and for many Serbian soldiers this image of heroic struggle and eventual victory gave meaning to the mass death of the war years. The creation of Yugoslavia in December 1918 meant that the wartime sacrifice of the Serbian soldier became one of 'liberation and unification' made on behalf of all South Slavs, and it was this trope which became central to self-legitimizing narratives amongst veterans of the Serbian army after 1918.

Although not on the same scale, Habsburg South Slavs had also endured suffering and sacrifice during the war. Losses for Habsburg Serbs, Croats, and Slovenes (civilians and soldiers) have been calculated at around 150,000.[4] Habsburg South Slavs fought on the Balkan front against the Serbian and Montenegrin armies,[5] on the Italian front, and against Russian soldiers in the East. The fact that so many Habsburg South Slavs had been in Russia during the October Revolution meant that these veterans were often suspected (occasionally with justification) of being Bolshevik sympathizers. Indeed the anarchic situation which engulfed the Croatian countryside in the autumn of 1918 was caused in large part by Habsburg military deserters and 'returnees', South Slav soldiers coming home from Russian captivity.[6] The fear of radicalization within the army led to the decision to disenfranchise soldiers on the active list in the newly-formed Yugoslav army, hoping to avoid the appearance of politicized soldiers' councils similar to those that had played such an important role in Russia's communist revolution. This meant that South Slav veterans were of political, as well as social and cultural significance to the new kingdom in 1918. In fact, only a minority of South Slav veterans who had fought in Russia became members of the Communist Party of Yugoslavia. For those soldiers, the war had brought socialist revolution a step closer, but for many Habsburg veterans it was unclear what had been gained from their wartime sacrifice. In this respect, they stood apart from veterans of the victorious Serbian army. With the end of the war and the creation of Yugoslavia, South Slav veterans needed to come to terms with sharing a state with soldiers formerly of an opposing army. Reconciliation between former enemies was an important part of cultural demobilization and the transition from war to peace in the Yugoslav kingdom.

Unification and the end of the war meant that expertise and skills of former enemies could now be pooled for the benefit of all. The Croatian orthopaedist Dr Božidar Spišić, for example, had worked with disabled veterans at a military barracks used as a school for disabled veterans in Zagreb during the war. He travelled to Belgrade in spring 1919 to deliver a lecture to his Serbian colleagues entitled 'How we can help our Invalids'. Spišić appealed for basic medical care and schooling to be provided free of charge, to ensure that disabled veterans would once again be capable of working and providing for themselves. 'Our invalids must not earn their daily bread by begging,' he warned.[7] Instead, he envisaged a reciprocal relationship between the state and its disabled veterans that would be beneficial to both parties. By re-training these men to become useful and productive workers in civilian life, the state would retain a large source of man-power. This was a vital consideration in Yugoslavia, where so much had been lost in material and human resources during the war.

A council of Serbian military doctors who had had experience of caring for disabled soldiers during the war responded with similar sentiments in May:

> Nobody today can think of the invalid question as merely a calculated percentage of disability, [and] then giving to those disabled the label invalid, along with financial support from the state. That would do almost nothing to help invalids and the state in which they lived.[8]

Like Spišić, the Serbian doctors saw no need for wounded soldiers to wear the 'invalid' label indefinitely in civilian life, 'Invalid means incapable, not of living, not of working, but of further fighting, for military purposes. Freed from the army, he must not be freed from all kinds of work'.[9] The council went on to suggest a programme of support, medical and financial, that would enable disabled veterans once again to earn money for themselves.

Outside the circle of military and civilian experts, many in Yugoslavia felt that the state was honour-bound to care for its veterans, especially those who were disabled.[10] This duty fell to the newly-formed Ministry of Social Policy. The officials and bureaucrats of this government department were responsible for weaving together the wartime strands of social and medical expertise and creating a welfare programme in Yugoslavia. It was a Herculean task, but the first Minister of Social Policy, Vitomir Korać, entered the debate with confidence. In November, he organized a conference on disabled veterans in Belgrade, attended by about 100 delegates from across the country. These included, *inter alia*, representatives of competent authorities, delegates of military and civilian groups, charitable organizations and families of missing, killed or interned soldiers. Participants were invited to offer opinions and suggestions pertaining to the resolution of the 'invalid question'. Some of these would be taken into account when drafting a unified law for disabled veterans. Items for discussion included medical treatment, organizational, administrative, financial, and socio-economic concerns for disabled veterans, housing, and programmes of professional training.[11]

The conference was intended as a comprehensive survey of the 'invalid question' and of the problems associated with it, and demonstrates both the energy and the ambition with which the Ministry of Social Policy initially confronted the challenges ahead of them. The delegates reviewed the situation from its war-time origins until the present day and discussed the direction they hoped it would take in the future. Suggestions were put forward that every single disabled veteran should be re-examined using the most advanced medical methods in order to ascertain their individual needs. Provisions were made for passing the concern of disabled veterans from military to civilian authorities, and there were calls for a review of all those institutions involved with disabled veterans to be unified into one single authority which would cover the entire country. The delegates also discussed how to ensure that within one year (eighteen months at most) every single disabled veteran who required a prosthetic limb would be supplied with one. Finally, provisions were made for the establishment of a department for social statistics since, at this time, the ministry did not have figures of its own.[12] Like Dr Spišić and the Serbian medical experts, the ministry was confident about how much could be achieved for disabled veterans; it was held that the 'invalid question' could be resolved by informed policy making and hard work. However, well-intended and positive statements handed over a number of hostages to fortune. The pledges which were made in official circles so soon after the war would resonate with disabled veterans throughout the country for many years to come. In the newly-unified state, a set of assumptions about post-war social policy and about what disabled veterans could expect from the government was established.

Initially, at least, the state was committed to providing for disabled veterans. As the discussion topics at the conference suggest, the Ministry of Social Policy stressed the concept that *re-training* disabled veterans for the workplace would lead to their *re-integration* into society, the latter a logical consequence of the former. To this end, wartime 'invalid schools' were maintained and expanded in the new state. At these institutions, disabled veterans could be trained by qualified experts in a range of trades appropriate to their reduced physical capabilities. In Zagreb, for example, the Holy Spirit Poorhouse was converted into an 'invalid school' and orthopaedic hospital (the only one of its kind in the region) in 1921, funded by the ministry. Disabled veterans could stay at a nearby dormitory (actually a converted army barracks) whilst they completed their apprenticeship. The state provided for accommodation, food, training, and even the necessary tools they would need for their new vocations (basket-making was considered suitable work, or disabled veterans could find employment at the orthopaedic hospital itself, making prosthetic limbs for amputee veterans). Schools for sightless disabled veterans were founded across the country, such as the one in Zemun, across the river Danube from Belgrade. Pupils at Zemun could learn Braille and make use of the school's well-stocked library.[13] 'Invalid' did not mean 'incapable of living' as the Serbian doctors had insisted in 1919, and re-integration started to look like the answer to the 'invalid question'.

The lack of data as to the number of disabled veterans was also a consequence of the transition from war to peace, and of the lack of integration in the state's legislation. The Ministry of Social Policy understood that in order to effectively tackle the 'invalid question' it would need to know its dimensions; in other words how many disabled veterans were in Yugoslavia, and what was the level of their disability. The ministry wanted to carry out a comprehensive survey which would process and categorize every single disabled veteran in the kingdom. This would create a corpus of knowledge that would allow the ministry to decide how many people were entitled to how much support. Disabled veterans were inspected at special tribunals throughout the country starting in spring 1921. The raw data could be used to make informed policy decisions, but it should be kept in mind that it also created the parameters of 'invalidity' in interwar Yugoslavia, parameters through which the state would define its responsibility (or lack of responsibility) to disabled veterans, and through which many disabled veterans would understand their own status. The language through which the 'invalid question' would come to be expressed in the Yugoslav kingdom was established by this process.

Despite these efforts, absolute numbers of disabled veterans are difficult to trace, the hunt for reliable figures is made harder by the condition of the archival collections of the Ministry of Social Policy in interwar Yugoslavia, of whose records only fragments remain. The historian is forced to look at less-reliable and sometimes conflicting reports. The Yugoslav delegates at the peace conferences in Paris supplied a figure of 264,000 disabled veterans *of the Serbian army*.[14] Given what is known about the chaotic situation at the end of the war and the difficulties encountered in quantifying disabled veterans at this time, the figure should be treated with due care. No doubt the number was inflated to ensure the best possible chance of receiving reparations from the defeated Central Powers. The most reliable figures in the first decade after unification were provided in an anthology published to celebrate the decennial of the formation of Yugoslavia. The author gave a figure, supplied by the Ministry of Social Policy, of 74,531, which broke down as follows: Serbs, 33,837; Croats, 21,850; Slovenes, 11,817; Germans, 2,657; Hungarians,

2,527; Romanians, 800; Czechs, 643; and others, 400. Thus the total amounted to 74,531.[15]

This is really the only figure that should pass the litmus test of historical scepticism, which means it is very difficult to trace the evolution of this aspect of Yugoslavia's social history in the first post-war decade. By the end of the 1920s, the number of disabled veterans had undergone several official reductions and re-calculations. It seems certain that, in the years preceding 1928, a number of disabled veterans were successfully re-integrated into society (which is to say re-trained and absorbed into gainful employment), perhaps many decided they were better off under the care of their families rather than the state, and some certainly died during this time (tuberculosis, for example, was a great killer in hospitals and invalid schools during and after the war). Nevertheless, it gives a sense of the scale of the problem facing the country in the years after the war. With its limited funds, some at the Ministry of Social Policy might have taken cold comfort in the knowledge that the war dead vastly outnumbered the war living. In fact, the figure did not include the large number of bereaved widows and war orphans created by the mass killing of the war, especially in Serbia. Their financial well-being was also the ministry's responsibility.

Disabled veterans' societies

Whilst the Ministry of Social Policy attempted to get to grips with the 'invalid question', a number of disabled veterans were themselves beginning to organize, the better to present their own demands to the state. After 1918, veteran societies and organizations were a significant and – in many cases – new development in associational life throughout Europe,[16] and Yugoslavia was not an exception. Unsurprisingly, veterans of the Serbian army were most active in this area, and their organizations were by far the largest in interwar Yugoslavia,[17] although smaller societies formed by veterans of the Habsburg army also emerged in the 'newly-associated' regions of the Yugoslav kingdom.

The disabled veterans' society differed significantly from most other veteran groups in so far as its membership could be drawn from throughout the kingdom, and included former soldiers of the Serbian and the Habsburg armies (not to mention the Montenegrin army).[18] However, cutting across tribal lines, or rather reconciling soldiers who had fought in opposing armies during the war, was no mean feat. The disabled veterans' movement in interwar Yugoslavia was an ambivalent creature, its members felt united by their shared fate as disabled veterans, and yet seriously divided by their wartime experiences. Their attempts at presenting a unified front to the government were hampered by the lingering iniquities in post-war legislation. Disabled veterans from all backgrounds agreed that those iniquities needed to be effaced by a single law, although the consensus broke down over the details of such a law. Most feared that they would be forgotten by the 'non-invalid' population, although there was much disagreement as to what they should be remembered for. The first disabled veteran organization was established by former soldiers of the Serbian army at the beginning of 1919, and based in Belgrade. A few months later, in June, the statute of a similar group was accepted by Zagreb authorities, and by 1925, there were disabled veteran organizations in Novi Sad, Kragujevac, Skopje, Ljubljana, Sarajevo, Podgorica, and Split, with a combined membership of about 38,000 members, over half of whom were from Serbia.[19]

In 1919, the Belgrade and Zagreb organizations, the two largest in the country, were in agreement over the urgent need for unity in order to raise the profile of the 'invalid question' and, most importantly, to put pressure on the government to pass a law for disabled veterans. At the end of the war Habsburg veterans were still being paid according to the laws established by the defunct monarchy, whereas veterans of the Serbian army were catered for by legislation dating back to the pre-war Serbian kingdom. This was yet another legal anomaly which needed to be ironed out by the new state's lawmakers. The unified Yugoslav kingdom was heir to a vast array of histor- ical, cultural and political traditions, legal and political headaches were a symptom of unifying those traditions into a coherent polity. Nevertheless, like many other such irregularities and misunderstandings concerning the military, voting quotas, and currency exchange rates, the lack of a single disabled veterans' law retarded the process of unification and, in this case, post-war reconciliation amongst former soldiers.[20]

Just as with the high politics of interwar Yugoslavia, disagreements and antagonisms amongst disabled veterans often revolved around the Belgrade/ Zagreb axis. The Belgrade and Zagreb societies differed over seemingly small details in the draft proposal. The polemics between the two organizations, however, revealed a deeper antipathy based on the memory of the war years. The disharmony in the Yugoslav parliament echoed in the meetings of the disabled veterans, as the Belgrade society complained that 'The representatives of Croatian invalids have the same attitude as their politicians [...] Many times we have made this futile attempt [at unification], always with sacrifices on our part'.[21] Such post-war sacrifices were a continuation of those made during the war, as the Serbian soldiers were keen to point out: 'we succeeded in freeing our brother Croats and Slovenes from the thousand-year slavery of Austria-Hungary [...] If the Croat and Slovene nations had trusted Radić and others [like him] they would not now be free.'[22]

The war years and the Serbian victory were sensitive matters for many Habsburg disabled veterans who resented the implication that they were soldiers of a defeated enemy. The Zagreb disabled veterans preferred the pacifistic solidarity of an 'invalid international' based on their shared suffering in the war and after. This meant unity 'not just with the comradely organi- sation in Belgrade, but with all war victims of all countries, since we are all victims one and the same'.[23] This was impossible at a national level, however, since 'our comrades in Serbia and Montenegro do not admit us as their comrades, they maintain that we are Austrian invalids'.[24] The corrosive impact of this kind of bickering on veteran relations should not be under-estimated. The memory of the Great War was interwoven into the fabric of the new state, and Serbia's struggle for the 'liberation and unification' of all South Slavs was the constituent myth of Yugoslavia. However, most Habsburg veterans did not recognize in it their own war experiences. The polemics between the Zagreb and Belgrade societies were a reflection of post-war culture in the Yugoslav kingdom and of the divisive nature of war memory.

Direct action

Interestingly, reconciliation between South Slav veterans was easier to achieve at an international level, as ex-soldiers looked beyond their own borders and saw that their fate was linked to the impact of the war throughout Europe. It was this international dimension, coupled with the notion of disabled veterans as victims of the Great War who were entitled to support and recognition, which facilitated the unification of all disabled veteran societies into a single organization, at the beginning of 1923. It also led to the most public display of veteran solidarity in the 1920s: a large rally held to express dissatisfaction at the perceived failures of the government to address the 'invalid question'.

The rapprochement between the feuding societies began in September 1922, and was prompted by the forthcoming 'Inter-Allied Invalid Congress', which was to be held in Ljubljana, bringing delegates from all formerly Allied states to Yugoslavia. The congress raised the profile of the 'invalid question' in the Yugoslav kingdom which, despite the earlier promises of the Ministry of Social Policy, was at risk of becoming submerged in the many other political and financial demands being made on the government. In what appears to be an exercise in public relations, the ministry set aside ten million dinars to adapt a tuberculosis clinic in Croatia, and a further three million dinars to build a disabled veterans' home in Belgrade.[25] The ministry also took the initiative in providing a draft for a disabled veterans' law, the lack of which was still the biggest complaint of many disabled veterans. After meeting with ex-soldiers from Belgrade, Ljubljana, Sarajevo, Split, and Novi Sad, the minister of social policy offered a generous proposal that was acceptable to all present.

On the eve of the 'Inter-Allied Invalid Congress' disabled veterans in Zagreb recognized that squabbling with the Belgrade society would jeopardize their tenuous link to Allied veterans, and offered 'fraternal' and 'patriotic' support to the central council.[26] The unity within the movement and the renewed interest in the 'invalid question' also convinced the Croatian contingent that it was time to take more decisive action to ensure that both the government and the general public knew about the suffering of disabled veterans in the new state. They suggested that a march or demonstration in Belgrade could achieve both of these goals. The strategy was approved by the central council (as it now was) in Belgrade, and a 'Section for Intervention' of about 100 disabled veterans was chosen for the purpose of lobbying the government.[27]

They arrived in Belgrade in November 1922 and a number of the veterans were received by the Prime Minister Nikola Pašić. Pašić had been with the Serbian army during its harrowing wartime retreat across Albania in 1915, and he expressed sympathy for the disabled veterans and their cause. He stated that the matter needed to be addressed immediately, but that due to the current parliamentary crisis it was very difficult for his government to act.[28] This was encouraging, and the disabled veterans decided to remain in Belgrade to see if the conditions in parliament would become more favourable.

Over the course of November the demonstration gained momentum and proved to have a broader appeal than the disabled veterans had expected, as civil servants and ex-volunteers joined the protests against the government. Like the disabled veterans, these men were dissatisfied with the way they were treated in the Yugoslav kingdom. By the beginning of December, around 6,000 disabled veterans, ex-volunteers, civil servants, and sympathizers had gathered outside the Yugoslav parliament. It was a huge public manifestation which happened to coincide with the fourth anniversary of the unification of Yugoslavia, on 1 December. Much to the chagrin of the Zagreb society, there seems to have been a hint of festivity within the ranks of the veterans of the Serbian army. The Croatian organization complained that some participants appeared to be more concerned with 'cinemas and concerts' than with the 'empty stomachs of invalids'.[29] Apparently, a number of veterans of the Serbian army combined protest with a celebration of the 'liberation and unification' of all South Slavs. The smaller Zagreb society was encouraged to see their ranks swelled on the streets by a large number of veterans of the Serbian army, but they were also worried that the focus of their protest would be lost. Nevertheless, tensions which had previously kept the societies apart were now firmly in the background, sublimated to the important task of getting a law passed. The disabled veterans, emboldened by the support they had received on the streets and in the press, promised an even larger demonstration if a law was not passed immediately. The Section for Intervention threatened to call every single ex-volunteer and disabled veteran in the country to the capital, and to block all exits out of the city, bringing daily life in the capital to a virtual standstill. They predicted that the call would bring up to 160,000 protestors onto the streets of Belgrade.[30]

During these weeks, it looked like the disabled veterans had caught the mood of a country dissatisfied with the lack of progress made in the four years since the end of the war. The threats to clog the streets of Belgrade with the country's malcontent proved empty, however, and the protest ended with a whimper rather than a bang. At the end of the year, Pašić's government was dissolved and new elections were called. Lobbying the government now became a moot point and the time spent on the streets and in council with the government had been wasted; disabled veterans would have to reformulate their strategy for a new political constellation. The announcement in parliament to dissolve the government was greeted by angry jeers from veterans in the public gallery, who heckled members with cries of, 'For shame!',

'National bloodsuckers!', and 'We will be waiting for you with sticks when you reconvene!'[31] A small consolation for their failed attempt at direct action was the definitive unification of all disabled veteran societies into one pan-Yugoslav organization, which was agreed upon at the beginning of 1923.[32]

Victors or victims?

The failed demonstration shows that the disabled veterans shared a sense of frustration at the lack of recognition their wartime sacrifice was given in the 1920s. The primary targets of this frustration were the state, the government, and its politicians. These were the men most directly responsible for the hardships the veterans now faced and also most directly responsible for compensating them in the post-war period. The government, for its part, was reaping what it had sowed immediately after the war. The politicians were measured against the promises they had made to disabled veterans in the first months after unification, and were found wanting. In addition to this, the disabled veterans wanted recognition from the general public. Non-veterans were not entitled to ignore the pleas of these men, and it was in search of this recognition that disabled veterans swelled on to the streets of Belgrade in their thousands. Veterans felt that the only alternative to this recognition was to be forgotten, to become invisible. For Serbian and Habsburg veterans alike this was their greatest anxiety. To become invisible was to admit that their wartime sacrifice, their invalidity, was meaningless, a burden on a society which did not care to be burdened by such matters. The demonstration of December 1922 was an attempt on the part of ex-soldiers to give meaning to their status as veterans by calling upon the state and society to acknowledge it.

It is also notable that the initiative for the demonstrations and the formation of a 'Section for Intervention' came from the Zagreb society. This is consistent with that society's aims to work exclusively for the purpose of gaining material and financial concessions for its members. This aim informed the decision to demonstrate outside the parliament in Belgrade, but it also created a tension with veterans of the Serbian army commemorating 'liberation and unification' with 'cinemas and concerts'. Many Habsburg disabled veterans preferred to reduce the 'invalid question' in Yugoslavia to its lowest common denominator, namely, that all disabled veterans in the new state were victims, and as such shared the same fate. Habsburg veterans embraced the notion of victimhood throughout post-war Europe (the notion which informed the Zagreb society's appeal that 'we are all victims one and the same') more enthusiastically than their Serbian counterparts, who saw themselves not just as victims, but also as victors. Veterans of the Serbian army wanted to combine such demands with a celebration of 'liberation and unification' and of their wartime sacrifice, celebrations which excluded Habsburg veterans. The social and cultural dimensions of the 'invalid question' were at odds: all disabled veterans protesting on the streets of Belgrade wanted support from the state and all agreed that solidarity amongst veterans was crucial.

Beyond this, mutual ground between Habsburg and Serbian veterans was harder to find, and there was no common language of mourning and commemoration between soldiers of such different backgrounds.

Throughout the 1920s conflicting centripetal and centrifugal forces were ever present within the South Slav disabled veteran movement. It seems, however, that after the protest in Belgrade, the forces of unity were in ascendancy. The unification of all disabled veterans groups into one 'Society for War Invalids' (*Udruženje ratnih invalida*) took place at the beginning of 1923. The decision was informed by the events in Belgrade at the end of 1922, where collective action was deemed more effective than working apart. The ability of South Slav disabled veterans to work together in spite of such divisive wartime experiences demonstrates that, at the very least, there was a potential for reconciliation in the post-war period (Similarly, it must also be noted that veteran movements throughout Europe were divided as to the meaning of the war and the best way to tackle their problems in the post-war period).[33] However, this unification did not create a *tabula rasa* which erased differences between disabled veterans of the Habsburg and Serbian armies. Neither did the law for disabled veterans, eventually passed in 1925, almost eight years after unification and having undergone 16 re-drafts.[34] The unambiguous sense of victory on behalf of the 'liberation and unification' of all South Slavs, felt by most veterans of the Serbian army, remained present throughout the 1920s.

Disabled veterans of the Serbian army, both before and after unification in 1923 and unlike Habsburg veterans, felt that their wartime suffering and sacrifice was at least partially redeemed by their victory and by the 'liberation and unification' of all South Slavs. In this sense, it is understandable that dates such as 1 December would resonate more strongly in their ranks. The war, as we have seen, had taken a far greater toll in Serbia than elsewhere in the Yugoslav kingdom. The commemoration and 'cinemas and concerts' of which the Zagreb veterans complained was part of an attempt by Serbian veterans to mediate the great trauma caused by the war. Invasion, defeat, retreat, occupation, and eventual triumph became elements of a national narrative from which the Serbian disabled veterans could find meaning in their wartime experiences. This epic ran like a red thread through Serbian national life in interwar Yugoslavia,[35] but it was not transferable to Habsburg veterans, and therefore had an exclusive quality which marred complete identity between disabled veterans.

In fact, it seems that this attitude of Serbian victory permeated deeper into post-war society in the Yugoslav kingdom. Sometimes it came with an attendant definition of Habsburg veterans as defeated enemies. Veterans in Zagreb made repeated claims that officials at the Ministry of Social Policy had insulted them on account of their war records. For example, at a meeting in Zagreb in 1920, a Croatian disabled veteran told of how, when he had been to see an official to request financial assistance, he was asked, 'were you at the front in Salonica?' and was told to 'go to [deposed Habsburg emperor] Karl, maybe he will give you something'.[36] No doubt former Habsburg soldiers were self-conscious about their wartime records, but official documents reveal similar prejudices. Croatian disabled veterans at an invalid school in Moslavina made frequent complaints about their treatment by staff during the 1920s. Disabled veterans, pupils at the school, told the Ministry of Social Policy in 1925 that so far complaints about their living conditions had been dismissed by the director, who on one occasion had told them 'if you don't like it, you can go to Franz Joseph'.[37] In 1930, an official report by the Ministry of Social Policy investigated numerous complaints made against the director, including the accusation that he had drunkenly called one pupil a 'kraut whore'. The comment referred to the ex-soldier's wartime record in the 'Austrian' army, and the director, who subsequently lost his job, did not deny making it. The ministry's investigation found that not only was the insult characteristic of the director's approach to his work, but that it reflected more generally the bad state of relations between staff and veterans at the school over the years.[38] In its willingness both to investigate the veterans' complaints and to dismiss the offending director, the Ministry of Social Policy showed sincerity in its attempts to treat disabled veterans in the Yugoslav kingdom fairly and equitably. Nevertheless, the history of this institute exposes lingering prejudices which went against the official line. These kinds of prejudices are very difficult to quantify, but can at least be highlighted.

Silent liquidation

Apart or together, the disabled veterans were swimming against the tide in the 1920s. In 1929, the Ministry of Social Policy re-defined – or rather restricted – its responsibility to disabled veterans. Initial optimism, so prevalent in the period immediately after the war, had evaporated in the face of scarcity and financial hard times. The law of 1925 was re-drafted in 1929 and a far less generous welfare policy was formulated, which included a reduction in the 'invalid fund' of 10 million dinars.[39] Invalid schools across the country were emptied of disabled veterans who no longer qualified for care. Support for the sightless, for example, was completely withdrawn, and disabled veterans at the Holy Spirit in Zagreb were moved to a smaller facility, as the building returned to its original function as a poorhouse.[40] The facts and figures about disabled veterans that the Ministry of Social Policy had gathered over the years now helped them to decide who was and who was not entitled to help from the state, essentially, who was and who was not an 'invalid'. In contradistinction to the line taken at the conference on disabled veterans so soon after the war, the ministry now decided that the responsibility for care of disabled veterans lay in the private sphere of the family, not in the public sphere of the state.

It is very difficult to gauge, in absolute terms, whether the Ministry of Social Policy made the right decision regarding disabled veterans towards the end of the decade. No doubt many wounded men had returned from battle and re-integrated into pre-war kinship groups, or at least their welfare had been looked after by such kinship groups, rather than in veteran organizations or by the state. The new, less-generous line taken by the Ministry of Social Policy might not have been entirely egregious, and it certainly made financial sense. Crucially, however, it was inconsistent with the approach the Ministry of Social Policy had taken towards the 'invalid question' immediately after the war. As elsewhere in Europe initial promises proved impossible to keep: there simply was not enough money to provide the conditions which disabled veterans, nevertheless, now expected to receive.[41] The Ministry of Social Policy had created an ideal image of welfare for disabled veterans which it was unable to realize, and within these relative terms, it can be judged as a failure.

This was certainly the attitude of many disabled veterans, as we have seen. They had from an early stage been critical of the state, whose responsibility it was to provide for disabled veterans, and who were therefore blamed by veterans when they failed to do so. The lethargy of the government in passing a law and its failure to provide financial care for veterans was regarded as nonfeasance by many disabled veterans. The budgetary restrictions of 1929 were hardly an abrupt turnaround; they merely confirmed what many veterans already believed to be true: Yugoslavia did not care about its disabled veterans. It was also a realization of the marginalization of disabled veterans from the public sphere, the 'invisibility' which lay at the roots of so much veteran angst in the interwar period, and which had galvanized them into taking action.

The despair which this caused was eloquently captured by a double amputee from Croatia, Josip Pavičić, one of the few disabled veterans to write about his experiences in the post-war kingdom. Unlike Krleža, Pavičić depicted the soldier's fate after 1918, recreating the atmosphere of invalid schools and hospitals in the post-war period, which he termed 'invalid catacombs'.[42] Whilst Vidović had died before the Armistice, Pavičić's protagonists survived the war, but the end of the conflict was merely the beginning of a new phase of their suffering. Their experiences in Yugoslavia were of neglect and hostility, from the state and from 'non-invalid' society, dreaming of pre-war life gave a temporary respite to the disabled veteran, but many, realizing they could not endure their post-war fate, turned to suicide. This caused a gradual but pronounced decline in the ranks of disabled veterans, and was thus the ultimate solution to the 'invalid question'. The process was barely noticed by the rest of society, and Pavičić termed it 'silent liquidation'. 'Silent liquidation' was the realization of the disabled veterans' worst fears: to be ignored and forgotten, to become invisible in a society which wanted to move away from the war years, a luxury which was denied to Pavičić and his fellow *ratni invalidi*.

Conclusion

Obviously, the melancholy trope of 'silent liquidation' was the antithesis of official policy towards disabled veterans, which aimed, if not to restore all disabled veterans to pre-war life, then at least to re-integrate them into the workforce, and to provide for them where this was not possible. This chapter has tried to show that the experience of disabled veterans in the 1920s was in part responsive to official policy. The Ministry of Social Policy, like the Yugoslav state, attempted to find its way in a new epoch, facing unprecedented challenges in the wake of the war. Disabled veterans took their cues from the state, negotiating with the government and with each other to find a meaning for their wartime experiences and a place in post-war society worthy of the sacrifices they had made during the war. For many veterans of the Serbian army, this was a straightforward matter of a debt of honour owed to them by Yugoslavia on account of their wartime sacrifice. The foundational narrative of the state acknowledged the important role soldiers of the Serbian army played during the war. This did not necessarily mean that the state would look after disabled veterans of the Serbian army in the interwar period, but it did mean that they had a convincing claim to the country's moral conscience. For Habsburg veterans, the matter was more complicated, and notions of victory and sacrifice were often eschewed in favour of a broader sense of suffering and victimhood in the post-war period. It should be remembered that Josip Pavičić, whose stories are marked by themes of the futility and hopelessness of war, was also a Croat who fought in the Habsburg army. This is perhaps an explanation for the absence of a positive message in the war stories of men like Miroslav Krleža and Josip Pavičić.

For Pavičić, the notion of a meaningful war did not come until after 1945. Like Krleža, he became a supporter of Tito (another veteran of the Habsburg army) and the Socialist revolution. Pavičić's stories about the 'invalid question' in the 1920s were re-printed in 1946, under the title *In Red Letters*, and with four new fictional tales of the Partisan struggle during the civil war in Yugoslavia. In a preface written especially for the new edition, the author spoke of his experiences as a disabled veteran in the interwar period:

> Those were difficult days […] Whilst the system concealed the tragedy with endless solutions to the 'invalid question', the problem was resolving itself – with alcohol, with the tuberculosis bacillus, with a bullet, a knife, with poison[…]And ten years later, whilst the 'invalid question' was still filling up sheets of paper, it had in reality resolved itself long ago […] Those [invalid] masses were for the capitalist order too much of an encumbrance, ballast which needed to be cast away so as not to hamper the rise of their balloon. And so the ballast was cast away.[43]

Pavičić and Tito, two Habsburg veterans of the Great War, had finally found a war worth commemorating, and socialist Yugoslavia, unlike its royalist predecessor, had found a more inclusive foundational narrative.

Notes

1 M. Krleža, *Hrvatski Bog Mars* (Sarajevo: Svjetlost, 1973), pp. 219–36. The stories were originally published together soon after the war, in 1922.

2 Including the Balkan Wars of 1912–13. For a comprehensive English-language history of Serbia in the First World War, see A. Mitrović, *Serbia's Great War, 1914–1918* (London: Hurst, 2007).

3 See J. Tomasevich, *Peasants, Politics, and Economic Change in Yugoslavia* (Stanford: Stanford University Press, 1955), pp. 222–23.

4 Ibid. Tomasevich notes how statistics are less reliable due to the decomposition of the Dual Monarchy at the end of the war.

5 Including a non-commissioned officer from the Croatian Zagorje named Josip Broz who, under his Comintern alias 'Tito', would preside over Socialist Yugoslavia after the Second World War.

6 See I. Banac, '"Emperor Karl has become a Comitadji": The Croatian Disturbances of Autumn 1918', *Slavonic and East European Review*, vol. 70, no. 2 (April 1992), pp. 284–305.

7 *Obzor*, 25 April 1919.

8 *Službene novine*, 17 July 1919.

9 Ibid.

10 The leading Belgrade daily *Politika*, for example, in an article published in September that year, wrote of how the state had a 'moral responsibility' to its veterans. The newspaper was thinking in similar terms to the Ministry for Social Policy at this time; the article goes on to note how the huge losses sustained in fighting added an economic urgency to the matter, and that the state should put as many disabled veterans back to work as possible. See *Politika*, 11 September 1919.

11 Arhiv Jugoslavije (Archives of Yugoslavia, hereafter AJ), Belgrade, Fond 39 'Ministarstvo socijalne politike i narodnog zdravlja, 1919–41', fasc. 7.

12 Ibid.

13 See *Politika*, 7 September 1919. The article also notes how the library's collection included the classics of Serbian, Croatian, and Slovenian literature, although pride of place was given to Serbian epic poetry.

14 M. Isić, *Seljaštvo u Srbiji 1918–1925* (Belgrade: Zavod za udžbenike i nastavna sredstva, Institut za noviju istoriju Srbije, 1995), pp. 25–26. Cited in Lj. Petrović 'Diskriminacija invalida u Jugoslovenskom društvu 1918–41. godine. Oblici socijalne represije nad osobama sa invaliditetom', *Tokovi istorije*, 3–4, 2003, pp. 21–38. Disabled veterans were designated as Serbian soldiers since the Yugoslav kingdom was not recognized by all powers until June 1919. See A. Mitrović, 'The Yugoslav Question, the First World War, and the Peace Conference 1914–20', in D. Djokić (ed.), *Yugoslavism: Histories of a Failed Idea 1918–1992* (London: Hurst, 2003), pp. 42–56.

15 M. Mrvaljević, 'Naše invalidsko pitanje' in *Jubilarni zbornik života i rada Srba, Hrvata, i Slovenaca 1918–1928* (Belgrade: Izdanje Matice živih i mrtvih SHS, 1928). Disabled veterans are categorized exclusively by ethnic criteria, so 'Serbs' in this table are veterans of the Serbian, Montenegrin, and Habsburg armies.

16 See, for example, A. Prost, *In the Wake of the War: Les Anciens Combattants and French Society 1914–1939* (Oxford: Berg, 1992).

17 See N. Šehić, *Četništvo u Bosni i Hercegovini 1918–1941: Politička uloga i oblici djelatnosti četničkih udruženja* (Sarajevo: Akademija nauka i umjetnosti Bosne i Hercegovine, 1971).

18 The only other large veteran society to do so was the Union of Volunteers, formed by veterans who had served in South Slav volunteer divisions during the war, and which had branches throughout the Yugoslav kingdom.

19 *Ratni invalid* (Belgrade), 18 January 1925.

20 The American historian John Lampe has studied the nature and the repercussions of some of these mistakes. See his 'Unifying the Yugoslav Economy, 1918–21: Misery and Early

Misunderstandings' in D. Djordjević (ed.), *The Creation of Yugoslavia, 1914–1918* (Santa Barbara: Clio Books, 1980).

21 *Ratni invalid* (Belgrade), 6 April 1922.

22 Ibid., 30 April 1922.

23 *Ratni invalid* (Zagreb), 1 August 1922.

24 Ibid., 15 November 1922.

25 Ibid., 30 September 1922.

26 *Obzor*, 29 October 1922.

27 The protest outside the *ban*'s palace was reported in *Ratni invalid* (Zagreb), 1 April 1920. The wisdom behind this demonstration and that which was about to take place in Belgrade is explained in an article in the same newspaper, 30 November 1922.

28 See D. Djokić, *Elusive Compromise: a History of Interwar Yugoslavia* (London: Hurst, 2007), pp. 54–55.

29 *Ratni invalid* (Zagreb), 15 December 1922.

30 Ibid.

31 Hrvatski državni arhiv (Croatian State Archives, Zagreb, hereafter HDA), Pravila društava, Zagreb, 4684, 'Udruženje ratnih invalida na području Hrvatske, Slavonije, Istre, Međumurja'.

32 Ibid.

33 See, for example, J. Bourke, *Dismembering the Male: Men's Bodies, Britain, and the Great War* (London: Reaktion Books,1996); R. W. Whalen, *Bitter Wounds: German Victims of the Great War 1914–1939* (Ithaca: Cornell University Press, 1984); Prost, *In the Wake of the War*.

34 *Ratni invalid* (Belgrade) 24 October 1926.

35 And beyond, the author Dobrica Ćosić would revive the story of Serbia's Great War, *mutatis mutandis*, to great effect in his multivolume novel *A Time of Death*, first published in 1972. See N. Miller, *The Nonconformists: Culture, Politics, and Nationalism in a Serbian Intellectual Circle, 1944–1991* (Budapest and New York: Central European University Press, 2007).

36 HDA, Pravila društava, Zagreb, 4684, 'Udruženje ratnih invalida na području Hrvatske, Slavonije, Istre, Međumurja'.

37 HDA, fond 1363, 'Politička situacija', box 16.

38 Ibid.

39 AJ, Fond 39 'Ministarstvo socijalne politike i narodnog zdravlja, 1919–41', fasc. 7.

40 A number of leading Croatian newspapers were in favour of the move, in a significant turnaround from the support they had given the disabled veterans earlier. *Obzor* suggested that the needs of the city's poverty-stricken children outweighed those of the veterans. See *Obzor*, 4 September 1928.

41 See, for example, Whalen, *Bitter Wounds*.

42 J. Pavičić, in his preface to *Crvenim slovima* (Zagreb: Matica Hrvatska, 1946).

43 Pavičić, *Crvenim slovima*, pp. 5–6.

4 National Mobilization in the 1930s

The emergence of the 'Serb question' in the Kingdom of Yugoslavia

Dejan Djokić

In January 1940, two important public gatherings took place in Yugoslavia. Speakers at the first event, held on 14 January – incidentally, New Year's Day according to the Julian calendar, kept by the Serbian Orthodox Church – praised the Crown and the government and expressed their belief that the country was at last united and going in the right direction. Prince Regent Paul, Princess Olga and Prime Minister Cvetković were present and witnessed in person the support they enjoyed, at least in one part of the country. Tens of thousands supporters came to greet them, despite cold weather. Speakers at the second event, which took place 12 days later elsewhere in Yugoslavia, criticized the government for favouring certain groups at the expense of others and expressed their dissatisfaction with the way the Yugoslav state was evolving, fearing for its unity.

One might imagine that the first meeting was organized by Serbs and the second by Croats. Interwar Yugoslavia was a Serb-dominated state: constitutions were Serb-style centralist, the Serbian Karadjordjević monarchy ruled the country, all but one prime minister had been Serb, the army was Serb-dominated. The list goes on. Under these circumstances, Croats boycotted state institutions in the early 1920s and demanded an equal treatment with Serbs throughout the interwar period. Serbs, on the other hand, seemed content with Yugoslavia – or so goes the conventional wisdom, according to which the interwar period could be best understood in terms of struggle between Serb governments and Croat opposition.

However, would such a conclusion be a correct one? Was the pro-regime rally organized by Serbs? Did Croats convene the anti-government gathering? The answer to both questions would be 'no'. The first meeting took place in Zagreb under the auspices of the Croatian Peasant Party (HSS) – a *de facto* Croat national movement – on the occasion of the high delegation's visit to the capital of the newly autonomous Croatia. The second meeting took place in Brčko, present-day Bosnia, and was convened and attended by local Serb leaders and clergymen.

The commonly accepted interpretation of interwar Yugoslavia rests on many 'truths', but does not explain developments such as these. This chapter offers an analysis of the 'Serb question',[1] and, more broadly, challenges some perceived notions about the Yugoslav kingdom. It is important to stress that in interwar Yugoslavia non-Serbs had been subjected to Serb domination; not just Croats and Slovenes, but also, and especially, Macedonians (officially regarded as 'Southern Serbs'), ethnic Albanians and even Montenegrins, most of whom, regardless of their political affiliation, viewed themselves as members of a wider Serbian nation.[2] This chapter does not attempt to argue otherwise. Instead, it suggests that divisions also existed within ethnic groups and that there were Serbs who opposed the government and non-Serbs who participated in it. Specifically, the chapter looks at the neglected issue of Serb dissatisfaction with Yugoslavia in the second half of the 1930s.

Context

In order to understand the emergence of the Serb question and, more specifically, to contextualize the two events of January 1940, it is worth revisiting earlier developments. Conflicting visions of Yugoslavia among Serb and Croat political leaderships appeared even before the country was formed in December 1918 and led to the emergence of the Croat question soon after the unification. However, the conflict between mostly-Serb centralists and mostly-Croat and other non-Serb federalists was but one aspect of the political contest. Inter-party and even intra-party rivalries and alliances – regardless of ethnic affiliation – were just as important, as were intra-ethnic conflicts, especially among Serbs. Serb-Croat conflict was one important dimension of the political dynamics of the period – this chapter acknowledges that – but was not the only one. Rather than view the period as one of a constant struggle between Serbs and Croats, interwar years might be seen instead as an era when a series of attempts towards an agreement between Serbs and Croats were made.[3]

Contrary to what is sometimes argued, views of leading Serb and Croat politicians had not been fixed in mutual antagonism by 1918, but had evolved during the interwar period. For instance, Stjepan Radić, leader of the Croatian Peasant Party, advocated republicanism and boycott of the Belgrade parliament in the early 1920s, but in 1925 entered government of his chief rival Nikola Pašić, of the Radical Party, and praised King Alexander. Two years later Radić left the government to form the opposition Peasant Democratic Coalition, together with another former rival, Svetozar Pribićević, leader of the Independent Democrats. This was essentially a coalition between Croats and Croatian Serbs and it lasted longer than any other political alliance in Yugoslavia. Radić had also previously briefly collaborated with Ljuba Davidović of the Democratic Party (Pašić, Pribićević and Davidović all had been ethnic Serbs). Following Radić's assassination in summer 1928 by a Radical Party deputy, Yugoslavia's democratic institutions entered a final crisis. On 6 January 1929 King Alexander abolished the Constitution, the parliament and political parties, and introduced a dictatorship.

In the early 1930s the regime unsuccessfully sought to reach a compromise with the Croats. Belgrade wanted Vladko Maček, Radić's successor, to publicly support the government, and, preferably, join it, before any changes within the existing order should be considered. Maček's position, on the other hand, was that a separate Croat identity must be recognized first, by granting Croatia self-rule.

As neither side was prepared to back down, a united Serb-Croat opposition began to emerge in the early 1930s, despite the regime's intimidation of the opposition and arrest of Maček and Pribićević, among others. Moreover, mistrust and disagreements, especially among the main Serbian opposition parties – the Democrats, the Radicals (Aca Stanojević's opposition faction) and the Agrarians – slowed down the formation of a common opposition front. After the assassination of King Alexander in October 1934, by Croatian and Macedonian revolutionaries, the dictatorship was relaxed by Prince Regent Paul, who ruled in the name of Alexander's minor son, King Peter II. At the (quasi democratic) elections of May 1935, the Democrats and the Agrarians presented a joint list with the Peasant Democratic Coalition and the Yugoslav Muslim Organisation – the main Bosnian Muslim party. The list was headed by Maček and, although it failed to win the elections, the opposition did better than had been expected. This prompted Prince Paul to bring about a change of government and start negotiations with Maček. The new government included the Radicals' pro-regime faction, the Slovene Clericals (the major Slovenian party) and the Yugoslav Muslims, who would soon merge into a single party – the Yugoslav Radical Union (JRZ). However, Milan Stojadinović, the new Prime Minister, was unable and possibly unwilling to persuade the HSS to join the new party or the government. Maček met the Prince Regent on several occasions during this period, but their clandestine talks came to nothing.

After the failure of negotiations with the regime, the Croat leader turned again to the Serbian opposition, while maintaining contacts with the Royal Court. The cooperation between the Peasant Democratic Coalition and Serbia's United Opposition would reach its peak in 1937–38: the (opposition) Bloc of National Agreement was formed in October 1937, demanding a return to democracy and a solution to the Croat question; Maček visited Belgrade in August 1938 to be greeted by some 100,000 Serbian supporters; the Serb-Croat opposition led by Maček nearly defeated the (Serb-Slovene-Muslim) government in another quasi democratic election of December 1938. This Serb-Croat collaboration in opposition contributed to the fall of Stojadinović in February 1939, although the Yugoslav Radical Union remained the government party, now led by Dragiša Cvetković.

Eventually, Maček reached an agreement (*Sporazum*) with Prime Minister Cvetković and the Crown in August 1939, but this resulted in the end of the united democratic opposition. The agreement was based on a compromise: there was to be no return to democracy, but an autonomous Croatia was set up and the Peasant Democratic Coalition entered the government. Prince Paul was widely seen as the most responsible for Belgrade finally granting Croatia self-rule. It was no surprise that his first visit to autonomous Croatia in January 1940 provoked such excitement and public approval. 'It is thanks to your wisdom that you realised that the Kingdom of Yugoslavia could only be saved by granting the Croats their demands, and it is thanks to your courage that you acted like a real man by cutting the Gordian knot in a single blow', Maček told Paul in Zagreb, before continuing: 'It is for these reasons that the Croatian people welcomes you today with open arms and wishes you, through me, a happy stay [in Croatia]. Long live the Prince Regent, long live Princess Olga!'[4]

The visit was meant to show popular support for the Croatian Peasant Party, the government and the Crown, but there were also genuine signs that Yugoslavia faced a more stable future. Yet, a careful observer might have noticed that the main reason for the Croats' newly-found enthusiasm was undoubtedly partly due to the Croatian *banovina* (province) turning into a quasi nation-state. Maček welcomed the Prince Regent to 'the capital of Croatia and all Croats, in the name of all Croats'.[5] Civil servants and teachers were being replaced by the new authorities – not so much because they were predominantly Serbs, often from prewar Serbia, but because they were associated with the previous regime; their replacements were mainly Croats loyal to Maček. In the first two months of 1940 over 20 new associations had been registered on the territory of the *banovina*, most of them with the prefix 'Croatian'.[6] At the same time, attacks on organizations and individuals closely connected with the previous regime, whether they were Serb or Croat, intensified.

By the time of Prince Paul's visit to Zagreb, many Serbs from the Croatian *banovina* had joined in what had grown into a pan-Serb 'movement', encouraged, if not organized, by the Serbian Orthodox Church, nationalist intelligentsia and most 'Serb' political parties. The movement was unofficially known as 'Serbs, rally together!'. The Brčko meeting, referred to above, was an example of the pan-Serb (re)action to the Cvetković-Maček Agreement. However, even during this period, a homogenous Serbian front failed to materialize.

It would be wrong to suggest that the Serb question emerged simply as a response to Croat autonomy. The first major conflict between Serb nationalism and the Yugoslav state took place two years earlier, during the 'Concordat crisis' of summer 1937.

Church vs. state: the Concordat crisis

In July 1935, 13 years after they had first started negotiations, the Yugoslav government and the Vatican signed a Concordat regulating the position of the Roman Catholic Church in Yugoslavia.[7] The government hoped to attract Croat support at the expense of the HSS and saw the Concordat as a way of solving the Croatian question. As Prime Minister Stojadinović told the parliament in summer 1937: 'the Concordat means agreement. Who with, gentlemen? With the Holy See. Who does the Holy See represent? It represents 400 million [Roman] Catholics, 5 million of whom live in our state'.[8]

However, when the document was finally submitted to the parliament for ratification in July 1937 the government nearly fell. The Serbian Orthodox Church instantly objected that the Concordat was concluded at its expense. It argued that although there were more Orthodox than Roman Catholic believers in Yugoslavia, the latter were placed in a favourable position by the state.[9]

Street protests led by Orthodox priests broke out in Belgrade and other Serbian towns. Particularly violent was the so-called 'bloody procession' of 19 July, when a procession praying for Patriarch Varnava's health (he was seriously ill at the time) turned into anti-government demonstrations. Serbian churches displayed black flags, church bells tolled intermittently, while crowds shouted 'the police have killed our bishop!', when the news spread that one of the bishops leading the procession was taken to a Belgrade hospital after a gendarme hit his metal Episcopal crown and allegedly damaged his skull.[10] The bishop luckily did not die – it turned out he only received minor injuries – but other casualties were reported. The gendarmerie responded with violence, charging with bayonets and firing guns in the air. Stojadinović and Serbian members of the government were excommunicated by the Church. Shouts of *djavo* ('devil' in Serbo-Croat, a play on *'vodja'* (leader), as Stojadinović liked to be called) and *Jereza* (a nickname for the JRZ, which sounds similar to Serbo-Croat for 'heresy') suddenly gained additional meanings.[11]

The Patriarch died only hours after the Concordat was ratified on 23 July. Although rumours that he had been poisoned by the regime were unsubstantiated, even traditionally good relations between the Church and the Crown were strained. A royal emissary who had enquired about the Patriarch's health was told by Metropolitan Dositej that the Patriarch's death was imminent, and that it was unfortunate he was dying on the same night when the Concordat was being voted in. 'But God is just!', Dositej added, raising his voice.[12]

The rumours, as is often the case in interwar Yugoslavia, played a major role in turning the public against the government; the difference this time was that the public was predominantly Serbian. The funeral was attended by thousands of mourners, including representatives of the Crown – but not government – as well as representatives of Yugoslavia's Muslim leaders, the Bulgarian Orthodox Church, and Serbian opposition parties. The authorities banned a proclamation issued by the Serbian Church on the eve of the funeral, in which the Patriarch's death was compared to that of King Alexander: two great patriots who died for their cause, at the time they were most needed by their people.[13]

Despite the brutal police action, Stojadinović believed that in dealings with the crisis an even firmer position should be adopted. Foreign newspapers reporting on the crisis were either bought off by the government or simply returned unsold, while a long-serving Belgrade correspondent of the Reuters was no longer welcome in the country. The government allegedly also considered a clampdown on opposition leaders.[14]

The government was forced to back down due to public pressure, withdrawing the document from further parliamentary procedure in late July. Stojadinović explained that by signing the Concordat the government 'sought to secure religious harmony in western regions of our country'; however, under the circumstances, 'it would not be wise to disturb religious harmony in eastern regions of the country'.[15] Nevertheless, tensions remained high and clashes between the gendarmerie and opponents of the Concordat continued throughout the summer. One such incident took place on 15 August in Mladenovac, a small town south of Belgrade. When a crowd besieged the house of a local government deputy who had voted for the Concordat, the gendarmerie intervened brutally, killing two or three people (depending on the source) and wounding several.[16]

Seen in retrospect, the Concordat crisis was a prelude to the emergence of the Serbian question two years later. However, although the demonstrations were partly at least inspired by Serbian nationalism, many demonstrators simply wished to express their dissatisfaction with the government.[17] Meanwhile, the crisis did not undermine significantly the relationship between the Croat and Serb opposition. The Serbian parties kept a relatively low profile during the crisis, careful to not antagonize their partners in Zagreb. Maček, on his behalf, sent a message to his Serbian counterparts, stating that if the opposition succeeded in forming a new government, he would propose the Concordat to be taken off the agenda. 'We Croats do not need a Concordat, nor do the Serbs', Maček stated.[18] Maček was aware that Stojadinović's tactics were to win sympathies among the Croats and erode the support for the HSS. When Stojadinović mentioned, during their meeting in January 1937, that he intended to ratify the Concordat, Maček replied: 'I am not interested in that issue, but can tell you in advance: if you support the Concordat, I shall oppose it'.[19] Moreover, the Croat leader did not regard the Serb-Croat conflict as a religious one, and believed that religion had no place in politics. In an earlier statement, he explained that Croats were 'a Catholic, but not a clerical nation'.[20]

An autonomous Serbia?

After August 1939 it became clear that eventually the rest of the country would be further divided up according to ethnic criteria, reversing King Alexander-inspired internal division of October 1929 (see Map 2). The same day the Cvetković-Maček Agreement was concluded a ruling on implementing the Decree on the Formation of *banovina* of Croatia in relation to the rest of the country was also issued. It stated that the decree 'of 26 August 1939 could be extended to other *banovinas* by royal decrees. In such a case, *banovinas* could [either] unite, or their territories could [be subject to] changes'.[21] The extent of the autonomy of future *banovinas* would equal the level of autonomy of Croatia. However, it was unclear how many new *banovinas* there would be and where their boundaries should be drawn.

The potential for disagreement in regard to the territory of the future Slovene unit was minimal, since Dravska *banovina* was a de facto Slovenia. Soon after the creation of the *banovina* of Croatia, Slovene leader Anton Korošec suggested that a Slovene *banovina* be proclaimed, as well, and a special working group was formed within the government to discuss the proposal.[22] However, nothing came out of this initiative because Croats and Serbs regarded all other issues as secondary to the Serb-Croat question. If Dravska was turned into Slovenia, then how could the government continue to postpone the creation of a Serbian *banovina*, and would not the rest of the country automatically become *de facto* a greater Serbia? Maček always believed that Serbs and Croats formed the main axis in Yugoslavia. Therefore, sorting out their relations was of utmost importance; all other issues could wait, including the question of Slovenia.[23] Similarly, Serb members of the government wanted to wait for an agreement on the Serbian *banovina* first, before 'upgrading' Dravska, possibly at the same time. Cvetković complained that Slovenes' insistence on a Slovene *banovina* was nothing less than 'blackmail' and that the Slovene leaders 'did not have a [wider] feeling for the state'. The Croats got their *banovina*, the Slovenes *de facto* have had theirs in the form of Dravska since 1929, but 'what have the Serbs got?', Cvetković wondered.[24] The Slovenes, however, felt in the late 1930s that their loyalty to the state had not been rewarded properly. Slovene leaders were allegedly criticized by their voters, who complained that 'the Croats are against this state, and still they got everything, whereas we are loyal to the state but got nothing!'[25]

The key question was where to draw the borders of the Serbian *banovina*. Would it include the whole of Yugoslavia, minus Slovenia and Croatia? This seemed to be Cvetković's plan, and many Serbs, though not all, argued in favour of such an outcome. On 16 December 1939 Mihailo Konstantinović, a minister without portfolio, delivered to Prince Paul a 'project on the *banovina* of the Serbian lands'.[26] The entity would be created by the unification of Vrbaska, Drinska, Dunavska, Moravska, Zetska and Vardarska *banovinas* into a single province, the capital of which was to be Skopje (Belgrade would remain the capital of Yugoslavia); the former *banovinas* would enjoy a semi-autonomous status within Serbia.[27] The future Serbian entity would enjoy the same level of autonomy from the central government in Belgrade as Croatia, where, however, there was to be no regional, ethnic or religious autonomy, despite large numbers of Serbs and Muslims living there. Just like Croatia, autonomous Serbia would be in charge of its finances, justice, education and social policies, while the central government would be responsible for defence, customs and foreign policy.[28] It remains unclear whether the authors of the document envisaged the inclusion into a future Serbian *banovina* of those territories previously parts of Vrbaska, Zetska and Dunavska which since August 1939 had formed part of the *banovina* of Croatia.

Maček repeatedly stated that the boundaries of the Croatian *banovina* were temporary and that he was looking to add more territory. He used the opportunity of Prince Paul's visit to Zagreb in January 1940 to raise this question, but it is unclear what was Paul's response.[29] Maček may have been under pressure from more radical elements within his party and from the Frankist opposition to try and further extend Croatia's territory. The pro-Maček press argued that the *banovina* of Croatia should incorporate Bosnia and parts of Vojvodina, although Maček was personally apparently satisfied with the terms of the 1939 Agreement.[30]

It was the status of Bosnia-Herzegovina that posed another major problem. Up until 1929 Bosnia had been fictionally preserved within the Yugoslav 33 administrative units system, but borders of King Alexander's *banovinas* put an end to this. As the Yugoslav Muslim Organization began to demand autonomy for Bosnia in 1939, was there going to be a fourth, Bosnian *banovina*, as the Democrats' leader Ljuba Davidović proposed in 1933, and as the government considered briefly in 1939?[31] Most Croats and Serbs seemed to prefer a division of Bosnia among themselves. The Croats believed that the so-called 'Turkish Croatia' (most of Vrbaska) should be joined to the Croatian *banovina*. Although the area did not have a Croat majority, the Croat 'state right' argument was used to justify Croat demands, as well as economic and geographic factors. The Independent Democrats supported this view, but because they believed that a greater number of Serbs in Croatia would strengthen the position both of the Serb minority and of their main party. The Democrats, on the other hand, seemed prepared to offer autonomy to Bosnia. Davidović repeated his argument of early 1933 that a Bosnian province should act as a buffer between Serbs and Croats, possibly together with southern Dalmatia. At the same time, the Yugoslav Muslims started a campaign for a Bosnian *banovina* and the restoration of historic Bosnia.[32]

Meanwhile, many Serbs argued that Bosnia should be part of a future Serbian *banovina*. The Serb Cultural Club, whose representative in Banja Luka was Stevan Moljević,[33] was most radical in this respect – according to Moljević and his colleagues, Bosnia was undoubtedly a Serbian ethnic territory. The Croatian Peasant Party demanded that parts of Vojvodina should be added to the Croatian *banovina*, on the basis both of ethnic and historic rights. Vojvodina had been another bone of contention during the negotiations between Cvetković and Maček, but because it had played an important role in Serbian nineteenth century history, and also because of a large number of Serbs living there, all Serb parties and groups regarded it as part of a future Serbian *banovina*.[34]

Discussion about and calls for the creation of a Serb entity in the post-1939 Yugoslavia was not confined to political parties: local politicians, Orthodox clergy, 'ordinary people', as well as an increasingly nationalist intelligentsia joined the debate.

Pan-Serb movement

On 11 March 1940, Zagreb authorities requested all civilian and police officials to report about the "'Serbs, rally together'" movement, that is about the movement for the secession of [predominantly] Serbian districts from the territory of the Croatian *banovina*.[35] The Brčko gathering, referred to at the beginning of this chapter, was organized as part of the 'movement', which emerged across the *banovina* soon after August 1939. Serbian Orthodox priests were often among its leaders, petitioning for the secession of predominantly-Serb areas or areas they perceived as Serb from the Croatian *banovina*. Father Zdravko Borisavljević, a priest from the village of Vinjska, was a key speaker at the Brčko rally. He claimed that in the post-agreement Yugoslavia 'Serb freedom is forbidden, the Serb *gusle*[36] are forbidden, the Serbian song is forbidden, even in Belgrade, but not by Serbs. Serbs must fight against being insulted and against being a minority', arguing also that there was an economic discrimination against Serbs, who were allegedly paid less than non-Serbs in Croatia.[37]

Local politicians, merchants and other leading Serbs from Derventa, Brčko, Bosanski Šamac and Gradačac also spoke at the rally. Most speeches were similar in tone, although none so blatantly nationalist as Father Borisavljević's. The opening speech by Milorad Kostić outlined the complaints and demands of those Serbs who opposed the 1939 Agreement, as well as their position vis-à-vis Yugoslavia. Kostić explained that the main reason for the meeting was to discuss 'the question of saving Yugoslavia's unity and [creating] a strong Serbdom, because without a strong Serbdom there would be no [Yugoslav] state.'[38] Kostić argued that Prime Minister Cvetković was not the Serbs' legitimate representative, adding that Serbs were not against an agreement with Croats, because without it Yugoslavia could not survive, but they wanted an agreement which would ensure they were equal to Croats. Therefore, they should be united in a Serbian *banovina* which would include all areas of Bosnia populated by Serbs and by Muslims, because, according to Kostić, the latter were in fact Serbs.[39] 'Dr [Juraj] Krnjević [a Croat leader] called the Serbs a minority, but they cannot be that in their own state', Kostić said, before rejecting any possibility of autonomy for Bosnia: 'the Serbs [of Bosnia] fought for the unification with Serbia, so there cannot be an autonomous Bosnia'.[40]

Where the 'ethnic' argument could not apply, those who called for the secession of areas they regarded as 'Serb' employed 'historic' arguments. For example, some Serbs from the municipality of Mostar called for the secession of the region and its inclusion in the Serbian *banovina* on the basis of Herzegovina's apparent mediaeval Serbian past. 'As the sons of the Vojvodina of St. Sava, we demand the secession of the city of Mostar from the Croatian *banovina*', an unpublished resolution drafted by a group of Mostar Serbs stated.[41]

The pan-Serb movement spread beyond Bosnia-Herzegovina. For instance, Serbs from the Glina area south of Zagreb, led by two local priests and a teacher, issued in November 1939 a resolution calling for the secession of the region from Croatia. The following month they held another meeting, but this time issued a more moderate statement, demanding merely full equality with Croats.[42] Serbs from Knin, Benkovac, Obrovac and Šibenik also petitioned for the secession of predominantly Serb areas and their unification with the Vrbaska *banovina*.[43]

Although the movement was widespread, its supporters often had local goals. Thus, the Serbs from Vukovar had, ever since the creation of autonomous Croatia, demanded the transfer of their district to the jurisdiction of the Dunavska *banovina*. Their leader was Nikola Teodorović, a secondary school teacher and a leading member of the local branch of the government party.[44] However, the pan-Serb movement failed to attract a mass following in the area,[45] just like it eventually failed to attract mass support elsewhere.

In those areas where the Independent Democrats – as noted, a pre-dominantly Serb party – had significant support there had been less opposition to the Agreement and Serb-Croat relations tended to be significantly better. This was not surprising, as the party genuinely supported a Serb-Croat agreement and had, publicly at least, always stood by the Croatian Peasants. On the day Croatia became autonomous, the Independent Democrats' leadership issued a statement praising the Agreement, describing it as the 'crowning of our efforts'.[46] In areas dominated by the Independent Democrats, even local priests, generally among the most radical advocates of the Serb cause, supported the Agreement. This was the case in the central Bosnian town of Bugojno, where, according to a contemporary account:

> Relations between Croats and Serbs are very good, even cordial. The leader of the local Serbs, most of whom are supporters of the SDS [Independent Democratic Party], is a priest, Jovo Popović, who has established an honest and brotherly cooperation with [local] Croat representatives [...] so that their relationship is virtually ideal.[47]

The same account noted divisions among local Muslims. Some were pressurized into joining the Croatian Peasant Party, while others, members of the Yugoslav Radical Union, simply did not know where their allegiances belonged anymore. In any case, many hoped that Bosnia would achieve some form of autonomy, perhaps even its own *banovina*.[48]

After the initial wave of protests across Serb areas in *banovina* Croatia the situation calmed down. Once it became clear that the Serb movement had failed to change the situation significantly, it lost its appeal. Contemporary accounts note that after the busy autumn, by spring 1940 activities of the 'movement' decreased markedly.[49] Once the initial shock was over, many Serbs came to accept the new order. However, this did not mean that dissatisfaction among them went away – it was still there, but was not as visible as had been the case during the first few months following the Agreement.[50] One of the reasons was a more sensitive approach by the Croat authorities. Aware that the politically motivated change of civil servants and other personnel had gone too far, Croatian *ban* [governor] Ivan Šubašić sent a circular in June 1940 to all local civilian and police authorities ordering them to cease firing staff without good reason.[51]

The Croat leadership had done little to prevent the often indiscriminate removal of Serb personnel from the local administration, police and schools. For example, the replacement of a Serb teacher by a Croat colleague in Veliko Korenovo, a predominantly Serbian village near Bjelovar, a town east of Zagreb, was hard to justify. It caused a small rebellion among the population of the village, who occupied the school and refused to leave until their old teacher was reinstated. The villagers insisted they had nothing against the Croats in general nor against the new, Croat, teacher personally, but were only protesting 'against those few [Croats] who wanted to get rid of [Serb teacher] Bogojević for their own, *personal* and *material* reasons'.[52]

The official report on the incident concluded that the villagers' protest was justified and that it was hard to understand why Bogojević was removed. The authorities were eventually able to end the protest by promising to investigate the whole case properly.[53] Although the Bjelovar authorities tackled the crisis with tact and fairness, Bogojević's case caused enough damage and gave credence to the frequently heard calls for Serbs to unite in common action.

There were cases where Serbs initially did not oppose Croatian autonomy, but the new authorities' insensitive policies created Serb resentment. 'We accept *banovina* of Croatia, we support the agreement of 26 August 1939 and accept it as the basis of the future reorganisation of the [Yugoslav] state', claimed Serbs from the Benkovac district. 'We accept and welcome every word by the Croatian *ban* Dr Ivan Šubašić, but we cannot accept what the [...] HSS activists are doing on the ground'.[54]

The new Croat authorities made unsuccessful attempts to re-Croatianize the language,[55] introduce a separate currency (*kuna*) and even a coat-of-arms. Not only Serbs, but moderate members of the HSS opposed such suggestions.[56] Although none of these proposals were implemented in practice, rumours that they would be led to a rise in tensions among the Serbs, already ultra sensitive following the formation of autonomous Croatia.

Economic factors contributed to the dissatisfaction of ordinary Serbs, as well as Croats, with the new authorities. In Croatia, like in the rest of the country, small landowners formed the vast majority of the land-owning peasantry. The percentage of small landowners in Croat areas was even higher than in Serb areas of the country.[57] The peasants were heavily in debt: the percentage of owners of land smaller than 10 hectares who were in debt was over 93 per cent in Savska and as high as 97 per cent in Primorska (by comparison, in Dunavska it was 83.4 per cent and in Drinska 84 per cent). On top of the problem of debt, the price of food in Croatia rose by between 50 per cent (beef) and 100 per cent (flour, potato, beans) in the period between August 1939 and August 1940.[58]

Remarkably, the new authorities did little to address this problem. Although the Croatian Peasant Party was above all concerned with the national question, functioning more like a national movement than a political party, it had also based its campaign against Belgrade and local gentry on the argument that Croatia, with its predominantly peasant population, was economically exploited. So, it was highly ironic that when a group of Croat peasants forcibly entered Maček's farm at Kupinec in August 1940 in order to cut forest trees, Maček called upon the once hated gendarmerie to get rid of intruders, his own Peasant Defence having refused to intervene against the peasants.[59] Later that year, a public rally organized by Maček's party in Podgora was disrupted by dissatisfied peasants who complained that the party had promised that, once the Croatian question was solved, they would not have to pay tax and that the number of bureaucrats would be trimmed down, but that in reality '[we] are today hungry and don't have enough bread'.[60]

The economic crisis and the failure of the Croatian Peasant Party to deal with social issues unsurprisingly made people sympathetic to the Communists. Reports from the period particularly note growing 'communist action'.[61] Some however went over to the other extreme, joining the *ustašas* in the case of Croats, or various Serb groups that were united under the 'Serbs, rally together' banner in the Serbian case. The regime's brutal measures against political opponents could not halt the growing dissatisfaction with the governing party in Croatia.

The situation was additionally complicated by the governing Yugoslav Radical Union's support of and even direct involvement in the Serb movement. Although the party formed the backbone of the Cvetković-Maček government, many of its Serb members worked to undermine the Croatian *banovina*. Teodorović, the aforementioned leader of the Vukovar Serbs, who campaigned for the secession of the town from Croatia, was a member of the party with close links to its senior members.[62] The support to the Serb cause by the Yugoslav Radical Union, which often contradicted the 1939 Agreement, was not limited to local party officials. Even Cvetković himself apparently sponsored and gave editorial suggestions to a newspaper of the Croatian Serbs that openly criticized the agreement he reached with Maček.[63] One of the reasons for Cvetković's action could be his dissatisfaction with the way the Croat press close to Maček reported Yugoslav politics, and the Agreement in particular, insisting that it was only a 'first step' – leaving it open to interpretation what the next step would be for Croatia.[64]

The rivalry between 'Serb' parties for leadership among Serbs, which intensified after the Agreement, was not limited to those parties participating in the government. Božidar Vlajić, a leading Democrat, believed that his party was best suited to unite the Serbs. At the time of Prince Paul's visit to Zagreb in January 1940, Vlajić conceded that gathering the Serbs in a united front was 'outside the scope of regular party business', but necessary under the circumstances. Vlajić suggested that the Democrats may be best suited for such a job, given their record in working toward 'the solution to our state problem in the form of a representative government and the agreement between the Serbian people and Croatian people'.[65]

The Serb Cultural Club

Serb dissatisfaction with the post-1939 order was due to several reasons, insensitive policies on behalf of new local (predominantly Croat) authorities, lack of legitimacy of the Cvetković-Maček government, and social-economic factors chief among them. As argued in the *Srpski glas* (*Serbian Voice*), the organ of the Serb Cultural Club (SKK) published in Belgrade, Serb dissatisfaction was not simply invented from above. While acknowledging that there were certain Serb advocates who were not well qualified to represent Serbian interests, the author of the article argued that 'those who think that the present mood among Serbs is an artificial product of the propaganda' are seriously mistaken.[66] However, Serb nationalism, not only of the type propagated by the Serbian Orthodox Church, played a significant role, too. Nobody represented this nationalism better than a group of intellectuals gathered around the SKK.

The SKK was registered in Belgrade in early 1937 (six months before the Concordat crisis and two and a half years before the *Sporazum*).[67] Its members included leading Belgrade intellectuals, such as Slobodan Jovanović. Initially its activities were mostly cultural, but this changed following the Agreement, when the Club's branches sprung up across the Serb-populated areas of Croatia, Bosnia and Vojvodina. At this time the Club's main, if not sole, aim was to define and defend Serbian interests in Yugoslavia. This 'think tank' of the Serbian intellectual and professional élite sought to overcome party divisions among Serbs and probably came closest to representing the pan-Serb cause in the late 1930s.[68]

The first issue of the *Srpski glas*, edited by the sometime left-wing writer Dragiša Vasić,[69] came out on 16 November 1939 and the last on 13 June 1940, when it was banned by the authorities, for its criticism of the Agreement.[70] While stating that it was not opposed to an agreement between Serbs and Croats, 'which has always been necessary', the newspaper criticized the Cvetković-Maček agreement for endangering the state unity and for being incomplete; it claimed that, unlike the Croats, the Serbs were not properly represented in the government. Moreover, the paper called on all 'Serb' parties to halt inter-party rivalry, for which 'there was a place in prewar Serbia, and which may have its place in a [future] separate Serbian unit, if Yugoslavia is eventually turned into a federation, but such rivalry does not have a place at the moment when the question of Serb-Croat relations is raised'.[71]

The newspaper argued that just like the Croats, who approach politics from a national point of view, the Serbs should agree on a single national programme, which may be possible without all the parties uniting into a single one.[72] This was not far from Maček's view that the Serbs, like the Croats, should have a single party or leader who would represent their interests. While the Croat press had often in the past accused the monarchy, the army and the government of being 'Serb', none of them had actually represented Serbs, certainly not the same way the Croatian Peasant Party represented Croats, as Maček was well aware.

The SKK rejected King Alexander's integral Yugoslavism, calling instead for Serb unity and a return to old 'Serbian' values – the same values which had apparently characterized the Serb nation before Yugoslavia had been formed. The editors of *Srpski glas* argued:

> Recently, one can hear from different sides the slogan 'Serbs, rally together'. We too believe that Serbs should rally together, but we hasten to add that merely rallying together is not going to be enough unless at the same time the old spirit does not wake up inside the Serbs, the same spirit which used to inspire their strength and greatness in the past, that same faith in the national ideals and that same manly decisiveness to sacrifice everything else for the sake of those ideals. What we need today is a moral revival. Within its limited powers, our paper will serve that revival.[73]

Despite an increasingly Serb nationalist discourse, the SKK did not reject Yugoslavia as a state. Its members argued that Yugoslavia could only be strong if 'Serbdom' was strong, not weak and divided. Indeed, the motto of *Srpski glas* was 'Strong Serbdom – strong Yugoslavia'.[74] Slobodan Jovanović, the Club's chairman, argued in an article published in the newspaper that Serbs had a twofold role in post-1939 Yugoslavia: to defend Serbian interests, but also to make sure that the central government functioned and that Yugoslavia became stronger not weaker.[75] In the same article, he also argued that Yugoslavism was not incompatible with Serbian and Croatian nationalisms. He saw Yugoslavism as a *state* idea, whereas Serbianism and Croatianism were *national* ideas.[76] Jovanović believed that Serbs and Croats should revert to the original Yugoslavism of the Illyrians, which was a reaction against a threat from an external enemy (Hungarians). According to him, Yugoslavia should be based on the self-interest of Serbs and Croats to live in a common state, which would best protect them from their neighbours and bigger powers.[77] Again, this was not unlike Maček's own view of Yugoslavia – a union of close, but separate peoples, not a Yugoslav nation-state.

Yet, even in the post-agreement atmosphere, when the Serbian question virtually replaced the Croatian one, the position *Srpski glas* took – another article began with 'It is time for a pure Serbian voice to be heard'[78] – provoked strong criticism from a number of prominent Serbs. The paper started a polemic with a rival publication *Napred (Forward)*, published by a group of Serbian federalists led by Mihailo Ilić, a constitutional expert who helped draft the Decree for the Formation of the *banovina* of Croatia and a vocal proponent of federalism. Arguing that most Yugoslavs – but particularly Serbs – did not understand the real meaning and advantages of federalism, the group around Ilić compared the situation in Yugoslavia to the one in the United States in 1787, when leading thinkers debated the federation and explained its meaning to the public.[79] Aware that most Serbs probably feared that the federalization would weaken the state unity and could even lead to disintegration, the editors of *Napred* argued that,

Conscious of all political, national and cultural components [that have formed] our country and [as] defenders of their rights and aspirations, we remain supportive of a single and strong state [...] which would preserve and encourage all different [identities]. We have always been, like the old *Federalist* once was in America, for this form [of state, i.e. federation], because it means a desire for unity of all those groups which do not want and cannot accept unitarism. Because now, as then [in 1787], 'federalism means a true unity and leads to a more complete national harmony', as [Alexander] Hamilton said.[80]

It was not just the Serbian federalist intellectuals around the *Napred* paper who opposed the SKK. For instance, Dragoljub Jovanović, one of the opposition leaders who had campaigned for an agreement with the Croats throughout the 1930s and who spent time in prison for criticizing the regime, argued with his former mentor and surname-sake Slobodan Jovanović over the post-1939 developments. Slobodan believed the Serbs made a mistake by not making any concessions to Croats for so long, but then conceded too much in 1939. He also complained that Croats looked down on Serbs as inferior. Dragoljub disagreed, telling the old professor: 'You are a great Serb, but you must not become a Greater Serb'. One of Dragoljub's younger party colleagues, who had studied in Paris where he met Julien Benda, published a pamphlet accusing Slobodan Jovanović of 'intellectual treason'.[81]

Conclusion

This chapter has offered a brief analysis of the Serb question which escalated following the creation of an autonomous Croatia in 1939, but had already emerged several years earlier. It became apparent from the mid-1930s that the Serbian Orthodox Church and members of intelligentsia were increasingly frustrated with developments in Yugoslavia. After the 1939 Agreement many Serbs – both those living in Croatia and those in the rest of Yugoslavia – sought to 'rally together' all their compatriots in an autonomous Serbian unit, while the Slovenes and Bosnian Muslims called for the creation of their own *banovinas*. By the tenth anniversary of the 1929 dictatorship, King Alexander's integral Yugoslavism was all but abandoned, even by many Serbs, normally seen as inherently integralist.

Three factors led to the escalation of the Serb question in the aftermath of the Cvetković-Maček agreement. Firstly, a large number of Serbs were included within the boundaries of the *banovina* of Croatia. Secondly, what started on 26 August 1939 was most likely the federalization of the country, which to many Serbs amounted to a prelude to disintegration. Thirdly, the agreement marked the *de facto* end of integral Yugoslavism. It is usually overlooked that not all Serbs embraced King Alexander's integralist ideology, not to mention the Serb parties' opposition to the royal dictatorship. However, the Serbs, as the largest and geographically the most scattered Yugoslav 'tribe', were generally happier than other Yugoslavs to live in a centralized state in which only one, Yugoslav, nation officially existed. With the abandonment of integral Yugoslavism, the question of a Serb identity within Yugoslavia arose. (It may be argued that the problem exists in present-day, post-Yugoslav Serbia.)

If the solution of the Croat question led to the opening-up of the Serbian one, and put an end to the democratization of the country, the beginning of federalization promised to bring long-term stability. By the late 1930s a decentralized state became acceptable to many Serbs, not only to non-Serbs. When Yugoslavia re-emerged in 1945, it was as a federation, albeit a non-democratic one. The South Slav state had never been a democratic federation in some 70 years of its existence, so it will never be known whether such form of government would have led to stability and ultimately to the preservation of the common state. However, it is probable that had the Yugoslav kingdom not been formed along such strict centralist lines, the interwar period may have been less volatile. If the enthusiastic reception in Zagreb, described at the beginning of the chapter, had taken place 20 years earlier, it is possible that things would have been different. Without the Croat question, the Serb question might not have emerged either. The South Slav state might not have survived the Axis' assault in 1941 in any scenario, but with a more harmonious interwar period, the Second World War in Yugoslavia may not have been so violent.

Notes

1 Terms such as 'Serb question' and 'Croat question' were used widely at the time, to refer to what may be described as a complex set of national and socio-economic issues and aspirations.

2 Bosnian Muslims' confessional autonomy was recognized, but many Croats and Serbs regarded them as Islamized members of their own 'tribe'. The classic, still unmatched study of various national questions in early twentieth century Yugoslavia, that is particularly good on Albanians, Macedonians and Montenegrins, is I. Banac, *The National Question in Yugoslavia: Origins, History, Politics* (Ithaca, NY: Cornell University Press, 1984). Another important work on the national question is A. Djilas, *The Contested Country: Yugoslav Unity and Communist Revolution, 1919–1953*, 2nd ed. (Cambridge, MA: Harvard University Press, 1996).

3 See my book *Elusive Compromise: A History of Interwar Yugoslavia* (London: Hurst and New York: Columbia University Press, 2007). The present work draws on Chapters 5 and 6 of the book.

4 'Zagreb je svečano i oduševljeno dočekao Nj. Kr. Vis. Kneza Namesnika i Kneginju Olgu', *Politika*, 15 January 1940.

5 Ibid.

6 Croatian State Archives, Zagreb (hereafter HDA) XXI/87/6021, Izvještaj o poslovanju za I tromjesečje 1940. i o političkim prilikama i dogadjajima u istom tromjesečju. Redarstveno ravnateljstvo, Zagreb, banskoj vlasti banovine Hrvatske, Odjeljenju za unutarnje poslove, Odjelku za državnu zaštitu u Zagrebu, Zagreb, 4 April 1940. New societies registered during the period included: The Croatian Football Association, The Association of Croatian Mountaineering Societies, The Croatian Table Tennis Association, The First Croatian Association of Newspaper Salesmen, The Assocation of Croatian Teachers' Societies, The

Croatian Library Association, The Association of Croatian Dance Teachers and the Croatian Association of Restaurant-owners.

7 Archives of Yugoslavia, Belgrade (hereafter AJ) 37/25/195, 'Projekt zakona o Konkordatu izmedju Sv. Stolice i Kraljevine Jugoslavije', Belgrade, 20 July 1937.

8 AJ 37/2/9–11, draft of Stojadinović's speech to parliament, [Belgrade], 23 July 1937.

9 For details, see *Primedbe i prigovori na projekat Konkordata izmedju naše države i Vatikana* (Sremski Karlovci: Patrijaršiska štampa, 1936). The Concordat crisis received significant attention in Britain, where some leading members of the Anglican Church sided with the Serbian Orthodox Church. See Nugent Lincoln's [The Bishop of Lincoln] letter to the editor, *The Times*, 7 July 1937.

10 'Black Flags in Yugoslavia: Concordat Bill Protests', *The Times*, 21 July 1937.

11 See D. Djokić, '"Leader" or "Devil"? The Ideology of Milan Stojadinović, the Prime Minister of Yugoslavia (1935–39)', in R. Haynes (ed.), *In the Shadow of Hitler: Personalities of the Right in Central-East Europe* (London: I.B. Tauris, forthcoming).

12 Bachmeteff Archives, Columbia University, New York, Papers of Prince Paul (hereafter BAR PPP), box 12, Vojislav Jovanović to Prince Paul, Belgrade, 23 July 1937.

13 'Angered Church in Yugoslavia: Funeral To-Day of Patriarch', *The Times*, 29 July 1937. Some leaders of the Islamic community in Yugoslavia openly sided with the Serbian Orthodox Church over the Concordat issue.

14 Hoover Institution Archives, Stanford University (hereafter HIA), Dragiša Cvetković Collection, Prince Paul folder, Stojadinović to Prince Paul, Belgrade, 18 August 1937; *The Times*, 'Church and Cabinet in Yugoslavia', 5 August 1937, 'Processions Banned in Yugoslavia: Journalist to Leave', 22 July 1937, and 'Alarmist rumours in Yugoslavia', 16 August 1937.

15 AJ 37/2/9–11, draft of Stojadinović's speech to the parliament, [Belgrade], July 1937. Stojadinović claimed that throughout the crisis he had full support from Archbishop Bauer and Archbishop-Coadjutor Stepinac. HIA, Dragiša Cvetković Collection, Prince Paul folder, Stojadinović to Prince Paul, Bled, 26 August 1937.

16 'Alarmist rumours in Yugoslavia', *The Times*, 16 August 1937.

17 M. Djilas, *Memoir of a Revolutionary* (New York: Harcourt Brace Jovanovich, 1973), p. 306.

18 M. Radojević, *Udružena Opozicija, 1934–39* (Belgrade: INIS, 1994), p. 176.

19 M. Stojadinović, *Ni rat, ni pakt: Jugoslavija izmedju dva rata* (Rijeka: Otokar Keršovani, 1970), p. 517.

20 V. Maček, 'Hrvati su katolički, ali ne klerikalni narod', *Vodja govori: Ličnost, izjave, govori i politički rad vodje Hrvata Dra. Vladka Mačeka* (Zagreb: Narodne Novine, 1940), pp. 243–44.

21 Lj. Boban, *Maček i politika Hrvatske seljačke stranke. Iz povijesti hrvatskog pitanja, 1918–1941*, 2 volumes (Zagreb: Liber, 1974), vol. 2, p. 227.

22 Boban, *Maček i politika HSS*, vol. 2, p. 231; M. Konstantinović, *Politika sporazuma. Dnevničke beleške 1939–1941; Londonske beleške 1944–1945* (Novi Sad: Mir, 1998), pp. 49–50.

23 Lj. Boban, *Sporazum Cvetković-Maček* (Belgrade: Institut društvenih nauka – Odeljenje za istorijske nauke, 1965), p. 262.

24 Konstantinović, *Politika Sporazuma*, p. 50.

25 Ibid., pp. 49, 51.

26 Ibid., p. 83. Historian Ljubo Boban published in 1965 a virtually identical document (Boban, *Sporazum*, pp. 412–18). Boban acquired the document from Vaso Čubrilović, also a historian and the younger brother of Branko, a minister in the Cvetković-Maček government. Vaso Čubrilović claimed he was given the document by Cvetković personally in 1943.

27 Skopje – or Skoplje in Serbian – was the capital of the medieval Serbian empire, designated as the future capital of the Serbian *banovina* most probably in order to emphasize the apparently Serbian character of 'south Serbia', although virtually no Serbs lived in the area.

28 Boban, *Sporazum*, pp. 412–18.

29 Boban, *Maček i politika HSS*, vol. 2, p. 158. Unfortunately Prince Paul's personal diary does not shed any light on this issue.

National Mobilization in the 1930s 79

30 M. Jovanović Stoimirović, *Dnevnik*, 1936–1941 (Novi Sad: Matica srpska, 2000), p. 323.
31 BAR PPP, box 2, Cvetković to Prince Paul, Belgrade, 2 May 1939. See also Konstantinović, *Politika sporazuma*, pp. 516–18.
32 See M. Radojević, 'Bosna i Hercegovina u raspravama o državnom uredjenju Kraljevine (SHS) Jugoslavije 1918–41. godine', *Istorija XX veka*, no. 1, 1994, pp. 7–41.
33 During the Second World War an advisor to the *četnik* leader Mihailović.
34 See M. Radojević, 'Srpsko-hrvatski spor oko Vojvodine 1918–41', *Istorija XX veka*, no. 2, 1996, pp. 39–73.
35 HDA XXI/89/6129, Naredba svim sreskim načelstvima, ispostavama, gradskim redarstvima i redarstvenim ravnateljstvima od banske vlasti banovine Hrvatske, Zagreb, 11 March 1940.
36 A single-stringed instrument traditionally played by Serbs, Montenegrins, and Croats and Muslims from the Dinaric regions of the former Yugoslavia.
37 HDA XXI/89/6129, Sresko načelstvo u Brčkom, banskoj vlasti banovine Hrvatske, Otsjek [sic] za državnu zaštitu, Brčko, 26 January 1940.
38 Ibid.
39 Ibid.
40 Ibid. Kostić conveniently ignored the fact that many Bosnian – and Croatian – Serbs fought against Serbia as soldiers in the Habsburg army. The argument that Serbs could not be a minority in Yugoslavia reemerged in the late 1980s and early 1990s.
41 HDA XXI/89/6129, Sresko načelstvo u Mostaru, banskoj vlasti banovine Hrvatske, Odjeljak za državnu zaštitu, Predmet: Pokret 'Srbi na okup', Mostar, 16 March 1940. Herzegovina means Duchy ('Vojvodina' in Serbo-Croat). The whole region – Herzegovina – was named after a fifteenth century Duke (*Herzog* in German), who assumed the title the Duke of St. Sava. Duke Stefan Vukšić Kosača is also 'claimed' by some Croats, who call him Stjepan Vukčić Kosača. Duke in Serbo-Croat is *vojvoda*, so Vojvodina and Herzegovina both mean a duchy. St. Sava (Rastko Nemanjić [ca.1175–1235] was the founder of the Serbian Orthodox Church).
42 HDA XXI/89/6129, Sreski načelnik u Petrinji banskoj vlasti banovine Hrvatske, Odjeljak za državnu zaštitu, Predmet: Pokret 'Srbi na okup'[,] otcepljenje i odvajanje pojedinih srezova sa područja banovine Hrvatske, Petrinja, 13 March 1940. Glina was the site of the infamous 'church massacre' of August 1941, when the *ustašas* gathered a large group of Serbs inside an Orthodox church and massacred them. The whole region around Lika and Knin witnessed some of the worst fighting in the Second World War and was also one of the areas where the Yugoslav war of the 1990s began.
43 HDA XXI/85/5784, Primorski žandarmeriski puk, Komandantu žandarmeriske brigade banovine Hrvatske, Split, 12 December 1939.
44 HDA XXI/89/6129, Sresko načelstvo u Vukovaru banskoj vlasti banovine Hrvatske, Odjelu za unutarnje poslove (Za odjeljak za državnu zaštitu) u Zagrebu, Predmet: Vukovar srez, političke prilike, Vukovar, 2 January 1940. Vukovar, with its mixed Croat-Serb population, was the site of one of the most brutal conflicts in former Yugoslavia in the 1990s.
45 Ibid.
46 I. Jelić, 'O nekim odjecima sporazuma Cvetković-Maček medju Srbima u banovini Hrvatskoj', *Historijski zbornik Slavonije*, vol. 3, 1965, p. 153.
47 HDA XXI/87/5979, Načelstvo sreza Bugojnskog, mjesečni izvještaj o javnoj sigurnosti i političkoj situaciji za mjesec prosinac 1939. g., Bugojno, 6 January 1940.
48 Ibid.
49 HDA XXI/89/6129, Predmet: Ocjepljenje [sic] i odvajanje pojednih [sic] srezova od banovine Hrvatske u vezi sa pokretom 'Srbi na okup', Zagreb, 13 April 1940.
50 Ibid.
51 HDA XXI/88/6053, Ban Šubašić Ispostavi banske vlasti Split, Redarstvenim ravnateljstvima, Zagreb, Split, svim sreskim načelstvima, etc., Zagreb, 7 June 1940.
52 HDA XXI/88/6048, Sresko načelstvo Bjelovar, banskoj vlasti banovine Hrvatske, Odjeljku za državnu zaštitu, Bjelovar, 2 March 1940. Emphasis added.
53 Ibid.

54 HDA XXI/89/6129, Načelstvo sreza benkovačkog, banska vlast, odjeljak za državnu zaštitu, Predmet: Pokret 'Srbi na okup' [,] otcepljenje i odvajanje pojediniih sreza [sic!] sa područja banovine Hrvatske, Benkovac, 16 March 1940.

55 Or, to de-Serbianize, or de-Yugoslavize it. I am grateful to Professor Sarah Kent for making this suggestion. Professor Kent's comments, Book panel: D. Djokić, *Elusive Compromise: A History of Interwar Yugoslavia* (2007), Association for the Study of Nationalities Convention, Columbia University, New York, 24 April 2009.

56 Jovanović Stoimirović, *Dnevnik*, pp. 314–15; Konstantinović, *Politika sporazuma*, pp. 105, 170. *Kuna* was the currency of the Independent State of Croatia (NDH) during the Second World War and is Croatia's currency today. When it was re-introduced in the early 1990s (following an earlier adoption of the old Croatian chequerboard flag, used in the NDH, but also long before), by the then government of Franjo Tudjman, it led to strong Serb objections.

57 In Savska land under 5 hectares formed 75.9 per cent of all land, while in Primorska it was as high as 86.5 per cent. By comparison, in Moravska it was 64.2 per cent and in Dunavska 62.8 per cent. Lj. Boban, 'O političkim previranjima na selu u banovini Hrvatskoj', *Istorija XX veka: Zbornik radova*, vol. 2, Belgrade, 1961, p. 227.

58 Ibid., pp. 227–31.

59 Ibid., pp. 238–39.

60 Ibid., p. 250.

61 For instance HDA XXI/87/6021, Redarstveno ravnateljstvo Zagreb, banskoj vlasti banovine Hrvatske, Izvještaj o poslovanju za I tromjesečje 1940 i o političkim prilikama i dogadjajima u istom tromjesečju, Zagreb, 4 April 1940.

62 HDA XXI/89/6129, Sresko načelstvo u Vukovaru banskoj vlasti banovine Hrvatske, Odjelu za unutarnje poslove (Za odjeljak za državnu zaštitu) u Zagrebu, Predmet: Vukovar srez, političke prilike, Vukovar, 2 January 1940.

63 Konstantinović, *Politika sporazuma*, p. 104.

64 Ibid., p. 171.

65 *Politika*, 14 January 1940.

66 S. M. D. [Slobodan M. Drašković], '"Velikosrpstvo"', *Srpski glas*, no. 3, 30 November 1939.

67 For its history and activities see Lj. Dimić, *Kulturna politika Kraljevine Jugoslavije*, Belgrade: Stubovi kulture, 1996–97, 3 vols., vol. 1, pp. 507–61, and N. A. Popović, 'Srpski kulturni klub (1937–41)', *Istorija XX veka*, vol. VII, no. 1–2, 1989, pp. 109–40.

68 St. K. Pavlowitch, *Serbia: The History behind the Name*, London, 2002, p. 134.

69 Like the lawyer Moljević, Vasić would eventually become a close collaborator of General Mihailović during the Second World War.

70 M. Jovičić, 'Reč unapred', in *'Jako srpstvo-jaka Jugoslavija'. Izbor članaka iz 'Srpskog glasa', organa Srpskog kulturnog kluba 1939–1940* (Belgrade: Naučna knjiga, 1991), p. 5.

71 Editorial, *Srpski glas*, no. 1, 16 November 1939.

72 Ibid.

73 Ibid.

74 Similar arguments could be heard in the 1980s, during the revival of Serbian nationalism in the last decade of socialist Yugoslavia.

75 S. Jovanović, 'Jugoslovenska misao', *Srpski glas*, no. 8, 4 January 1940. For Jovanović's wartime political career and his views on the 1939 *Sporazum* see St. K. Pavlowitch's chapter in this volume.

76 Ibid. It is unclear whether Jovanović believed that state idea was possible without 'state nation' (*Staatsvolk*). I thank Dr Aleksa Djilas for pointing out to me this apparent contradiction in Jovanović's argument.

77 Ibid. See also A. Pavković, *Slobodan Jovanović: An Unsentimental Approach to Politics*, (Boulder, Co. and New York: East European Monographs, distributed by Columbia University Press, 1993), pp. 199–204.

78 [Ed.], 'Naša reč', *Srpski glas*, no. 1, 16 November 1939.

79 [Mihailo Ilić], 'Smisao i zadaci federacije', *Napred*, 28 October 1939.

80 Ibid. Hamilton, together with James Madison and John Jay, was the editor of *The Federalist*, and one of the authors of the US Constitution (the *Napred* article also refers to Madison and Jay). For more on the views of the *Napred* group see also [Mihailo Ilić], 'Federacija, nacija i nacionalizam', *Napred*, 13 December 1939.

81 For details see Djokić, *Elusive Compromise*, pp. 253–58.

5 Ethnic Violence in Occupied Yugoslavia

Mass killing from above and below

Tomislav Dulić

Following the failed attempt to co-opt Yugoslavia into joining the Tripartite Pact, German, Italian, Bulgarian and Hungarian forces invaded the country on 6 April 1941. Within a matter of days, the Axis forces succeeded in destroying the main parts of the Yugoslav Army. On 18 April, the Yugoslav government capitulated. In the period that followed, Nazi Germany annexed the northern part of Slovenia, while the southern part of Slovenia together with Dalmatia and the Bay of Kotor were annexed by Italy (see Map 3). Hungary received Bačka and Medjimurje in northern Croatia, Bulgaria occupied parts of Serbia and the bulk of Macedonian territory, while Kosovo south of Mitrovica and parts of western Macedonia were attached to Italian-dominated Albania. Montenegro was placed under Italian administration, while the rest of Serbia including the Banat was occupied by Germany. However, the dismemberment of the country had already started before the Axis victory. On 10 April, the Independent State of Croatia (*Nezavisna Država Hrvatska*, NDH) was proclaimed in Zagreb; it comprised the rest of Croatia, Bosnia-Herzegovina and parts of present-day northwestern Serbia.

Following the establishment of the NDH, the *ustašas* (who at the time had a following of a mere few hundred) and their *Poglavnik* (Leader) Ante Pavelić immediately embarked on an ambitious state-building scheme that aimed at achieving an ethnic homogenization of state territory. This was to be done through physical annihilation of Jews and Roma, as well as by removing all traces of Serbian presence through mass killing, deportations to Serbia proper and forced conversions to Catholicism. However, the terror soon provoked spontaneous rebellions that gradually merged with either Josip Broz Tito's People's Liberation Movement (*Narodnooslobodilački pokret*, NOP) or Draža Mihailović's Yugoslav Army in the Fatherland (*Jugoslovenska vojska u otadžbini*, JVUO).[1]

This analysis will not pay much attention to the NOP, since the primary aim is to provide some insights into how the ethnically motivated mass killings[2] perpetrated by *ustaša* and *četnik* forces were organized by the leaderships and then implemented on the ground. For this purpose, I will compare the *ustaša* and *četnik* campaigns to Raul Hilberg's model of a 'modern' destruction process. He has argued that all campaigns of systematic mass murder consist of three 'organic' steps, which are essential for group destruction to be effective. These include a) defining the group to be annihilated, b) concentrating (or seizing) members of the group and c) annihilating them through mass murder. A 'modern' destruction process differs from a pre-modern one in the respect that it contains three sub-steps that follow each of the 'generic' phases and 'are required not for the annihilation of the victim but for the preservation of the economy'.[3] The sub-steps include a) dispossessions, removals from work-places and nationalization of property following definition, b) starvation measures and forced labour following concentration and finally c) confiscation of personal effects following death. Following the analysis of the destruction processes 'from above' the article shifts focus to the local mechanisms of violence, with a particular emphasis on the behaviour of perpetrators, victims and non-participating members of the perpetrators' respective in-groups sometimes referred to as 'bystanders'. For reasons of space and since the JVUO did not have any concentration camps, emphasis will remain on the mobile killing operations, and the very specific dynamics that developed in Jasenovac and other camps will largely be left out, as well as the counter-insurgency killings that occurred in response to partisan attacks on Axis forces.

Disposession, deportation and mass killing 'from above'

Within a fortnight of the establishment of the NDH, the *ustašas* adopted racial laws that were modeled on the Nürnberg Laws in Nazi Germany and targeted the Jewish and Roma communities. Soon, however, the persecution of Roma sparked protests in Bosnia and Herzegovina. The reason was that many Roma had assimilated with the Muslims (today's Bosniaks), which led to confusion as to why Muslims were attacked when officially they were an integral part of the Croatian nation. In August 1941, the authorities in Zagreb therefore decided to exempt the settled Roma (as opposed to the itinerant group that travelled or lived in settlements called *čerge*) from racial persecution since they had become 'Croatianized'.[4]

The *ustaša* policy vis-á-vis the Serbs differed in a fundamental way from the measures undertaken against the Jews and Roma, since the Serbs were not subjected to the racial laws and could – frequently in theory only – escape death by converting to Catholicism. Instead, they found themselves at the mercy of a xenophobic ideology that described them as a mortal threat to the Croatian nation, embodied in a 'Serbdom' characterized by 'Byzantinism', 'easterness' and a 'specific soul' that was incapable of productive work.[5] In late May 1941, Foreign Minister Mladen Lorković declared that,

> the Croatian nation needs to be cleansed from all the elements which are a misfortune for that nation, who are alien and foreign in that nation, who melt down the healthy strength of that nation, who for decades have been pushing that nation from one disaster to another. Those [elements] are our Serbs and Jews.[6]

Even if 'easterness' was considered a very negative trait, the *ustašas* had an ambivalent attitude towards the East. This is illustrated by the fact that on the one hand they emphasized the role of the Croats as the *Antemurale Christianitatis* of Europe,[7] while at the same time arguing that the Muslims of Bosnia and Herzegovina were the 'flower of the Croatian nation', since they were considered to be descendants of the Croatian nobility that had converted to Islam in the late Middle Ages.[8] This somewhat inconsistent reasoning was necessary, because it provided the *ustašas* with a demographic argument for the inclusion of Bosnia-Herzegovina into the NDH.

For the Serbs, however, there was no place in the NDH, as became clear very early on from statements such as those by a leading *ustaša* Viktor Gutić. In April 1941, Gutić received the task of 'liquidating' 'former Vrbaska *banovina*' [see Map 2], since Pavelić contemplated moving the capital of the NDH to Banja Luka. After a visit to Zagreb in late May he declared in *Hrvatska Krajina* (*Croatian Krajina*) that all 'undesired elements will soon be destroyed in our [Bosnian] Krajina, so that soon all trace of them will be wiped out and only a bad memory of them will remain'.[9] Two days later he gave the following statement:

> The Serbian army is no more. Serbia is no more. There are no *gedžas* [derogatory term for Serbs], our bloodsuckers, the gypsy Karadjordjević dynasty has vanished and here the roads will soon wish for *Srbalja* [archaic term for Serbs, here used sarcastically], but the Serbs will be no more. I have ordered drastic measures for their complete economic destruction and new [orders] are following for their complete annihilation. Do not be soft on any of them. Always keep in mind that they were our gravediggers. Destroy them whenever you can and you will not fall short of my and the *Poglavnik*'s praise.[10]

Gutić's statement is important not least because he referred to a process by which the Serbs would first become economically dispossessed and then murdered or deported, which is in line with the phases in Hilberg's model. Following the establishment of the NDH, the *ustašas* immediately embarked on a policy designed to remove Serbs and Jews from public administration and other government jobs,[11] while at the same time preparing for the nationalization of Jewish businesses through the adoption of a 'Decree Regarding the Change of Jewish Surnames and Denoting of Jews and Jewish firms'.[12]

The nationalization of Serbian property began following the agreement on 'population exchanges' concluded with Nazi Germany on 4 June. It stipulated that some 200,000 Slovenians were to be deported from German-occupied Carinthia and Lower Styria in Slovenia to the NDH in exchange for an equivalent number of Serbs that were to be deported from the NDH to German-occupied Serbia.[13] In late June, the authorities continued institutionalizing the attack on the Serbian community by establishing the State Office for Revision (*Državno ravnateljstvo za ponovu* – *Ponova* for short), which received the task of registering and nationalizing the assets of Serbian deportees and Jews.[14] The activities of the *Ponova* were closely coordinated with the Office for Public Order and Security (*Ravnateljstvo za javni red i sigurnost*, RAVSIGUR) and the *Ustaša* Supervisory Office (*Ustaška nadzorna služba*, UNS), which supervised the 'undesirables' through its subsection I (*Ustaša* Supervision) and organized the concentration camp system through its section III (*Ustaša* Defence).[15] In addition, the Office for Colonization (*Ured za kolonizaciju*) was to use the real assets of the deportees for the resettlement of Slovenes and Croatian nationals from neighbouring countries.[16]

Legal aspects of the nationalization were finalized during autumn 1941 through the adoption of two decrees, which in effect stipulated that all assets of those who left the country would become state property.[17] The *ustašas* finalized the nationalization in late 1941 and early 1942 by closing down the *Ponova* and transferring its assets to the Office for Nationalized Property (*Ured za podržavljeni imetak*) at the Ministry of Finance.[18] Finally, the state solved the question of inheritance rights by adopting a decree in early 1942, according to which all inheritance of Jews who had died after 10 February 1941 became state property.[19]

The 'legal' deportations of Serbs began in mid-July with the rounding up of the Serbian elite, including priests, teachers and well-to-do farmers, none of whom were allowed to convert to Catholicism.[20] After that, the *ustašas* gradually widened the net and deported an increasing number of ordinary people until they had filled their quota. Throughout the process, victims were stripped of all their assets and the *Ponova* head Josip Rožanković even instructed his officials to 'pertinently suggest' that the deportees bring all their personal valuables with them to the collection centres so that one would not have to search for them.[21]

The Četniks: grand schemes and limited capabilities

Mihailović primarily viewed the JVUO as a military organization and he was therefore initially reluctant to allow political activities within the organization.[22] In autumn 1941, however, he agreed to the creation of a political body, the Central National Committee (*Centralni nacionalni komitet*, CNK), headed by Mladen Žujović, Dragiša Vasić and eventually Stevan Moljević.[23] During the summer of 1941, Moljević wrote a memorandum on the postwar reconstruction of Yugoslavia, entitled 'Homogenous Serbia'. By ascribing the military disaster in April 1941 to a 'treason' committed by the non-Serbian, particularly Croatian, parts of the population, he concluded that it was the ethnic composition of Yugoslavia that prevented the Serbs from assuming their allegedly 'leading role' in the Balkans. Consequently, the Serbian nation had to constitute itself in an ethnically homogenized territory before joining in a federation with Slovenes, Croats and possibly Bulgarians.[24] In September 1941, Mihailović wrote a memorandum for the government-in-exile, according to which one should make preparations and, when the Allies win the war,

> punish all those who have served the enemy in a criminal way and who have been willingly working towards the annihilation of the Serbian people; to draw the *de facto* borders of the Serbian lands and ensure that only Serbian inhabitants remain; to pay particular attention to the swift and radical cleansing of the towns and their settling with fresh Serbian elements; to prepare a plan for the cleansing or moving of the Serbian peasant population in order to achieve the goal of the homogeneity of the Serbian state community; in the Serbian community, to pay attention to the question of the Muslims in particular and solve it in this phase.[25]

Even if Moljević's memorandum was written months before he joined the CNK, leading *četniks* shared his vision. In May 1942, Dragiša Vasić referred to Moljević's writing in a letter, hailing it as a very interesting idea. Speaking about the forced resettlement after the war, he said that one should not be too worried since he remembered the anarchic situation after the First World War when 'one could have annihilated a considerable amount of one's own population, while nobody would care'.[26] Most official *četnik* documents envisaged the 'punishment' of those 'guilty' of treason, which indicates selectiveness as opposed to wholesale massacre. Nevertheless, empirical evidence and in particular the killing of women and children shows that the interpretation of 'guilt' was extremely wide, in effect giving the perpetrators a *carte blanche* to kill anyone they pleased.[27]

The *četniks* displayed an ambivalent attitude towards the Muslims. On one hand, they refused to recognize them as a nation, while on the other hand, they did not envisage their assimilation into the Serbian nation through forced conversions. Rather, they argued that the 'guilty' Muslims should be 'punished', while the rest were seen as apostates of Christianity that should be deported to Albania and Turkey.[28]

Finally, the *četniks* did try to establish various administrative bodies in the regions that they controlled for some period of time, for instance court-martials and provisional local governments. The difference in comparison to the *ustašas* was that these institutions were very rudimental due to, among other things, a lack of administrative personnel and an inability on the part of the *četniks* to effectively combine legislative with executive powers over territory. Over and above everything else, the *četniks* lacked the means to organize specialized institutions for the destruction of their 'undesirables' similar to the *Ponova* or the UNS with its system of concentration camps.[29]

Destruction 'from below'

The example of Goražde, which was occupied by *četnik* forces under Major Jezdimir Dangić on 1 December 1941, serves as an archetypal example of *četnik* atrocities in the region. Upon arrival, Dangić gave a speech in front of a group of assembled Serbs, Croats and Muslims, which contained references to a 'Greater Serbia' and finished with the laconic conclusion that 'we cannot be together anymore, we and the *balije* [derogatory term for Muslims]'.[30]

Following the speech, *četnik* bands spread out in town and began burning, pillaging, raping and killing in a pattern that characterized their atrocities. A large proportion of victims were murdered on a bridge, their bodies dumped into the river. This suggests that the *četniks* did not appear to divide the destruction process into sub-steps, whereby the initial killing of the elite is followed by more indiscriminate murder. Neither did they as a rule care much about transporting the victims to secluded localities before murdering them. In fact, the *četnik* behaviour indicates that they actually sought to use the killings, arson and other crimes as a way of signalling to the rest of the local Muslim population that their only salvation lay in escape to *ustaša*-controlled areas. The *četnik* behaviour can also be explained by the fact that they did not control a state apparatus. Consequently, they did not have 'state property', so pillaging and arson served the dual purpose of 'paying' the soldiers, while at the same time preventing the return of the 'undesirables'.[31]

The dumping of corpses into the Drina river proved an effective tactic, floating bodies serving as a chilling reminder to others of what awaited them. According to an eyewitness account written in Višegrad in February 1942:

> On the 7th, 8th and 9th of this month from early morning through the night, a crowd of people would stand and watch as corpses passed under the bridge over the Drina ... I had the opportunity of seeing how a son recognised his father or a mother her son and similar things. Being present during such occasions is a terrible experience; there was not a dry eye. During those days, we saw how the Drina carried six, four and most frequently two [victims] who had been tied together and had their throats slit. These were, as I told you, only the first victims and the refugees say that there are many more in the countryside, for instance in the forest, creeks, etc.[32]

Whether the result of a conscious calculation or not, the *četnik* flaunting of their misdeeds appears to have worked well, since thousands of Muslims took to the roads in an attempt to save themselves, although some did not get far. Fehim Sijerčić from Čajniče, for instance, was caught and incarcerated together with a smaller group of Muslims in the school in Raščići. At night, the Serbian local Kojo Vuković approached the building and called on the prisoners to come outside, saying that they had nothing to fear and that they would be served brandy. After leaving the school building, the Muslims were all beaten and taken to a cliff for execution – an event that Sijerčić probably remembered for the rest of his life:

> Kojo brought us to the cliff and with his company started shooting at us, one after another, after he had taken all our clothes. A bullet grazed my

head and I fell down the cliff, badly injuring my groin [...] At the bottom, I fell into the water. Later I regained conscience. I felt pain. When I stood up, [I heard] a rifle shot. Then, a second rifle shot. I heard someone screaming 'Diko, Diko!' and calling out for his wife. Then, the third rifle shot.[33]

Turning to *ustaša* atrocities in the Herzegovinian town of Stolac, we encounter an event that had a profound impact on the life of the Serb Desimir Mihić. In the municipality where he lived, Croats and Muslims made up a 75 per cent majority of the population. As a result, the NDH authorities did not have much of a problem establishing control over the area after the withdrawal of Italian occupation forces in early June 1941.

After assuming power, the *ustašas* set up a local 'Ustaša Advisory Board' that consisted of members of the municipal administration, tradesmen and a couple of Catholic clerics. Over the next few days, they mobilized members of the local community into *ustaša* units that began arresting well-to-do farmers, teachers and other prominent Serbs in a pattern that was repeated throughout the region.[34] Even if the arrests created an acute sense of insecurity for Serbs, the initial killings of able-bodied men did not begin until a couple of weeks later when *ustaša* detachments spread out in the countryside and began arresting civilians. In the village Šćepan Krst, for instance, a group of Serbs were brought to a place called Masline, where they were killed and thrown into a sinkhole.[35]

By late June, Mihić learned that his father had passed away in Zagreb and succeeded in procuring a travel pass to attend the funeral. Unfortunately, an *ustaša* in Čapljina recognized him and decided to imprison Mihić together with a group of 60–80 Serbs from Čapljina municipality. Mihić asked his fellow prisoners whether they had been interrogated, since he knew that the Serbs in Stolac had also been arrested under that pretext and then killed. When the prisoners answered that no one had interrogated them, Mihić,

> understood the fate that was awaiting us. They thought that this massive arrest only was a preventive measure, because the *ustašas* are afraid we would start an uprising on St. Vitus Day [28 June] and that they will release us after St. Vitus Day. I did not want to worsen their suffering, but I was frank and told them we would have our lives ended that night.[36]

This was a crucially important moment in Mihić's life, but it also serves as an illustration of the psychological processes that frequently worked against the victims' ability to escape murder. The prisoners simply refused to believe him and instead accepted the perpetrators' promise that they would be released after interrogation. Mihić, however, had access to information that placed him in a different psychological situation compared to his fellow prisoners. He used previous experience to make a correct appraisal of the situation and prepared his escape by struggling to loosen the chain around his wrists while being transported to the killing ground in the vicinity of Modriča. Consequently, one should not be surprised that it was him and not the others who jumped into the Neretva river while the prisoners were being unloaded from the lorries.[37]

On occasion, disturbances contributed to pulling the victims out of a state of 'numbness' similar to the one experienced by the victims in Čapljina. Seconds prior to the shooting of Muslims near Foča, for instance, several gunshots nearby startled those present and opened a window of opportunity for escape through nearby cornfields.[38] Similarly, a massacre in Ljubinje turned into a disaster for the perpetrators when they tried to 'effectivize' the killing process by tying a dozen or more Serbs with a long rope, shooting the first ones and then pulling the rest down into a sinkhole. When a group of prisoners were stuck in the entrance of the sinkhole, the killing process ground to a halt. At that moment, many victims who until then had obeyed their guards while standing in line at the massacre site suddenly were pulled from their paralysis and began running from the scene. Some were killed, but 50 or so managed to survive.[39]

The relationship between political decision-making and local violence

One question that always comes to mind when analyzing local violence is whether and to what extent the central perpetrators had control over the killings on the ground. In the case of the *četniks*, one can easily establish a direct relationship between the leaders and most of the crimes committed in south-eastern Bosnia, since the massacres happened in their immediate vicinity. Nevertheless, massacres on occasion did occur even though they for tactical reasons appear not to have been desired. This, for instance, seems to have been the case with the second attack on Foča in August 1942. Fearing that a *četnik* massacre would provoke German and Italian countermeasures, the local commanders ordered that civilians should be spared. Unfortunately, the soldiers did not adhere to the order, and some 400 men, women and children were killed.[40]

As for the *ustašas*, their leaders were often based tens or even hundreds of kilometres from where violence occurred. Even so, there appears to have existed a surprisingly strong correlation between events on the ground and decision-making at the top, which is perhaps best illustrated if we return to Stolac. At the time when Mihić was busy dodging *ustaša* patrols in the vicinity of Modriča, things in Stolac were developing along a familiar pattern with a substantial part of the Serbian elite finding itself incarcerated in the district courthouse. What neither the prisoners nor the *ustašas* knew was that a most unexpected guest was observing everything they did. Danilo Režina, a former employee of the court, was hiding in the attic of the courthouse where he remained for three months until the Italian re-occupation of the Croatian littoral in September. It is unclear how he reached the daring decision, but it was facilitated by the fact that his Croatian wife took over his job and could bring him food packages (in his postwar statement Mihić said that he slept under a floorboard).[41]

In the night of 27–28 June, Režina allegedly witnessed a highly interesting, albeit tragic event from his hideout. Outside, a group of Stolac *ustašas* were preparing for a massacre when a postal worker suddenly arrived with a telegram saying that the killings should stop. After some deliberations, the perpetrators nevertheless decided to go ahead with what they had intended. They brought out the victims, loaded them onto vehicles, drove them outside of town to a prepared mass grave, and killed them.[42]

What happened in Stolac was an exception to the rule, since most of the killings ended abruptly on 28 June as a result of orders coming from Zagreb, which shows that the central actors had considerable influence on local developments. For Mihić, this fact and his own remarkable ability to assess human behaviour once again saved his life. In the morning of 28 June, he found himself stranded on the banks of the Bregava River (a tributary of the Neretva). Suddenly and without an opportunity to escape, he was discovered by a group of *ustašas*. In Mihić's words, one of them called out to him:

> 'Go at once to the other side […] because if you do not obey and just move to the side, I will kill you like a rabbit. But if you do as I say and if you haven't done anything wrong, I swear by God and the holy Mohammed that nothing will happen to you. Yesterday, an order came and the bells were ringing, telling that no one can be killed without sentencing. The people are already returning to their homes, so give up and do not die in vain'. If they had been Catholics, I would not believe them and would have been killed. But, knowing that this oath still is powerful to the Muslim peasant, luckily I listened to them, crossed the Bregava and surrendered.
>
> We went to the opposite hill, where seven or eight *ustašas* were waiting for us. We walked slowly, me in front and those two behind me with rifles on the ready: 'God, you are lucky', one of them said to me, 'had we only captured you yesterday at this time, we would have buried you somewhere, so that you would not stink'.[43]

Pavelić's decision to temporarily halt the persecution was taken as a result not of empathy, but because the *ustaša* violence had sparked a rebellion that threatened to engulf eastern Herzegovina. As a result of the deteriorating security situation, the German authorities pressured him to do something, since they feared the rebellion might spread into neighbouring Serbia. In addition, the *ustaša* leader seems to have been dissatisfied with the fact that local administrators frequently tried to 'solve' the 'Serbian question' in their regions without taking due account of the overall plan for a resettlement policy. He summoned the county heads on 30 June and lectured them about the need to cease with 'extralegal' deportations, since,

[f]or such undertakings there are certain ministries and their offices. The state and national revision, that is, the revision of national life of resettlement and emigration, has before its eyes an entire set of those questions. We have over one million Croats abroad. We will make possible for them to return to their homeland. But to do that we need to prepare everything here. It has to be done within a system.[44]

There was a relative calm from late June to the initiation of the first 'legal' deportation of priests and other intellectuals in mid-July. By late July and August, however, the violence resurfaced with a vengeance, but also went into a new phase. Instead of primarily attacking military-aged men, the *ustašas* began targeting an increasing amount of women, elderly and children. The fate of Prebilovci near Čapljina offers an illustration of the effects that violence had on some localities. In 1941, the village had 116 households with 994 inhabitants. In 1946, only 21 households remained with a total of 164 inhabitants; 33 families had been completely wiped out and another 33 reduced to one member each.[45]

Perpetrator motives

Turning to the issue of perpetrator motives, we reach an aspect of the violence that has caused considerable debate since the publication of Daniel J. Goldhagen's *Hitlers Willing Executioners*.[46] The author argued that participation in the Holocaust was contingent upon a backdrop of 'eliminationist antisemitism' that was endemic to German culture and ideological indoctrination. In *Ordinary Men*,[47] Christopher Browning used the same sources as Goldhagen to reach the conclusion that it was not primarily ideology but a set of social-psychological mechanisms that drove the men. His conclusion was highly disturbing, since it meant that many of us, providing the confluence of a set of circumstances, could become perpetrators.

The NDH provides a particularly interesting example of a place where ideology probably had even less to do with the perpetrators' decisions to participate in massacre than on the Eastern Front. First, there simply was no time to indoctrinate the perpetrators, since the killings began within a couple of weeks after the *ustašas* took power.[48] Secondly, the *ustašas* lacked the means to influence the perpetrators beyond Croatia proper and the urban centres in Bosnia, since print media had problems reaching the countryside and the authorities did not establish radio coverage until after the most violent periods had already passed.[49] And the *četniks* for their part hardly had any print media to speak of, except leaflets, until well into the war.[50] Thirdly, even if print media would have reached remote areas, widespread illiteracy would have prevented the population from reading newspapers, let alone understand the complex ideological message of *ustaša* ideology or antisemitism.

This does not mean that propaganda was pointless, or that none of the perpetrators acted out of ideological conviction. Even if research shows that perpetrators more often participated as a result of psychological mechanisms than ideology, recent studies suggest that there is a correlation between the 'degree of participation' and ideological conviction.[51] In the case of the *ustašas*, one could find those who shared the extremist world-view of the leadership among 'the races' (the veterans of the organization that had been trained in Italy and Hungary in the 1930s). Ante Vrban, an officer who organized the killing of children in Jasenovac, belonged to this group. After the war, he joined the 'Crusaders' (*Križari*), a terrorist cell that tried to instigate a rebellion in Yugoslavia. He was caught by the Yugoslav secret service after an incursion into the country in 1947. During interrogation he said that he 'agreed with the liquidation of Serbian and Jewish prisoners, because they were a danger to Croatian statehood, since they were tearing it down'.[52] When asked about motives, he stated that,

> I joined the *ustašas*, where I also became an officer and as such I carried out orders that were given to me by my superiors. Nothing of that which I did during the NDH did I do under anyone's influence, but only because of my patriotism for Croatian tradition and independence. I wish to say that if any of my deeds have been to the detriment of the Croatian people then I am sorry and I regret that.[53]

Overall, there is no single explanation as to why individuals murdered their neighbours. Moreover, there might not even have to exist an 'objective' reason for participation in violence, since the context within which the perpetrators found themselves, and which was characterized by peer-pressure, obedience to authority, and a 'culture of cruelty', contributed to and carried out atrocities regardless of motive.[54] For some, the prospect of material gain appears to have been important, often in combination with other motives. When describing the activities of *četnik* commander Aćim Babić, for instance, witnesses mention that he 'sought revenge on the criminals',[55] but refused to participate in military combat since his main interest lay in pillaging. The problem of arbitrary pillaging was at the centre of concern among NDH officials, which is illustrated by *ustaša* commander Marko Roša's instructions to the units in the Bribir and Sidraga county, dated 18 June 1941. After instructing his subordinates not to torment the Serbs in public, since that might provoke reactions by the Italian forces, he demanded that '[p]illaging of Serbian property has to be prevented and all requisitions have to be carried out lawfully, so that all property is noted [unreadable] which will become state property and which has to be accounted for'.[56]

'Bystanders' and rescuers

So why, then, did the state engage in the dissemination of propaganda, one may ask, if not to motivate the perpetrators? The answer is that it probably was not even the primary of aim of propaganda to mobilize the perpetrators,[57] even if such effects of course were welcomed. Research seems to suggest that propaganda served the purpose of identifying and placing the out-group beyond the 'universe of obligation' of the perpetrators' in-group.[58] Through this process of identifying the 'undesirables', the state also signaled that those who belonged to the in-group had nothing to fear if they did not interfere with policy. Those who did protest became isolated as outcasts, no 'better' than the victims.[59]

Moreover, the fact that an armed conflict erupted in the NDH provided the *ustašas* and *četniks* with an opportunity to signal that one could not trust one's neigbour. Consequently, it was better to strike first instead of risking being attacked. By fomenting strife and fear, the leaderships took advantage of a human tendency to create positive feelings about the in-group by contrasting it to another group that automatically is depicted in a more negative light.[60] Thus, they succeeded in creating a psychological distance that facilitated passivity and prepared the ground for murder.

This strategy worked on most ordinary civilians, who concentrated on trying to muddle through in the business of everyday life, while a minority decided to intervene for the benefit of their fellow humans. Among these were communist revolutionaries such as Svetozar Vukmanović-Tempo, who in Rogatica tried to prevent *četnik* pillaging by appealing to local Serbs. Others included the former judge and Muslim Muharem Sadiković from Prijedor, who played an important role in the drafting of protest letters that would eventually carry the signatures of over 200 Muslim clergy and intellectuals;[61] and Diana Budisavljević, who organized a relief effort that would save thousands of Serbian children from an almost certain death.[62] These individuals represent a category of people that empirical research suggests were over-represented as rescuers, since they had a background that was different from the mainstream in their societies. In the case of Vukmanović-Tempo, it was probably ideological conviction and his standing as a leading revolutionary that made him intervene, while the fact that Sadiković had worked in Belgrade and was married to a Serbian woman made it very difficult for him to accept the *ustaša* view of Serbs.[63] Diana Budisavljević was even more interesting, not only because she was an Austrian-born woman who had married a well-known Serbian lawyer in Zagreb, but because at first she was reluctant to organize aid. After fearing that the task would be too difficult since she had no experience,[64] Budisavljević became drawn into a process that made it possible for her to fetch orphaned children from the Jasenovac–Stara Gradiška camp complex and bring them to safety.

Notwithstanding the fact that some of those who rescued others were gradually drawn into the process of saving innocent civilians, one must remember that others acted on the spur of the moment at the risk of losing their own lives. Such, for instance, was the case with Rajko Srndović, who in full sight of the perpetrators would save Muslims 'who already had been tied with wires and brought under the knife on the bridge' in Goražde.[65] These men and women did not have the same social background as Budisavljević or

Sadiković and their actions are difficult to explain as anything other than expressions of a deep resentment towards persecution and massacres.

Conclusion

This chapter has shown that the violence in the Independent State of Croatia for the most part occurred not due to irrational 'Balkan hatreds', but as a direct result of political decision-making. By comparing *četnik* and *ustaša* atrocities to Hilberg's model referred to at the beginning of the chapter, it has been shown also that the destruction processes took different forms due to the fact that the *ustašas* had the infrastructural capacity of a state at their disposal, while the *četniks* were a guerrilla organization. As a result, it was primarily the former that fully included the substeps that according to Hilberg characterizes a 'modern' destruction process. The institutionalization of the destruction process and its division into distinct phases testifies to the fact that the *ustašas* viewed their project of ethnic homogenization as precisely the form of 'social engineering' that Zygmunt Bauman refers to when describing what happened during the Holocaust as an effort 'to bring about a social order conforming to the design of the perfect society'.[66]

Another issue that set the *ustaša* destruction process apart from the *četnik* one was that the authorities frequently disapproved of pillaging and destruction of property, unless it was done in accordance with law and the regulations pertaining to anti-partisan warfare. This difference is also explicable by the fact that the *ustašas* controlled a state, and governments as a rule do not take kindly to the destruction of state property. The *četniks*, on the other hand, could not hope to control territory over a prolonged period of time. Instead, they appear to have used pillaging as a way to co-opt the soldiers into participation, while the burning of non-Serbian homes served the purpose of preventing returns.

However, this should not be interpreted as a devaluation of the *četniks* to a horde of barbarians or – even less so – as a ranking of the crimes that were perpetrated. The *četniks* tried to be as organized as they possibly could and they sought to realize a modern 'national utopia'. The problem was that they simply did not dispose of the military and infrastructural capacity to organize and maintain a coherent destruction process throughout Yugoslavia over a prolonged period of time (which, incidentally, they appear to have understood and therefore thought that most non-Serbs would be deported after the war). Such a conclusion has important theoretical implications. Scholars specializing in the study of genocide and other forms of mass killing have debated whether there is a correlation between the magnitude of group destruction and the level of organization on the part of the perpetrator, in other words whether it takes a state to destroy a targeted minority *in toto* or in a very substantial part. Evidence from the NDH suggests that it might. Even if one takes the differences in intent and the size of the victimized groups into account, the destruction of some 75 per cent of the Jews and almost

100 per cent of the itinerant Roma serves as perhaps the most persuasive confirmation of the hypothesis.

The fact that the level of organization on the part of the perpetrators has very little to do with the suffering of the victims is perhaps best illustrated by the micro-level analysis of mobile killing operations. Empirical evidence suggests that *četnik* violence affected the victims irrespectively of gender and age from early on (even if a majority nevertheless were able-bodied men), and it is difficult to discern specific phases in the killing process. In contrast, the *ustašas* more often tried to sub-divide the killings into phases and transport the victims outside of urban centres before murdering them. For the individual victim, however, it mattered very little if s/he was a Serb, Croat or Muslim, since all had to adapt to the circumstances and make difficult choices. It was this interaction between the victims and the perpetrators that decided the fate of so many innocent people, irrespectively of the perpetrators' motives for participating in the murders.

Finally, the analysis has also shown that most Yugoslavs concentrated on the self-absorbing task of muddling through everyday life, while some intervened on behalf of their fellow humans, even at the risk of losing their own lives. On occasion, some of the nameless, unknown individuals who felt helpless or were afraid to do anything at least tried to show sympathy for the victims. This, for instance, occurred in Jastrebarsko in the beginning of 1942. When a group of Serbian women and children from Ljubinje passed through the town, they noticed how many ordinary Croats watched them with grief and sorrow, while 'many even wept bitterly'.[67] Even if these tears saved no one, they serve to remind us of the compassion and humanity that many ordinary citizens felt for their fellow humans.

Notes

1 For more on the political developments in Yugoslavia during the Second World War, see St. K. Pavlowitch, *Hitler's New Disorder: The Second World War in Yugoslavia* (New York: Columbia University Press, 2008); J. Tomasevich, *War and Revolution in Yugoslavia 1941–1945: The Chetniks* (Stanford: Stanford University Press, 1975); J. Tomasevich, *War and Revolution in Yugoslavia 1941–1945: Occupation and Collaboration* (Stanford: Stanford University Press, 2001).

2 By the generic term 'mass killing' is meant genocide, 'ethnic cleansing', 'democide', 'politicide', massacre and other forms of lethal violence directed against civilians and non-combatants. For more on the sometimes irreconcilable definitions, see I. W. Charny, 'Toward a Generic Definition of Genocide', in G. Andreopoulos (ed.), *The Conceptual and Historical Dimensions of Genocide* (Philadelphia: University of Pennsylvania Press, 1994), pp. 64–93; H. Huttenbach, 'Locating the Holocaust on the Genocide Spectrum: Towards a Methodology of Definition and Categorization', *Holocaust and Genocide Studies*, vol. 3, no. 3 (1988), pp. 289–303, p. 294; N. Naimark, *Fires of Hatred: Ethnic Cleansing in Twentieth-Cetnury Europe* (Cambridge, Mass. and London: Harvard University Press, 2001), pp. 3–4; F. Chalk. 'Redefining Genocide', in Andreopoulos (ed.), *Genocide: Conceptual and Historical Dimensions*, pp. 47–63; R. J. Rummel, *Death by Government* (New Brunswick, N.J.: Transactions Publishers, 1994), p. 31.

3 R. Hilberg, *The Destruction of the European Jews*, 3 volumes (New Haven and London: Yale University Press, 2003); reprint, 3rd ed., vol. III, p. 1065.

4 N. Lengel-Krizman, *Genocid nad Romima* (Zagreb and Jasenovac: Javna ustanova spomen-područje Jasenovac, 2003), p. 37. Subsequently, the Ministry of the Interior ordered that one should not persecute the settled Roma; see Croatian State Archives, Zagreb (hereafter HAD), Ministarstvo unutarnjih poslova NDH, 223/104/II-A/32661, 'Ministarstvo unutarnjih poslova NDH kotarskoj oblasti Derventa po pitanju rasne pripadnosti bijelih Cigana', Zagreb, 30 August 1941.

5 *Hrvatski Narod*, 31 July 1941. For more on the propaganda in the NDH, see F. Ademović, *Novinstvo i ustaška propaganda u Nezavisnoj Državi Hrvatskoj: štampa i radio u Bosni i Hercegovini (1941–1945)* (Sarajevo: Media centar and Nezavisna unija profesionalnih novinara Bosne i Hercegovine, 2000), pp. 339–77. In the literature on the war, it is sometimes claimed that a leading *ustaša* (Eugen Kvaternik, Mile Budak and Andrija Artuković have been mentioned in this context) once said that one-third of the Serbs were to be killed, one-third deported and one-third converted to Roman Catholicism. However, there is no documentary evidence to give unequivocal support to such claims. Moreover, it is unclear whether the *ustaša* in question is supposed to have said 'one third' – thus giving a precise number as to how many would be killed – or just said 'some'.

6 *Hrvatski Narod*, 28 July 1941.

7 A. Pavelić, *Die kroatische Frage*, K. C. Von Loesch (ed.) (Berlin: Institut für Grenz-und Auslandstudien, 1941), p. 18.

8 A. Pavelić, *Poglavnik govori* (Zagreb: Naklada Glavnog ustaškog stana, 1941), p. 13.

9 *Hrvatska Krajina*, 28 May 1941, transcribed in Archives of Yugoslavia, Belgrade (hereafter AJ), Državna komisija za utvrdjivanje zločina okupatora i njihovih pomagača u zemlji 110/276/242/1466.

10 *Hrvatska Krajina*, 30 May 1941, transcribed in AJ 110/276/241/1466. For details of the anti-Serbian and antisemitic propaganda, see Ademović, *Novinstvo i ustaška propaganda*, pp. 339–86.

11 F. Jelić-Butić, *Ustaše i NDH* (Zagreb: SN Liber Školska knjiga, 1977), p. 102.

12 Naredba o promjeni židovskih prezimena i označavanja Židova i židovskih tvrtka, *Narodne novine*, br. 43, 4 June 1941.

13 *Zbornik DNOR*, ser. XII, vol. 1, doc. no. 5, 'Telegram nemačkog poslanika u Zagrebu Ministru vanjskih poslova Rajha o preseljavanju Slovenaca i Srba', Zagreb, 4 June 1941. At a conference in September, it was agreed that 118,000 people had been deported by then; Archives of the military-historical Institute, Belgrade, Archives of the NDH (hereafter AVII, ANDH), 233/28/7–2, 'Niederschrift über die am 22 September 1941 in der Deutschen Gesendschaft in Zagreb unter Leitung der Deutschen Gesandten stattgefundene Besprechung über die Umsiedlung as dem Reich nach Kroatien und aus Kroatien nach Serbien', Zagreb, 22 September 1941.

14 Goldstein, I., *Holokaust u Zagrebu*, Zagreb: Novi liber, 2001, p. 177; Jelić-Butić, *Ustaše i NDH*, p. 168.

15 Jelić-Butić, *Ustaše i NDH*, pp. 112, 185.

16 Ibid., p. 168.

17 Zakonska odredba o imovini osoba koji su napustili područje Nezavisne Države Hrvatske, *Narodne novine*, 7 August 1941, articles 3 and 4; Zakonska odredba o imovini osoba izseljenih s područja Nezavisne Države Hrvatske, *Narodne novine*, 7 August 1941, articles 3, 4 and 6. According to the decrees, there was a possibility of filing a complaint in Zagreb within fifteen days after the decrees were adopted. Failing to do so meant that one forfeited ownership rights.

18 Jelić-Butić, *Ustaše i NDH*, p. 184; N. Kisić-Kolanović, 'Podržavljenje imovine Židova u NDH', *Časopis za suvremenu povijest*, vol. 30, no. 3, 1998, p. 441.

19 Zakonska odredba o podržavljenju židovske imovine, 30 October 1942.

20 N. Novaković (ed.), *Zločini Nezavisne Države Hrvatske, 1941–45* (Beograd: Vojnoistorijski institut, 1993), doc. no 169, 'Okružnica Ministra unutarnjih poslova Andrije Artukovića i Ministra pravosudja Mirka Puka Velikim Županama', Zagreb, 30 July 1941.

21 Novaković (ed.), *Zločini NDH*, doc. no.106, 'Okružnica Državnog ravnateljstva za društvenu ponovu Velikim župama', Zagreb, 9 July 1941.
22 Pavlowitch, *Hitler's New Disorder*, p. 103.
23 Ibid., p. 55.
24 *Zbornik DNOR*, ser. XIV, vol. 1, *Dokumenti četničkog pokreta Draže Mihailovića, 1941–1942* (Beograd: Vojnoistorijski institut, 1981), doc. no. 1, 'Memorandum "Homogena Srbija" Stevana Moljevića', 30 July 1941.
25 *Zbornik DNOR*, ser. XIV, vol. 1, doc. no.6, 'Program četničkog pokreta DM od Septembra 1941, September 1941, poslat Emigrantskoj vladi u Londonu', September 1941. It has been debated whether it was Mihailović himself who wrote this letter. However, in instructions to Pavle Djurišić from 20 December 1941, he used similar words when writing that one should 'cleanse' Sandžak from minorities; *Zbornik DNOR*, ser. XIV, vol. 1, doc. no. 34, 'Instrukcija Draže Mihailovića Pavle Djurišiću', 20 December 1941.
26 *Zbornik DNOR* ser. XIV, vol. 1, doc. no. 85, 'Pismo Dragiše Vasića Draži Mihailoviću', May 1942.
27 It has been argued that the *četniks* with the term 'cleansing' actually meant 'physical liquidation': Z. Dizdar and M. Sobolevski (eds.), *Prešućivani četnički zločini u Hrvatskoj i Bosni i Hercegovini* (Zagreb: Dom i svijet, 1999), p. 93. Even if euphemisms frequently were used, this appears to be an overly narrow interpretation of the document, since it would mean that the *četniks* also intended to kill those Serbs that were to be deported from Croatian areas. It is more likely that they meant forced expulsions by a method that also included the commission of massacres if and when that was thought to be necessary. Such an interpretation would better explain why they discussed deportations of Croats to Croatia and Muslims to Turkey or Albania; had 'cleansing' *per se* meant physical annihilation, such plans would have been unnecessary.
28 *Zbornik DNOR* ser. XIV, vol. 1, doc. no. 85, 'Pismo Dragiše Vasića Draži Mihailoviću', May 1942.
29 Momčilo DJujić's *četniks* had a jail that sometimes is referred to as a 'camp' in Kosovo, Croatia; see Dizdar and Sobolevski, *Prešućivani četnički zločini*, pp. 70–71. However, the facility was something rather different from concentration camps like Jasenovac or the Nazi Camps in Europe.
30 AVII, ANDH/72/5/2–6, 'Ministarstvo unutarnjih poslova NDH glavnom stožeru Ministarstva domobranstva', Zagreb 8 June 1942. The origin of *balije* is unclear, but it might have its roots in the Serbian, Croatian and Bosnian word *balav* (snotty); A. Škaljić, *Turcizmi u srpskohrvatskom jeziku* (Sarajevo: Svjetlost, 1989), p. 118.
31 Vladimir Dedijer noted in his memoirs that the *četniks* would paint signs on the Serbian houses in southeastern Bosnia, to avoid mistakenly burning them down; V. Dedijer, *Dnevnik* (Beograd: Jugoslovenska knjiga, 1951), p. 66.
32 AVII, ANDH/75/47/5–2, 'Zapovjedništvo Vojne Krajine, pismo Kareić I. iz Višegrada rodjaku u Sarajevu', Sarajevo, 2 April 1942.
33 M. Zečević (ed.), *Dokumenta sa sudjenja Ravnogorskom pokretu 10 juni – 15 juli 1946. god.*, vol. 2 (Belgrade: SUBNOR, 2001), p. 1437. Sijerčić apparently fell 200 metres through a thick layer of snow. When the *četniks* left with the victims' clothes, Sijerčić found one of his friends sitting on a stone and helped him cross a nearby creek; M. Zečević, (ed.), *Dokumenta*, p. 1438.
34 AJ 110–487/537/55152, 'Zapisnik sastavljen 17. 6. 1946. godine u Stocu po delegatu Zemaljske komisije za utvrdjivanje zločina okupatora i njihovih pomagača', Stolac, 17 June 1946.
35 AJ 110–487/537/55237, 'Zapisnik sastavljen 2. jula 1946. godine u Stocu po delegatu Zemaljske komisije za utvrdjivanje zločina okupatora i njihovih pomagača', Stolac, 2 July 1946.
36 Archives of Serbia, Belgrade (hereafter AS), Komesarijat za izbeglice Nedićeve vlade, G-2, f. 7 (Stolac), statement by D. Mihić, 19 March 1943, p. 5.
37 Ibid., p. 6.

38 HDA, Zbirka mikrofilmova Ministarstva oružanih snaga NDH [fond 1450], roll D-2205, fr. 273.
39 AJ 110–488/566r/55192, 'Zapisnik sastavljen dne 16. jula 1946. godine pred delagatom Zemaljske komisije za utvrdjivanje zločina okupatora i njihovih pomagača u Vlahovićima, srez Stolac, okrug Mostar', Stolac, 16 July 1946; AJ 110–488/568r/55192, 'Zapisnik sastavljen dne 16. jula 1946. godine pred delagatom Zemaljske komisije za utvrdjivanje zločina okupatora i njihovih pomagača z Vlahovićima, srez Stolac', okrug Mostar, Stolac, 16 July 1946.
40 AVII, Ča/ 231/44/6, Pitanje Foče', izveštaj majora Petra Baćovića i Dobrosava Jevdjevića s kraja Avgusta 1942 Draži Mihailoviću', August 1941.
41 AJ 110–491/489/52548, 'Zapisnik sastavljen kod Opštinskog odbora u Stocu, srez Stolac/ za rejon gradski/ Okrug Južno-hercegovački, dana 9 maja 1945. g.', Stolac, 9 May 1945.
42 Ibid. During postwar criminal proceedings, the district court in Mostar rejected Režina's claim that he had seen the accused carrying wires into the courthouse, presumably to tie the victims with. The reason was that he first said he had witnessed the *ustaša* preparations from the attic, and then claimed to have seen them from 'the office' of the court. Nevertheless, the court did not question that he actually spent months in the attic of the building (in 1946, Režina was employed by the Mostar disctrict court); AJ 110–818/593, 'Okružni sud u Mostaru, broj KO: 302/46, Presuda', 3 July 1946.
43 AS G-2, f. 7 (Stolac), statement by D. Mihić, 19 March 1943.
44 Pavelić, *Poglavnik govori*, p. 44.
45 AJ 110–480/56731, 'Zapisnik sastavljen pred Zemaljskom komisijom za utvrdjivanje zločina okupatora i njihovih pomagača, 7. jula 1946. u Prebilovcima', Prebilovci, 7 July 1946.
46 D. J. Goldhagen, *Hitler's Willing Executioners: Ordinary Germans and the Holocaust* (London: Little Brown & Company, 1996).
47 C. R. Browning, *Ordinary Men: Reserve Police Battalion 101 and the Final Solution in Poland* (New York: HarperPerennial, 1993).
48 It was in Croatia proper that the first massacres of Serbs occurred, in late April 1941. Jelić-Butić, *Ustaše i NDH*, p. 166.
49 In an important contribution to a better understanding of the propaganda in the NDH, Fadil Ademović notes that the war severed contacts between Zagreb and the interior of the country, which made it very difficult for local newspapers to fulfil their propaganda mission. He also shows that Sarajevo did not have its own radio station until January 1942, while noting that there were only 87,000 radio licenses in the NDH in early 1943; Ademović, *Novinstvo i ustaška propaganda*, pp. 124–30, 171.
50 *Sloboda ili smrt* was the first paper of the JVUO. It was first published in September 1941, but was discontinued after just four issues. The second paper, *Ravna gora*, was first published in early 1943. In addition, larger *četnik* military units issued the 2–4 pages long bulletin *Vidovdan*, beginning in late 1941 and early 1942. However, most of the units did not begin publishing the bulletins until 1943; M. Matić, *Ravnogorska ideja u štampi i propagandi četničkog pokreta u Srbiji 1941–1944* (Beograd: Institut za savremenu istoriju, 1995), pp. 66–69, 81–126.
51 S. Straus, *The Order of Genocide: Race, Power, and War in Rwanda* (Ithaca, NY and Bristol: Cornell University Press, 2006), p. 247.
52 HDA, fond 1561, Služba državne bezbjednosti republičkog sekretarijata za unutrašnje poslove SRH, Saslušanje A. Vrbana, 013.2.18, p. 45.
53 Ibid., p. 47. The reference to superior orders was a commonplace argument by perpetrators in order to avoid punishment, but it is also illustrative of what Henri Zukier and others refer to as 'instrumentalization', by which the perpetrator casts 'himself as the instrument of another's will or higher purpose'; H. Zukier, 'The Twisted Road to Genocide: On the Psychological Development of Evil during the Holocaust', *Social Research*, vol. 61, no. 2, 1994, pp. 423–55, p. 449.
54 For more regarding the psychological aspects of participation in atrocity, see J. P. Sabini and M. Silver, 'Destroying the Innocent with a Clear Conscience: A Sociopsychology of the

Holocaust', in J. E. Dimsdale (ed.), *Survivors, Victims, and Perpetrators* (Washington, New York, and London: Hemisphere Publishing Corporation, 1980), pp. 329–58; S. Milgram, *Obedience to Authority* (New York: Harper & Row, 1974); E. Staub, *The Roots of Evil: The Origins of Genocide and Other Group Violence* (Cambridge and New York: Cambridge University Press, 1989), pp. 67–88; J. Waller, *Becoming Evil: How Ordinary People Commit Genocide and Mass Killing* (Oxford: Oxford University Press, 2002).

55 AJ 110–460/510/57551, 'Zapisnik sastavljen dne 23.4.1946 pred Zemaljskom komisijom za uvrdjivanje zločina okupatora i njihovih pomagača u Sarajevu, Sarajevo', 23 April 1946.

56 AJ 110–577/42/10/41, 'Marko Roša, ustaški logornik Velike župe Bribir i Sidraga, bratskom ustaškom logoru: Knin, taboru Drniš, taboru Promina', Knin, 18 June 1941.

57 As Bauman notes, 'the perpetration of the Holocaust required the neutralization of ordinary Germany [sic] attitudes toward the Jews, not their mobilization'; Bauman, *Modernity and the Holocaust*, p. 185.

58 H. Fein, *Genocide: a Sociological Perspective* (London; Newbury Park; New Delhi: SAGE Publications, 1993), p. 43.

59 During the Holocaust, the Nazis made use of this method to achieve a 'social atomization' of the German population, by which they also succeeded in controlling those few who objected to the anti-Jewish measures; S. Gordon, *Hitler, Germans and the 'Jewish Question'* (Princeton: Princeton University Press, 1984), pp. 148–49.

60 H. Tajfel, 'Social Identity and Intergroup Behaviour', *Social Science Information*, vol. 13, no. 2, 1974, pp. 65–93.

61 For more on the letters of protest, see E. Redžić, *Muslimansko autonomaštvo i 13. SS divizija: autonomija Bosne i Hercegovine i Hitlerov Treći Rajh* (Sarajevo: Svjetlost, 1987), p. 16.

62 AS, G-2, f. 5 (Prijedor), statement by M. Sadiković, p. 6; S. Vukmanović-Tempo, *Revolucija koja teče: Memoari*, vol. 1 (Beograd: Komunist, 1971), p. 246. The local *ustaša* commander Marko Vrkljan in a subsequent report confirmed that the partisans played an important role in the preventing of a large-scale massacre in Rogatica; AVII, ANDH/64/1/2–4.

63 Staub points out that some rescuers, not unlike Tempo, were 'unusually fearless, self-confident and adventurous', while others were characterized by 'being members of a minority religion ... being new to the community, having a parent from another country' or had another background that made them separate from the community at large; Staub, *The Roots of Evil*, pp. 166–67.

64 *Dnevnik Diane Budisavljević*, ed., J. Kolanović (Zagreb: Hrvatski državni arhiv and Javna ustanova Spomen-područje Jasenovac, 2003), p. 14.

65 AVII, ANDH/72/5/2–6, 'Veliki župan kod Ministarstva unutarnjih poslova Glavnom stožeru MINDOM-a; izvješće o općem stanju u Goraždu', Zagreb, 8 June 1941.

66 Bauman, *Modernity and the Holocaust*, p. 91.

67 AS, G-2, f. 7 (Ljubinje), statement by F. Toholj.

6 Yugoslavia in Exile

The London-based wartime government, 1941–45

Stevan K. Pavlowitch

When King Peter II and the nucleus of the Yugoslav government arrived in London at the end of June 1941,[1] they were received as heroes who had sacrificed all to defy Hitler three months earlier, on 27 March. In spite of the rapid collapse of Yugoslavia's defences, its government's declaration, as soon as it had left the country, that it was still at war, followed by news of risings in the summer, boosted British public morale. The 18-year-old monarch became the symbol of Yugoslavia's struggle to keep its freedom in alliance with Great Britain. The exiled cabinet was a coalition of parties that strove for a solution of the country's problems in a parliamentary system. Assembled under General Dušan Simović, apparent leader of the coup, it symbolized a yearning for a fully representative leadership in an hour of need.

The moral assets that the King and his ministers found in London rested on weak foundations. Composed of the leaders of all the parties that had, at one time or another, been in opposition since King Alexander had suspended the original Constitution in 1929, the government had been legalized under the later Constitution of 1931 granted by Alexander and which made ministers responsible to the sovereign alone. The politicians subscribed to a theory formulated by the constitutional theorist, historian and deputy Prime Minister Slobodan Jovanović, according to which the coup had, in intention, restored parliament as a constitutional factor equal to the Crown. Until such time as it could be elected, its rights were deemed to be vested in the parties represented in government. Jovanović's theory notwithstanding, constitutional legality was, for the time being, vested in the King alone.

Theories could be advanced, for the Constitution of 1931 had, in fact, been all but destroyed. As a result of the bargain (*Sporazum*) struck in August 1939 between Prince Paul and the Croatian Peasant Party (HSS) leader Vladko Maček, an autonomous Province (*banovina*) of Croatia had been set up, parliament had been dissolved, and the restructured government empowered to prepare a new electoral law. Although they had in fact initiated a revision of the Constitution, these measures had been enacted on the basis of the Crown's reserved emergency powers and were ultimately to be submitted to parliament. The new parliament, which would presumably have had a constituent role, was never to be. Peter II assumed the royal prerogative six months before his statutory majority. Maček, who suspected that the coup had, in part, resulted from resentment against the *Sporazum*, had made a further extension of the *Banovina's* competence a condition to his staying on in government. Accepted by Simović, not given formulation for lack of time, this was confirmed along with the *Sporazum* itself by a government declaration issued in Jerusalem in May.

Simović's government had been conceived as a representation of parties, but it was a disparate collection. The whole political spectrum was there, except for the subversive fascist and communist extremes and the time-servers of the makeshift government Yugoslav Radical Union of the late 1930s: politicians of the HSS and of its Independent Democrat (SDS) allies, Slovenian Populists (SLS) and the Yugoslav Muslim Organization (JMO), Radicals (NRS) and Democrats (DS), Agrarians (SZ) and the Yugoslav National Party (JNS). There were some who had opposed the manner of the *Sporazum* and the Pact with the Axis Powers, and others who had been for the *Sporazum* but against the Pact; there were regional leaders, ethnic leaders, and parliamentary party leaders without a parliament; a couple of distinguished non-party personalities, and the generals who had emerged at the head of the coup. It claimed to be a revolutionary government, but had to be legalized under what remained of the existing Constitution. In their few days of effective power, the ministers had had no time to tackle any of the country's problems.

When the government reassembled in exile, the acknowledged spokesmen for the Croats, the Slovenes and the Muslims were no longer with it. The JMO leader Džafer Kulenović had gone over to the newly-proclaimed Independent State of Croatia (NDH), and there had been no one to take his place. Fran Kulovec of the SLS had been killed in the bombing of Belgrade, and had been replaced. Maček had decided to stay and share the ills of war with his own people in Croatia. He had delegated to the government the HSS secretary general Juraj Krnjević, who had only in 1939 returned from ten years of self-imposed exile.

How to continue the war: the politicians and the military

Reunited in Athens, the government had issued statements, repeated solemnly in Jerusalem, that it would continue to fight until victory. It had not yet realized that only a few hundred officers and men had been able to leave Yugoslavia and join the British, or the extent to which the renown of the Yugoslav army had been shattered during the short April campaign. However, Simović must already have known more about the extent of the military defeat than he was willing to admit.

There had been disagreement between the generals involved in the coup as to what form the new government should take. Whereas General Borivoje Mirković had favoured a military government, Simović had wanted to preside over a 'government of national salvation' with 'distinguished personalities'. Radoje Knežević, the civilian link between the military conspirators and the opposition who had become minister of the Royal Household, had argued that the new government had to be made up of representatives from all the parties.[2] On the whole, the generals had had to give in, but the rivalry between them and the party leaders remained.

Simović was a patriotic general but a politically inept prime minister, who wanted to play a great rôle and did not trust politicians. On the grounds that they had lost their following in the turmoil of the collapse, he counteracted the 'Jovanović theory' with his own: for the duration of the war, the only real expression of legitimacy was a government led by him, surrounded by distinguished personalities of his choice. No sooner in London than the hero of 27 March tried to reorganize the government as a smaller team in which he would himself take over the main portfolios. By exploiting the differences between the politicians, he soon got them to agree that he was ill-suited to preside over them. His value as the hero of the March coup, already impaired by his part of responsibility for the military defeat, was now practically ruined by his scheming. Because the British feared that his replacement would damage the cohesion of the government in London and threaten continued resistance in Yugoslavia, the ministers, under Jovanović's influence, postponed his downfall, in the hope that he could be made to mend his ways – to no avail. Eventually they addressed a collective letter of resignation to King Peter, motivated by Simović's mishandling of government. He had to be dismissed by the sovereign on 11 January 1942, and withdrew into bitter resentment.

Paradoxically, Simović had created a measure of agreement. The ministers believed that it was time to consider some of the political problems they had brought out with them and that they stood a better chance of doing it without the generals. They took over as a new government under Professor Jovanović, their respected senior whose original appointment as vice-premier had been meant to provide a Serb counterpart to Maček. Jovanović looked at politics through scholarly spectacles tinted with old-fashioned positivism.[3] Ironically he was the only civilian non-party 'distinguished personality' left in the cabinet. Along with the exclusion of Simović, the only other change was the inclusion of General Dragoljub (Draža) Mihailović as war minister to replace General Bogoljub Ilić. Since Mihailović was in Yugoslavia, the government was safely in the hands of civilians.

Another source of conflict was the division between the generals and the younger officers who had actually carried out the coup. The war minister General Ilić had been left in Cairo, with the additional post of chief of staff to a resurrected Supreme Command, to oversee what existed of the Yugoslav 'forces' in the Near East. The émigré command had started off with dreams of creating an army in exile by enlisting volunteers from Yugoslav immigrants in America, to add body to the few hundred officers and men who had actually been able to join the British in Egypt. In the end, it had to settle for volunteers from Slovenian-Italian POWs. An infantry battalion had been formed by the beginning of 1942, but Yugoslavia was to be the least important of the Allies in terms of military forces available outside the occupied national territory.

When Simović and Ilić were dropped from the government, so was General Mirković, the commander of Yugoslav troops in the Near East. All the stresses latent in the small officer corps there suddenly emerged. The junior executants of the March coup, resentful of the ineptitude of their seniors during the April campaign, sided with the politicians. The generals in Cairo refused to relinquish their posts, generally supported by the air-force officers who sided with Simović. The government in London was powerless to enforce its will except through the British. As the crisis of the Yugoslav military in Egypt occurred during the summer of El Alamein, and the chief mutineer was Mirković who enjoyed British sympathies, the affair was not settled until November 1942. Its consequences were far-reaching. The military were even more demoralized, their chances of contributing to the Allied war effort even more remote, and the prestige of 'Yugoslavia in exile' had fallen sharply.

Until October 1941 the government had not been able to obtain precise information about events at home, let alone exert any influence over them. When Colonel Mihailović was first heard of in the summer, his movement was reported as consisting of officers resentful of the ministers and generals who had brought about the defeat and fled. The military in exile were quick to perceive that he could be a help and a threat. The generals needed to tie him to the government, to defuse the potential subversion in his movement, and to make up for the capitulation and the lack of military contribution to the Allied case. This led to his promotion and to the first approaches to the British for help. But the younger conspirators of the March coup now abroad were classmates of their colleagues in the resistance whose grievances against the generals they shared. They too were anxious to support Mihailović.

The news of the uprising in Yugoslavia was a morale booster for the Allies. Mihailović expressed his allegiance to the Yugoslav government. Even though he asked for discreet support rather than propaganda, and London urged restraint, stirring stories emerged about the Yugoslav resistance, and he was soon built up by British and Yugoslav propaganda into an Allied superman. The politicians no longer needed Simović. They had found another figure. Mihailović's appointment, on 10 June 1942, as chief of staff of the Supreme Command, transferred back to the occupied homeland, coupled with his promotion to full general, resurrected the Yugoslav army and reduced to scale the awkward affair of the military in the Near East. There was no other instance of the leader of a resistance movement in the occupied homeland being symbolically taken into an exiled government. The territory from which he operated seemed to have become important for the outcome of the war in Africa. The Yugoslav government contributed his organization to the Allied cause, while it gained a military arm at home.

The new prime minister wanted to strengthen the link between Mihailović and the government so as to improve the standing of both partners and of their country's cause. Jovanović feared that, as a result of the collapse and its aftermath, the Serbs had lost faith in their government, in the possibility of restoring a Yugoslav state, in the Western Allies, in democracy perhaps, in themselves even. Mihailović's views and aims seemed to correspond to Jovanović's: a pro-Western, anti-fascist and anti-communist line, and the defence of Serb interests in a restored state community with the other Yugoslavs. Mihailović could help to restore some of the confidence that had been lost.

Both partners were to be disappointed. The government could not be sure it had successfully bound Mihailović's movement, with its important element of resentment against all politicians, let alone the various fellow-travelling *četnik* groups that had hitched themselves to his reputation. Anyhow Mihailović himself was soon the subject of accusations of collaboration, and charges of *četnik* vindictiveness made his movement suspect to non-Serbs, all of which compromised the government through its association with him.

Co-operation between the government and Mihailović was made difficult by the fact that the British denied the Yugoslavs the right of uncontrolled radio communications. This did not create any immediate military difficulty since in 1942 there was, on the whole, no difference between the British and the Yugoslav government's conceptions of Mihailović's military rôle. But whereas the government for a long time saw Mihailović's movement mainly in its military aspect, in Yugoslavia it was quickly also perceived as a political movement and the government was not able to obtain enough information about that aspect. Jovanović, as prime minister and acting war minister in London, did try to provide Mihailović with guidelines, but that was at a time when its stand generally agreed with the British. Premature action was to be avoided. Mihailović was to prepare for D-Day when the Allies would land, either in the Balkans or elsewhere in Europe, when he would launch a general rising. In the meanwhile he was to link the various underground groups so as to keep under pressure a greater number of Axis forces, but in such a way as to minimize reprisals on the population or the disruption of his own forces.

Jovanović was conscious of the danger involved in the break between Mihailović's men and the partisans. His policy was to try to stop the civil war from developing and to reconcile the two rival movements under Mihailović's command. If that were impossible, fighting between them should at least be prevented and some sort of co-ordinated action obtained against the common enemy. The government could hope to influence Mihailović to a degree, but not the partisans, and so it tried to enlist the help of the Soviet government who, at that time, was interested in any guerrilla action so long as it kept German troops busy outside Soviet territory. This relatively conciliatory attitude towards the partisans was kept by the Jovanović government until the communist propaganda campaign began against Mihailović in late 1942.

It is not clear when the government realized all that was going on under cover of nominal allegiance to Mihailović, particularly in Italian-occupied territories. Not before the summer of 1942 was direct but tenuous communication established. Mihailović notwithstanding, Jovanović's ministers were indeed all civilian politicians, but each group of ministers listened only to what it could interpret optimistically from its own intelligence. Jovanović's own tenure of the war ministry in London was barely more than nominal, exercised as it was through the military private office of the war minister, which was headed by Major Živan Knežević, the most influential of the younger officers who had carried out the coup of 27 March and who also interpreted intelligence and instructions according to his wishful thinking.[4] Although collectively the government did not know enough about what was happening at home, it did by the turn of 1943–44 have a clearer idea of what was going on. Its denials then of accommodations and passivity (although no better or worse than misinformation issuing out of the partisan movement and its supporters abroad) were to be a powerful factor in the erosion of its credibility among Allied governments and opinion.

The attitude towards the resistance adopted at the end of 1941 still appeared legitimate to the Yugoslav government in 1943, at a time when the British had changed theirs to one of activism. As they argued that they were in no position to impose anything on Mihailović,[5] his supporters in the government came round to the opinion that it would be no bad thing if the armed communist movement were destroyed before the end of the war. Mihailović was never openly told of any new line. This was partly because the government could not have told anything by radio that went against the British line, even if it wanted to, and partly because it could no longer, from the end of 1942, agree on any policy whatever. By the time that radio contact outside British control had been established under the Purić administration, it was too late to do either partner any good. The question of communications was only one of the problems on which divergences developed between the British and the émigré government. While the ultimate British consideration was one of military efficiency, for the exiled leaders it was primarily one of political importance. Any communication on vital but delicate matters, not for British ears, between the expatriate government and its supporters in the occupied homeland was almost out of the question.

Bearing the brunt of the struggle for the survival of Europe, the British assumed a total identity between their own war aims and those of their lesser and dependent allies. For a long time they did not realize that resistance movements were not only concerned with liberation, but also and increasingly with the seizure of control in the wake of an Allied victory. They insisted on overall control until at least the end of 1942, but were more generous in promises than in actual supplies. This was mainly due to technical reasons, and to the fact (which the Yugoslavs did not realize and the British never told them) that Yugoslavia was never more than a side-show in the overall context of the war.

Foreign policy: relations with the great allied powers

The very impotence of the exiled Yugoslavs, living off their rapidly diminishing moral credit with the British, allowed the latter to adopt a far more proprietary attitude towards them than towards other allies. The Yugoslavs never took British actions at face value, always explaining them by hidden motives or political manoeuvres. The British, who had at first built up the government of 27 March 1941 into gallant heroes and Mihailović's men into a powerful Allied force, by 1943 laid their disappointment exclusively at the door of the Yugoslav government.

The atmosphere still had much of the original trust and admiration when the Yugoslav and Greek governments signed, in London on 15 January 1942, a treaty laying the groundwork for one of the regional projects the British were promoting at the time. It established the basis for a post-war Balkan community, but the friendship between the two exiled governments was to have little effect on their occupied homelands. It did, however, fit right into Foreign Minister Ninčić's views. Momčilo Ninčić was anxious that his country should become part of a wider bridge between the opposing interests of the Great Powers, and not the instrument of any one of them.

His policy also led him to want good relations with the USSR. Yugoslavia was already linked to the Soviet Union by a non-ratified treaty, signed early on the day of the invasion of Yugoslavia to demonstrate Stalin's displeasure with increased German involvement in the Balkans. The Soviet government had then returned to a policy of accepting *faits accomplis* in German-held lands until its own territory had been invaded. After that, anything which tied down Axis troops was welcome. Resentment at the potential anti-Soviet implications of the British-sponsored Balkan plan was an additional reason for its approach to the Yugoslav government about a revival of the April 1941 agreement. Only when the drafting stage was reached, to what turned out to be a treaty of mutual assistance between the USSR and a government devoid of territory or armed forces, did the British Foreign Office object, and the proposal was dropped.

The Soviets' apparently friendly attitude towards the Yugoslav government was nevertheless maintained. In August 1942 legations became embassies on Soviet initiative, following similar British and American moves. Even though this coincided with its first accusations against Mihailović, Moscow was careful not to identify him with his government. The party coalition government believed that the Soviet government could, if it so wished, get the Yugoslav communists to take orders from Mihailović, or at least desist from the civil war. The Soviet leadership, who did not yet expect a communist revolution to succeed in Yugoslavia, retreated into an equivocal attitude until mid-1944.

The Yugoslav government similarly hoped to get American help to break away from its dependence on the British. It invested much energy to obtain trans-Atlantic support and to mobilize the Yugoslav-Americans. King Peter's visit to the USA in June 1942 was followed by a lend-lease agreement. In the latter half of 1943 the government also began to look to the United States for protection against British pressure to discard Mihailović. It obtained expressions of sympathy, but little real benefit. Ambassador Fotić was liked, but he seemed to be losing faith in the very concept of Yugoslavia, and part of his government wanted him dismissed. From November 1941, when the news of the massacres in the NDH split the Yugoslav-American community into bitterly feuding factions, Yugoslav officials in the US were themselves divided by the same issue. From the summer of 1942 a new split appeared on the issue of communist charges against Mihailović. All of this had repercussions on the attitude of American public opinion to Yugoslavia. The US were anyhow not interested enough in the Balkans to want to get involved in a side-show which they accepted as being a British responsibility. In trying to obtain American interference, the Yugoslavs were never told the truth about their chances, and they incurred British displeasure.

The main 'domestic' issue: the Serb-Croat question

Tension had dropped as soon as the government had passed firmly into the hands of the party representatives. So, 1942 was relatively the best year for the émigré government. The ministers had some reason to be satisfied. Jovanović had a long experience of chairing academic bodies. The British had been pleasantly surprised to see that Serbo-Croatian concord had not only been preserved, but actually seemed to have improved with the removal of the generals. The belief that Anglo-American influence would be decisive was helped by British-sponsored programmes of reconstruction and federation. Serbs tended to think that Mihailović was their defence against the dangers that threatened them. Croats were satisfied that they could weather the storms of the war by sitting it out in the government until the end, after which the Serbo-Croatian problem would be sorted out on a new basis with Allied blessing.

There was the rub. In exile and under the shock of events in the occupied homeland, party leaders were faced again with the pre-war Serb-Croat issue, hideously magnified. The first clashes had occurred in Athens and Jerusalem. Maček's decision to stay behind had been accepted with some distrust by Serb ministers. By not adding his weight to the government that had left the country, he had contributed to reducing its prestige. Croat ministers had reacted nervously to accusations that they had favoured the Pact, and that treachery of Croat military personnel was one of the causes of the débâcle. Then, in London, contradictory reports arrived about developments at home until they were clear enough to create an atmosphere of desperation among Serbs generally, including ministers. The Croat ministers suspected their Serb colleagues of wanting to use the news as a means of discrediting Croats. The Serbo-Croatian problem turned into one about the existence of the state itself during the stormy cabinet meetings of October and early November 1941. All then realized that such recrimination could only worsen the situation at home. On 15 November Simović repeated in a broadcast that the programme of the government remained the restoration of Yugoslavia. The three deputy prime ministers, the Serb Jovanović, the Croat Krnjević and the Slovene Krek, got together to draft a declaration on the future constitutional pattern of Yugoslavia.

Not all the Serb ministers had been keen on that part of the Jerusalem Declaration of 4 May 1941 which had stated that the 1939 *Sporazum* was a 'cornerstone of state policy'. The agreement had not actually federalized the authoritarian Constitution of 1931, but simply introduced a Croat *corpus separatum* in an otherwise centralist state. The HSS ministers had enjoyed a position of strength under Cvetković's prewar premiership, since they could claim to represent the Croatian nation in a cabinet otherwise bearing the colours of an artificial government movement. Under Simović they faced the leaders of other truly political parties. They realized that the March coup had been carried out partly in reaction to the *Sporazum*, and that the partners with whom they had struck the bargain (Prince Paul and Cvetković) were no longer there. So they had to press for a public confirmation from their new partners.

Yet the picture was constantly being altered. The Axis Powers had granted extreme Croatian nationalists a state of their own. Before the Yugoslav government had even flown out to Greece, Maček had appealed to Croats to obey the new authorities, who thereafter kept him isolated or even interned. The HSS was effectively leaderless. Krnjević and the finance minister Šutej were the only two HSS ministers abroad with the government. They were on the defensive, feeling outnumbered. When *ustaša* atrocities became known, Krnjević seemed to believe they had been grossly exaggerated in order to blacken the Croats in the eyes of the Allies. He found it difficult to speak out against the massacres, yet at the same time continued to insist on obtaining an ironclad constitutional guarantee of the postwar status of Croatia.

Many émigré Serbs became convinced that Krnjević, who had belonged to the more intransigent wing of his party, also aspired to a separate Croatia. Thus was created a gulf of suspicion that proved impossible to bridge. Most Serb ministers had been converted to a postwar federal reorganization, made up of only three units – Serbia, Croatia and Slovenia. They had confirmed the Sporazum in Jerusalem, and felt that to revalidate it again would lose them the confidence of outraged Serbs at home. They now saw reorganization in terms of making sure that no important number of Serbs would ever be again under Croatian rule. The Sporazum was anyhow no more than a temporary measure to be looked at again after a postwar general election. Even those still willing to understand their Croat colleagues' point of view deemed it essential that the latter should condemn the massacres without qualifications. The more they insisted on this, the more outnumbered Croats fought back with charges of 'Serb chauvinism'.

In the absence of any direct evidence of Krnjević's thinking, one has to surmise on the basis of indirect evidence.[6] It seems that he wanted to keep all options open for the future through a recognized Croatian political unit. If Yugoslavia were to be restored, it would be renegotiated, and since the Serbs would once again be in an advantageous position, as initial victims and final victors, Croats should stand on a well-acknowledged position. If Serbs and Croats parted company, then again a well-established starting position would be an advantage for Croatia.

He considered himself to be the plenipotentiary representative of the Croatian nation in the Allied camp, but he could only act as such as vice-president of the Yugoslav government in London. The impressive unity of the HSS had been shattered. It was difficult to know what the Croats at home wanted. The extreme right of the HSS had been taken over by the *ustaša* Movement. Krnjević too had his communication problems. He had to try and contact party cadres at home without British or Serb control, and get to know what Serb ministers would not trust him with. Fearing that Mihailović's movement could become an instrument of Serbian predominance if not revenge, he tried to discredit it. He would not engage in any genuine debate about the future of Yugoslavia, and ended up in an intransigent posture which greatly contributed to the paralysis of the émigré government.

Serb ministers did not form a monolithic bloc. The NRS defended Serb interests and attacked the Croats, but it did not conceive of a Yugoslav government without HSS representatives, even though it would gladly have done without some of the all too 'Yugoslav' JNS and SDS intermediaries. The DS too stood for Serb interests, but it wanted to build bridges, and thought that it was imperative not to make the conflagration worse. All agreed that it was not the time to go back on the Sporazum, or to deny it, but that it was not the time either to make what they saw as new concessions to the HS, such as binding themselves publicly again to that document. All believed that Yugoslavia was still in the interest of the Serbs (and of the Croats and Slovenes too). Most wanted it as a three-unit federation. Some talked privately of Serbia as Yugoslavia's Prussia.

The horrors of war did cause some of the Serb members of the government to become increasingly assertive in their nationalistic approach. A few probably began to hesitate between a three-member federation and rejection of any further association with the Croats, since the latter probably did not want it either. This in turn led to a split between these Serb ministers and others who feared for the survival of Yugoslavia, but the split was hardly along party lines, and some Serb politicians did co-operate with Croats against other Serbs throughout 1942. Attempts to get a compromise afloat were usually blown off course by attacks on the Croats in the Allied press believed to be inspired by Serb colleagues, before being wrecked by what was seen as the intolerance of the HSS vice-premier.

As chairman of the Serb Cultural Club, founded in 1937 as an opposition pressure group to work in favour of Serb interests within Yugoslavia, Jovanović had been against the *Sporazum*, but he had wanted to reach a negotiated compromise between Serb and Croat interests acceptable to both. The war had reinforced his belief. It was in the interest of Serbs, Croats and Slovenes alike to salvage the concept of a common state, for it was only in a Yugoslav community that the three groups, now dismembered and disunited, could be reunited in one same country to advance their respective and their collective interests. Little hope was left if Yugoslavia's exiled politicians were to fall out among themselves. He agreed with the British government that it was essential for the Yugoslav government to issue a declaration placing above any doubt that it was the government of Yugoslavia. To state clearly its commitment to federation and democracy would answer criticism from the Croats that the Serbs wanted Yugoslavia as no more than a cover for Serb hegemony, and from the communists that the exiled politicians just wanted to go back to the *status quo ante bellum.* Jovanović is on record as saying that he would not continue as prime minister unless he succeeded in obtaining agreement on this basic policy issue, and an assurance that there would be teamwork.[7]

The issue dragged on. Jovanović proved unable to create a team spirit where none existed. The Yugoslav politicians had taken with them into exile all their unresolved conflicts. By the end of 1942, as no progress had been made on the Declaration, the prime minister went ahead with a number of measures to make it clear that the government was committed to renewing the Yugoslav state, in the interest of its components and of Europe as a whole. Such was the gist of the King's speech broadcast on Unification Day (1 December 1942), of Jovanović's firm directives to Mihailović on 5 December, and of his strongly worded instructions of 14 January and 11 February 1943 to Ambassador Fotić in Washington. By that time, however, the two extremes had hardened to the point where the Serb end was confident that the Americans would intervene to let the Serbs decide on the future of Yugoslavia, and the Croat end, that the British would arbitrate, and do so in favour of the Croats. The attempt to make the Declaration acceptable to all produced only generalities, and the debate over its formal approval degenerated into clashes over words.

The result was that the cabinet could not put an end to mutual recriminations, or put forward a single propaganda line to occupied Yugoslavia, or attempt to co-ordinate its policy with that of the Great Allied Powers. It was unable to give Mihailović the guidance he was entitled to expect, or the population at large anything to counteract the psychological impact of the partisans. It failed to provide leadership for the pro-Yugoslav moderate forces in many quarters of the occupied homeland, wedged between fascists and communists, which looked to their exiled leaders. Messages reached the government in London, urging it to speak with a single voice and to adopt policies designed to put an end to the wars of mutual extermination. But the émigré government was fast losing the possibility of doing anything constructive to that end, or even to establish a common front against the communists, and all the time it was losing prestige in British eyes.

The cabinet crises of 1943 and King Peter

Such a climate produced cabinet crises only remotely connected with developments in Yugoslavia or in the councils of the Allies. It eventually destroyed the Jovanović government – ironically at a moment when Tito's movement, also going through a crisis, was willing to stop fighting the Germans in order to concentrate its energies against its native opponents and, if necessary, oppose a landing by the Western Allies.

In the first week of 1943 the cabinet was thrown into a crisis from which it emerged with a feeling of sobered satisfaction. It was reduced to ten members: Jovanović president, Mihailović war minister, Krnjević and Šutej for the HSS, and one each for all the other parties. It was realized that the partisan movement had obtained a hold on the mixed areas, that it was necessary to repair the government's prestige, and to try and bring together Mihailović and Maček. A divided and confused Yugoslav government was losing the sympathy of the British government, which increased its pressure in the spring with a formal plea for concord, a unified resistance, and a declaration on the future of Yugoslavia.

In May Jovanović completed the draft 'Declaration on the War Aims and the General Aims of the State Policy of the Yugoslav Government'. This committed it to the liberation and reunification of Yugoslavia, and its federal and democratic reorganization. It was submitted to the cabinet, debated at length, and approved by all – in principle. Krnjević then added that Jovanović was not the right man to carry out the policy embodied in the Declaration. Disillusioned, Jovanović resigned on 17 June. The British had by then decided to establish relations with the partisans.

The King's consultations with the party leaders on the formation of a new cabinet took almost a fortnight. He eventually chose the Radical Miloš Trifunović, who had been out of office between 1927 and 1941. He had opposed the *Sporazum* and constantly put Serb interests first in the émigré government, but the NRS had been the largest party in the days of parliamentary rule. Krnjević had actually expressed his preference for Trifunović, saying that at least he knew where he stood with that former opponent. On 26 June 1943 Trifunović assembled two representatives from each of the parties except the SDS,[8] with Mihailović again as war minister. The new government then formally adopted the Declaration, only to be faced with a set of HSS amendments, including a reference to the *Sporazum* as 'one of the cornerstones of state policy'. Krnjević justified them with the argument that the new prime minister had stated privately that he did not recognize the *Sporazum*. It all had to start from scratch again.

The main issue was complicated by side issues taken over unsolved from Jovanović – ambassadorial appointments, the British request for the government to go to Cairo, and King Peter's wish to marry Princess Alexandra of Greece. It was impossible to settle other problems raised by the British government, such as demands concerning the resistance. The Croat ministers eventually stated that any further collaboration with their Serb colleagues was impossible, but that they would not withdraw. Trifunović resigned on 10 August 1943; a new cabinet was sworn in two hours after he had handed in his resignation. United against the generals at the beginning of 1942, the politicians had found themselves divided over other issues, and their cabinets had survived at the whim of an immature monarch who had inherited the shadow of the powers of his father's made-to-measure statute.

King Peter was both exploited and flattered. Serb ministers were, on the whole, unable to resist him, and the Croats showed every signs of wanting to continue the practice of dealing directly with the Crown. Peter II appears to have enjoyed the shadow play of 'ruling', as much as he disliked the duty of 'reigning'. It was because he resented Simović's paternalism that he readily dismissed him. If the full 'parliamentary' ritual of consulting party leaders was observed on Jovanović's resignation, no such forms were observed after Trifunović's fall. The British government, having lost confidence in the sense of reality of the Yugoslav politicians in exile, had decided to neutralize them by exploiting, in its turn, the King's position.

Peter II contributed powerfully to the chaos by insisting on getting married. He wanted to get rid of those who opposed his plans, and complained about them to all who, for other reasons, were ready to exploit his dissatisfaction. A paradoxical *conjuncture* of reasons advanced by the King of Yugoslavia, the Prime Minister of the UK and the Secretary General of the HSS brought about the demise of the émigré political administration. Trifunović's cabinet was no more than a transition. As Krnjević was coming up with his amendments to the Declaration, King Peter asked his prime minister to make at least an announcement of his engagement, which Trifunović did in order to gain time. No sooner had the royal engagement been announced at the end of July 1943, than Trifunović and Krnjević had outlived their usefulness to the King. The British insisted on the appointment of an emergency, purely administrative, government, ready to follow their advice. With Trifunović's cabinet stuck in an impasse, the King's personal government of civil servants emerged, sanctioned by Churchill.

The King's government: marriage and liquidation

The new prime minister was Božidar Purić, a senior diplomat. The King wanted him to underwrite his marriage. Churchill wanted him to drop Mihailović. Purić accepted that there was nothing he could do against King Peter's determination to marry, except to stall, but it was on the express condition of keeping Mihailović that he took on the job. His was the most thoroughly committed to Mihailović of all the émigré cabinets. Mihailović was reappointed, along with a naval officer and four civil servants. With no political authority whatsoever, the government suffered a further fall in prestige. Its existence depended entirely on the confidence of a 20-year-old monarch in exile and on the toleration of the British prime minister. The first acts of the Purić cabinet were to shelve the Declaration with the argument that it would be worthless coming from a small team of civil servants; to decide to go to Cairo; and to appoint an ambassador to London. Then complications started. The Yugoslav political establishment in èxile was alive with opposition to Purić. It was not difficult for the King to threaten to get rid of him, no sooner had Purić tried to advise the monarch to postpone his marriage until his return to Yugoslavia.

Peter II had met Princess Alexandra, niece of King George II of the Hellenes, in April 1942 and had immediately proposed. The government did not object to the choice, but all the Serb ministers considered an engagement, let alone a wedding, would be inopportune in time of war. The King did not raise the question again until April 1943, when he asked all members of the government for their opinions in writing. The Serb ministers repeated their objections. Mihailović answered that no announcement should be made until he had time to prepare public opinion. Having obtained the announcement of his engagement from Trifunović, King Peter took the matter up again with Purić in Cairo. It was only when he had been asked back to London for talks with the British government that Purić relented. The wedding was performed in the British capital on 20 March 1944.

After the Cairo and Tehran conferences there had been, in December 1943, another change in British policy towards Yugoslavia. Pressure on Purić increased to come to an arrangement with the partisans, but he would not budge. British pressure then switched to King Peter, to appoint a more reasonable prime minister and to ditch Mihailović. Churchill believed that he could, through the King, retain a measure of continuity and a measure of British influence in Yugoslavia. Afraid of what he had done, King Peter returned for advice to the senior party leaders, but Churchill had suggested Ivan Šubašić, HSS *ban* of Croatia since 1939 who was in the USA, in a state of self-proclaimed breach of relations with the government, though not with his King or with his *Banovina* budget. The King summoned him for consultations. Churchill informed Tito that Šubašić would be prime minister; then the Commons that King Peter had accepted the resignation of the Purić cabinet, and that he was forming a new one, with Šubašić and without Mihailović – at a time when Purić had neither resigned nor been dismissed. Broken, King Peter gave in.

The young monarch now became a simple instrument. Šubašić was sworn in on 1 June 1944 as a one-man government. Along with the King, as the royal-appointed *ban* of Croatia, he represented the continued legitimacy of the state. He was willing to talk with Tito, secretary general of the Communist Party of Yugoslavia and head of the partisans' Communist-led Peoples' Liberation Movement. A prominent member of the HSS, Šubašić was more tractable than Krnjević. Just as he had once acted as intermediary between Prince Paul and Maček, so now he was to act as intermediary between Churchill (nominally King Peter) and Tito. Ten days after his appointment, he left for the island of Vis to begin negotiations with Tito on the formation of a coalition government. The issue of the monarchy would not be raised before the war had come to an end; the partisans' administration would be the only authority in Yugoslavia, and their army the only acknowledged fighting force. The royal government's task would be to organize support for the partisans, and Tito put forward the names of two personalities to be included in the joint government. Such was the gist of the Šubašić-Tito agreement signed on 16 June 1944. Šubašić had consulted nobody. Except for a few temporary concessions of form obtained from Tito, it was a capitulation.

On his return, Šubašić appointed five other ministers – Tito's two nominees and three émigré politicians drifting to a policy of compromise with Tito. Mihailović, who had not been included, refused to recognize the new government, but he proclaimed his loyalty to the King and did not organize a counter-government. There followed a purge of the émigré administration. Mihailović was dismissed as chief of staff of the Supreme Command on 29 August. Finally on 12 September, the King broadcast an appeal to all Serbs, Croats and Slovenes to rally round Tito, adding that 'the stigma of treason' would stick to those who did not answer the call. Having joined Tito in liberated Belgrade, Šubašić signed another agreement with him on 1 November. Pending a plebiscite to be organized after the complete liberation of the country, the King would delegate the royal prerogative to a regency appointed in agreement with Tito. A provisional government would be set up from Šubašić's cabinet and from Tito's national committee. When the prime minister returned to London, the King refused to accept the new agreement, and dismissed him on 23 January 1943, only to reinstate him under strong British pressure six days later, having swallowed the regency. Šubašić and the members of his cabinet then went to Belgrade for good. When on 7 March 1945 Tito formed his new provisional government, with a majority of 25 to 3 in the merger, the 'Royal Yugoslav Government in exile' was no more.

Conclusion

The Yugoslav government that went into exile had been formed in the eleventh hour as a broad representation of disparate parties. It had had no time to agree on a programme. It was not a working team, let alone a war cabinet. The party leaders who had made their way to the safety of the British shore were unable to face the disaster that had destroyed Yugoslavia. They were frozen by defeat and exile into the attitudes which they had had on the eve of having been brought together. Indeed, for most of the time most of them acted as if they could survive the war together only by avoiding the real issues. Reduced as they were trying to save acquired positions, for which they considered themselves to be sacred depositories, their only real policy could be one of wait-and-see, paralyzed by the use of the *liberum veto.*

For long out of office, then all together in office in exile, they were already politicians of another age who did not realize that their achievements, ideals and followings were being destroyed by the war. They were 'royalists' to the extent that they were the Government of HM the King of Yugoslavia, and also to the extent that their political culture knew of no other constitutional form. Royal authority was soon no more than a word to be bandied about by various factions. The British were perhaps the most ruthless exploiters of the concept, the more so since the exiled Yugoslavs believed that the Allies, and the British in particular, would settle all their difficulties for them. They admired but did not love the 'English', and in order to gain their confidence, took to revealing their secrets and dissensions to them, in exchange for which they were despised, misled, and kept in deliberate ignorance of many aspects of British policy. Different Yugoslav politicians had different contacts with British officialdom, and every one of them believed that 'British policy' was what his contact told him. Cut off from their homeland, they relied on distorted scraps of information, which were not collated, so that each one of them came to believe only that which fed his wishful thinking.

The exiled Yugoslavs were alien to the milieu and to the mentality of the British. Most of them never really understood why, having been overwhelmed with expressions of British gratitude on their arrival, they were shoved off the stage as irrelevant nuisances three years later. They were projected and then rejected by issues that were over, above and behind them.

Notes

1 They had flown out of Yugoslavia on 14 and 15 April and, by way of Athens and Jerusalem, had arrived in Great Britain on 21 June – the eve of the German attack on the USSR. In addition to the sources cited in the endnotes, this chapter has drawn on the following works: Lj. Boban (ed.), *Hrvatska u arhivima izbjegličke vlade 1941–1943* (Zagreb: Globus, 1985); M. Grol, *Londonski dnevnik, 1941–1945* (Belgrade: Filip Višnjić, 1990); M.A. Kay, 'The British Attitude to the Yugoslav Government-in-exile, 1941–45', unpublished doctoral thesis, University of Southampton, 1986; M.A. Kay, 'The Yugoslav Government-in-Exile and the Problems of Restoration', *East European Quarterly*, vol. 25, no. 1, 1991; M. Konstantinović, *Politika Sporazuma. Dnevničke beleške 1939–1941; Londonske beleške 1944–1945* (Novi Sad: Mir, 1998); B. Krizman (ed.), *Jugoslavenske vlade u izbjeglištvu, 1941–1943. Dokumenti* (Belgrade: Arhiv Jugoslavije and Zagreb: Globus, 1981); K. St. Pavlović, *Razgovori sa Slobodanom Jovanovićem, 1941–1945* (Windsor, Ontario: Glas kanadskih Srba, 1972); K. St. Pavlović, *Ženidba kralja Petra II* (Belgrade: Otkrovenje, 2002); St. K. Pavlowitch, 'Out of Context. The Yugoslav Government in London, 1941–45', *Journal of Contemporary History*, vol. 16, no. 1, 1981; B. Petranović (ed.), *Jugoslovenske vlade u izbeglištvu, 1943–1945. Dokumenti* (Belgrade: Arhiv Jugoslavije, and Zagreb: Globus, 1981); D. Šepić, *Vlada Ivana Šubašića* (Zagreb: Globus, 1983); D. Tošić, 'Antagonizam izmedju nauke i politike. Beseda u Srpskoj akademiji nauka i umetnosti 17. februara 1997. u povodu rasprave o S. Jovanoviću', *Istorijski zapisi*, 1, 1997. It has also drawn on the unpublished papers of the Conference on governments exiled in London during the Second World War, held in London in October 1977 (Imperial War Museum), and on the diary of Kosta Pavlović for the period 1941–45 currently being edited for publication in Belgrade.

2 J.B. Hoptner, *Yugoslavia in Crisis, 1939–1941* (New York & London: Columbia University Press, 1962), pp. 263–64.

3 Earlier in March 1941, SOE officials in Belgrade had suggested that, in the event of Yugoslavia teaming up with the Axis, he should leave for London to organize there a Free Yugoslav Committee on the pattern of the Free French. D. Djordjević, 'Slobodan Jovanović', in W. Laqueur and G.W. Mosse (eds.), *Historians in Politics* (London and Beverly Hills: Sage Publications, 1974), p. 261.

4 The war minister had a military administrative office beside the civilian one that all ministers had. This has often been mistakenly, if literally, translated as 'Military Cabinet'. The French-style *cabinet* was the minister's advisory administrative staff. Major Knežević was the brother of Radoje Knežević who headed the Royal Household.

5 Jovanović told the Soviet ambassador at the beginning of 1943 that the government could only take away from Mihailović what it had conferred on him – the position of war minister – but not his leadership of a movement in the occupied homeland. Slobodan Jovanović, *Zapisi o problemima i ljudima, 1941–1944* (London: Society of Serbian Writers and Artists Abroad, 1976), p. 36.

6 The closest is M. Martinović, 'Mukotrpni rad d-ra Krnjevića za vrijeme rata u Londonu', in P. Stanković (ed.), *Kalendar Hrvatski Glas 1955*, xxv, (Winnipeg, 1955), pp. 66–79

7 I. Jukić, *The Fall of Yugoslavia* (New York and London: Harcourt Brace Jovanovich, 1974), p. 119.

8 The SDS did not want to sit with General Živković, King Alexander's prime minister of 1929, included as leader of the JNS and deputizing for General Mihailović.

7   Reassessing Socialist Yugoslavia, 1945–90

The case of Croatia

Dejan Jović

This chapter argues against the popular view that Croats and Croatia were forced back into Yugoslavia at the end of the Second World War by some external power and that socialist Yugoslavia was one long and dark 'prison' for the Croatian nation.[1] On the contrary, a combination of factors, including the legacy of the Second World War and the ability of Yugoslav communists to successfully address the Croatian question, led to Croats and Croatia accepting the new state. The role of Josip Broz Tito – the founder and main leader of socialist Yugoslavia and an ethnic Croat through his father's side – was of crucial importance in this process. Moreover, it is argued in this chapter that Croatia was amongst the last Yugoslav republics supportive of the Yugoslav status quo, even in the late 1980s when Kosovo, Slovenia and Serbia had already significantly challenged not only the communist political system but also the purpose and sustainability of any Yugoslavia. In the last years before the break-up of the Yugoslav federation, Croatia remained one of the most conservative (i.e. pro-communist) and the most pro-Yugoslav parts of the former Yugoslavia. Furthermore, even after declaring independence from Yugoslavia (in June 1991) Croatia has continued relying on what it interpreted as a letter and spirit of Yugoslavia's 1974 Constitution. Not only that, the official discourse claimed that declaration of independence (25 June 1991) was legal because the Constitution confirmed the right of all Yugoslav nations to self-determination, but in a more contemporary context (in 2008) Croatia justified its recognition of Kosovo's unilaterally declared independence by its own reading of the 1974 Constitution.[2] Much of the communist interpretation of recent history – especially of the character of the interwar Yugoslavia – survived as the official discourse in the new independent Croatian state. The first president of the Croatian Republic, Franjo Tudjman remained largely positive in his several assessments of the role of President Tito, especially with regard to the status of Croatia in socialist Yugoslavia.[3] Hence, it is not surprising for example that Marshal Tito's Square in Zagreb survived several attempts by more extreme nationalists in Tudjman's government to rename it. This is all in sharp contrast to what is today often heard as interpretation of Croatian history in the twentieth century, including by some of Croatian leading nationalist historians.

Legacy of the Second World War

At the end of the Second World War, the newly formed People's Republic of Croatia was ideologically, politically and ethnically divided; perhaps to a greater degree than any other Yugoslav republic. Due to the burden the new Croatian republic inherited from the Independent State of Croatia (hereafter NDH) and its *ustaša* institutions, Croatia was in a distinctive position with respect to all other republics, even compared to the newly-created Bosnia and Herzegovina, which had also been part of the NDH. The *ustaša* regime had been one of the most brutal in occupied Europe.[4] The system of repression (which included *ustaša*-run concentration camps) was established, organized and supervised by the local fascists (although under the general political, military and ideological umbrella created by the external occupying force) and used almost exclusively against the local population: Serbs, Jews, Roma and anti-*ustaša* Croats. Because the main perpetrators were local, the issue of responsibility for mass murder and expulsion (which in today's terminology could be labelled ethnic cleansing and genocide) had to be addressed in a different way from countries where the blame could be assigned to outsiders (in most cases Nazi Germans and Fascist Italians).

During the war, a strong partisan movement emerged in Croatia, fighting both the occupying and local forces (the *ustašas* and *domobrani* (Homeguard), and in some areas also the *četniks*). The head of the People's Liberation Movement (NOP), was Josip Broz Tito, General Secretary of the Communist Party of Yugoslavia (KPJ). Tito was half-Croat, half-Slovene, but he rarely refered to himself as belonging to either of these (or any other) ethnic groups, and insisted instead that he was primarily a Yugoslav.[5] More importantly, his political identity was defined by his Marxist ideology and communist political identity. Before the war, Croatia was a relatively fertile ground for the activities of the Communist Party, culminating in 1937 with the founding of the Communist Party of Croatia (KPH) as a distinctive organizational unit within the Communist Party of Yugoslavia (KPJ). During the interwar period, discontentment with the authorities in Croatia was significant. Although the Croatian Peasant Party (which in principle favoured the politics of compromise within Yugoslavia) was by far the strongest party in Croatia, there existed radical political programmes seeking an opportunity to rebel, including revolutionary ideologies based on separatism (*ustašas*) and class revolution (communists).[6]

As opposed to the exclusively Croatian and ideologically fascist *ustaša* movement, communist ideology was internationalist, which was one of the reasons that in Croatia the communist party members included both ethnic Croats and ethnic Serbs. This bi-national nature was a characteristic of the Croatian communist party more than any other Croatian party. In the first two years of the war (1941–43), the partisan detachments in Croatia were primarily composed of Croatian Serbs, many of whom fled to mountains to escape *ustaša* terror.[7] At the end of 1941, of 7,000 partisan fighters from Croatia, 5,400 (77 per cent) were ethnic Serbs, and 800 ethnic Croats.

Among those who died that year, 78 per cent (927) were ethnic Serbs, and 19 per cent (231) ethnic Croats.[8] In 1942 and until September 1943, the share of ethnic Croats increased to 32 and 34 per cent respectively.[9] The initial imbalance in the ethnic composition of the partisan units in Croatia changed after the fall of Italy in September 1943 when Croats were mobilized in the liberated areas of Dalmatia and Istria. As a consequence of this, at the end of 1944, 60.4 per cent of the total partisan force in Croatia (which had 121,351 fighters) were ethnic Croats, and 28.6 per cent were Serbs.[10] According to official figures from 1964, among those partisans who were killed in Croatia during the four war years, 53 per cent (31,805) were Croats, and 44 per cent (26,715) Serbs.[11] Thus, at the end of the war, the Croatian partisans too (and not only the communist party membership) were a fully multinational (though primarily bi-national, Croatian and Serbian) political and military formation. The share of both ethnic Croats and ethnic Serbs from Croatia in the units of the victorious Yugoslav Army in 1945 was higher than the share of these two ethnic groups in the total population of Yugoslavia. Ethnic Croats from Croatia were 16 per cent of the Yugoslav population, but they were 22 per cent of the Partisan armed forces. Ethnic Serbs from Croatia were less than 5 per cent of Yugoslavia's general population, but they were about 20 to 25 per cent of the Partisan forces in 1941 and about 10 per cent in 1945. Croatian historians Ivo and Slavko Goldstein emphasize these numbers to conclude that the 'below average participation in partisans of the Serbs from Serbia was to some way compensated with above average participation of Serbs from Croatia (and Bosnia-Herzegovina)'.[12]

As a consequence of this joint participation of ethnic Croats and ethnic Serbs from Croatia in partisan activities during the Second World War, it comes as no surprise that the policy of ethnic equality – promoted by Yugoslav communists (the ideological and military leaders of the partisan movement) – reflected realities on the ground probably more closely in Croatia than in other parts of the newly re-established Yugoslav state. The Yugoslav partisan movement, and subsequently the new socialist federation, was based on the politics of brotherhood and unity, which was predicated on the equality of all peoples in Yugoslavia at that time. This was partly for ideological reasons (the internationalism inherent in all communist movements' ideologies aims at erasing differences between small and bigger ethnic groups, at least symbolically) but also for reasons of Croatia's recent historical experience and its ethnic and political structure. Since Croats and Serbs were both indeed South Slavonic nations (and thus were by new socialist discourse declared *brothers*), their 'brotherhood' was also seen as a condition for any Yugoslavism to succeed. Croats and Serbs both showed little solidarity or even care about the fate of non-Slavonic groups that were forced to leave Croatia in the immediate aftermath of the war: ethnic Italians from Istria and Dalmatia[13] and ethnic Germans from Slavonia and Bosnian Posavina. They viewed them not only as non-Slavonic minorities, but also as fundamentally disloyal to Yugoslavia. In sharp contrast, neither Serbs nor Croats treated each other as 'minorities' or 'foreigners'. In the light of their joint participation in the Partisans, they viewed each other – at least within the public, i.e. official discourse – as equal to one another.

This equality featured also in the interpretation of the recent past. The new authorities developed an ideological discourse that emphasized the immense sacrifices made by all the Yugoslav peoples equally. This referred not only to the sacrifices made in recent clashes against the occupying force and the 'domestic traitors' (collaborators), but also the sacrifices (real or only mythical) made during a longer period of more or less continuous struggle against foreign domination and authority. Not surprisingly for the elite that wanted to move away from the ambys of fratricidal warfare into offering a 'bright future' to all Yugoslav nations, the collective merits were acknowledged and emphasized, but collective guilt was rejected. It helped that the *ustaša* regime was not an elected authority (like the Nazis in Germany), but it was instead installed by the occupying forces. Accordingly, there was no reason why a majority (or even a significant part) of ethnic Croats should be held responsible for the *ustaše's* actions against the Serbs, Jews and the Roma. Any attempt to blame the whole of Croatia, or all Croats, for genocide against these groups met with fierce opposition by the new Croatian communist authorities. Furthermore, all such attempts were disqualified as malicious, and sometimes even as symptoms of anti-Croatian intentions of those who argued along these lines. The new Communist authorities, of course, accepted that there were collaborators to be found among Croats, just as among all nations, but – according to the official interpretation of the events from the Second World War – they were a minority. The majority consisted of antifascists and national liberators.

In the first post-war years, the distinction between 'majority' and 'minority' was thus in no way based on some ethnic principle, or on political orientations and preferences of the (non-existent) electorate. The new socialist Yugoslavia soon after 1945 abolished political parties and electoral democracy, and thus the concepts of 'majority' and 'minority' could not reflect the real popularity of certain political options with voters. Rather, the concept of 'minority' referred to defeated forces of the Second World War in Yugoslavia – equally to the former bourgeoisie and to defeated domestic fascists. Examples of sacrifice, as well as examples of heroic co-operation and brotherhood among the partisans (and the civilian population) of various nationalities were emphasized with the view of presenting a bi-ethnic Croat-Serb (and in a wider sense: Yugoslav) population as victims of foreign occupation and foreign-born ideologies of fascism and Nazism. The Yugoslavs – and for most Croats this primarily meant Croats and Serbs – were historical victors over their own treacherous non-national (*nenarodne*) minorities. This victory was possible only because of their co-operation, such as it was in the Partisans.

Partly because of the sensitivity of broaching the subjects from the recent past, and partly because of the ideological vision, the new socialist authority found the key to stability of the new order in a formula brought forth by Tito in his first speech in liberated Zagreb, on 21 May 1945: 'Enough with the past!'[14] For the new socialist authority, Yugoslavia was only possible as 'New' Yugoslavia, radically (in other words, revolutionarily) different as compared to the previous, 'Old', royal Yugoslavia. Instead of a monarchy, in 1945 Yugoslavia became a republic. Instead of becoming a unitary country, Yugoslavia became a federation. Instead of attempting to build a Yugoslav nation, the new communist elite promised to protect, preserve and develop the existing national identities of all its Slavonic nations. However, it was of great significance to change the character of what constitutes national identity of each of the Yugoslav nations. In line with Tito's announcement of a complete break with the past, the nationality policy aimed at enhancing *socialist* (*communist*) aspects of identity, and thus Yugoslavia actively engaged in repressing the influence of the clergy and religious organizations, as well as of various *retrograde, bourgeios* groups. Instead of becoming a country whose political system was built on pluralism, Yugoslavia decided to abolish political parties, which it saw as potentially divisive and too 'quarrelsome', and set up a single – communist – party as a political hegemon.[15] Even this party was then (in 1952) renamed the League of Communists, in a move that was consistent with the idea of developing a new, previously unseen and untried non-party system. Instead of accepting those aspects of tradition that generated or facilitated conflicts among the peoples, socialist Yugoslavia attempted to reinterpret the past so as to eliminate controversies. But, the Yugoslav communists were not wizards. They knew – from personal experience among others – that nationalism was and could continue to be the main threat to the project of a *New Yugoslavia*. However, they also knew that after a long war with such horrible atrocities, many were tired of conflicts. With the global defeat of Nazism and local defeat of the *ustaše*, nationalism too was defeated. The anti-nationalist programme of Yugoslav communism was thus not without a chance.

In addition, communism in 1945 became the main global alternative to both nationalism and liberal democracy, which further strengthened the position of Yugoslav communists too. Where controversies over the interpretation of the recent past persisted, they were placed *ad acta*. The past too often divided the Yugoslav peoples, while the future, expressed as a vision of joint development of socialism and as a transitional period between a class nationalist society and a classless internationalist society, was to re-connect them. This vision of the future – expressed in the ideological image of a desired goal to which the reality was to be adjusted in a long-lasting process of permanent reforms – would remain at the very core of the Yugoslav political, and all other, identities for the next 40 years.

Serbs and other non-Croats in socialist Croatia

During the war, the partisans had been the only organized military-political formation opposing the ethnic cleansing and genocide conducted by the *ustaša* against the Serbs, Jews, and Roma. After the war, a policy of full acceptance and affirmation of these groups was practised, especially regarding the Serbs in Croatia, who indeed were the main victims of the *ustaša* regime. In the new classification of national groups, the Serbs were given the status of a 'constitutive people' of Croatia, and thus nominally equal to Croats.

However, during the war, the number of Serbs, Roma and Jews significantly diminished, while in the period immediately following the war many ethnic Italians and Germans were forced to leave. As a result, in the second half of the twentieth century, Croatia was one of the most ethnically homogenous Yugoslav republics. Only Slovenia had fewer 'minorities' than Croatia. Later, especially in the 1980s, this fact served as a foundation for an argument that emerged in Serbia that socialist Croatia was some sort of a 'continuation' or even the 'successful conclusion' of the project of ethnic homogenization organized, in its most brutal form, by the *ustaša* regime.

On the other hand, perhaps to avoid further controversies regarding the position of non-Croats in Croatia, the political elite of socialist Croatia tolerated a higher-than-average representation of Serbs in political and state institutions, the military and the police. This was done also in response to ethnic homogenization of Croatia, for which Croatian communists blamed only and exclusively their wartime opponents, *ustaše*. The new post-1945 authorities made deliberate efforts in order to demonstrate that new, socialist Croatia was radically different from its *ustaša* predecessor. The above average representation of Serbs in the political elite can also be explained by their greater representation among the partisans, especially the early resistance fighters, who were regarded throughout the entire socialist period as 'guarantors' and 'controllers' of the ideals and achievements of the revolution.

Aside from ideology and founding principles, the position of Serbs in socialist Croatia was also defined by certain pragmatic, i.e. political, compromises on both federal Yugoslav and Croatian levels. It was indeed the case that Serbs were genuinely over-represented in the party (which now became the *real sovereign* of Yugoslavia) although the vast majority of top positions were still occupied by Croats.[16] In addition, the ideological concept that insisted on the equality of the larger and smaller communities within Yugoslavia recognized their status as that of a 'constitutive people', thereby formalizing their constitutional and political equality with the far more numerous ethnic Croats. The Yugoslav system was based on the idea that nobody could be treated as a minority, but as equal to the majority. On the request of representatives of Hungarian ethnic group, in 1962 Tito agreed to declare the concept of 'minority' as politically incorrect, which lead to its subsequent exclusion from the official discourse.[17] For example, non-Slavic minorities were proclaimed 'nationalities'.[18] Since Serbs amounted to the largest group living in the other republics – in other words, outside Serbia-proper – this recognition of the status was especially favourable for them. However, it was also favourable for other national minorities, such as Croats in Bosnia and Herzegovina, Montenegrins in Serbia and so on. Recognition of equality between Serbs and

Croats in Croatia was also at least in part the result of a sense of historical responsibility for the *ustaše* genocide, which reduced the number of Serbs in Croatia by between 125,000 and 137,000.[19] This recognition, however, was never explicit since Croatian Communists refused to accept any responsibility either for themselves or for the Croat nation as such for crimes committed by *ustaše* on behalf of Croats. *Ustaše*, they claimed, never represented Croats or Croatia, and thus neither Croats nor Croatia should bear responsibility for their acts.

On the other hand, notwithstanding proposals to this end, Croatia always refused to have a special 'autonomous region' established on its territory where the Serbs would constitute a majority. Until the early 1970s, relatively little had been done to rebuild the settlements in areas that had been damaged in the Second World War, and where the greatest number of victims had been of Serb ethnicity. The regions of Lika, Kordun and Banija, for example, remained among the least developed parts of Croatia, unlike Istria and the Dalmatian islands, which, thanks primarily to tourism, and although previously under-developed, after the war became among the richest parts of the country. This had an effect inasmuch as the Serbian population did not see itself as a privileged group. Instead, they took the opposite view, largely based on the perceived economic inequalities in Croatia. An attitude developed among some Serbs (especially those who lived in rural and under-developed regions, not so much those from urban centres) that they were the main victims and the main victors of the war – yet, somebody else (ethnic Croats) bene-fitted more than themselves from that victory. However, many Croats dis-agreed. Since the Serbs relied on state support and state jobs more than Croats (also because some of the Croats – especially those whose relatives were *ustaše* – could not pass through strict post-war political vetting due to parti-cipation of their relatives in *ustaše* or their own association with the NDH), they were often seen to be unfairly advantaged. This issue, along with other sensitive issues, was not much publicly debated. After all, this was the time of authoritarian communism, which did not favour openess and ideological pluralism. Instead, it 'smouldered' in alternative discourses, in parallel and private 'histories' only to surface later (especially at the end of the 1960s and in the 1980s). Sensitive issues were discussed among the partly leadership, but were not open to public debate.

Why did Croats accept socialist Yugoslavia?

In the light of this rather complex post-war reality, one should ask also: why did so many Croats accept socialist Yugoslavia? Was this acceptance genuine or was it just that there was simply no alternative either to Yugoslavia or to communism? When, in the late 1980s, a wave of calls for serious reforms was already shaking the whole of Yugoslavia, particularly Kosovo, Slovenia and Serbia, Croatia remained relatively calm and passive; in fact, it may be argued that Zagreb stood out as a factor of stability and compromise. From a permanent cause of instability, by continuously emphasizing the 'Croatian question' in the earlier history of Yugoslavia, Croatia in the 1980s became a republic providing what might have been the final serious attempt at preservation of some form of socialist Yugoslavia. (One might think of the examples of Ante Marković, the last Yugoslav prime minister (1989–91) and Stipe Šuvar, a member of the Yugoslav collective presidency (1989–90), the two most prominent Croatian politicians at the time.) Was such a position enforced? Was it due to political pragmatism or ideological dogmatism? Or was it also an expression of the conviction of those leading Croat politicians – and many others, who until 1990, supported them – that socialist Yugoslavia after all offered a satisfactory solution for Croatia, or that it fulfilled as much as, or almost as much as, was possible in the existing circumstances?

Socialist Croatia accepted Tito's concept of socialism not only because all other concepts were defeated (and it seemed that this defeat was historical, i.e. that neither liberal democracy nor Nazism could ever be resurrected), but – at least in part – also because the new concept promised to deliver on some of the main Croatian political demands of the twentieth century. Firstly, the post-war situation ensured conditions for stability and peace within Croatia – and peace and stability was much needed in a country with such traumatic experiences. In this process, Tito played a very important role. Many Croats – and especially those who participated in *domobrani*, or were employed by the wartime authorities, feared that with the end of the war they would become targets of revenge. Others thought that Croatia's position in Yugoslavia would worsen compared to the interwar situation, largely due to the role that the *ustaše* had during the war. None of this happened. Instead, a Croat – Tito – emerged as the main leader of new Yugoslavia. Tito was not a representative of Croatia, nor did he treat Croatia any differently from other Yugoslav republics. He was not a nationalist, and certainly not a Croatian nationalist. However, his understanding of socialism emerged in the context of the time and place in which he lived, and that was – for the major part of his life before coming to power – Croatia within the multinational context of, first, Austria-Hungary and, later, the Yugoslav kingdom. It was on these grounds that Croatia's main interests were also included in Tito's vision of Yugoslavia; a vision which absolutely dominated the Yugoslav communist movement until at least the mid-1970s, and (although in its somewhat distorted form) possibly even until the end of Yugoslavia, in 1990. New Croatia was built not only as an antithesis to *ustaša*-controlled Croatia, but also as an alternative to the interwar Yugoslav kingdom. It was no longer a *banovina* but a *federal state* and a *republic* of its own. The recognition of the *Croatian statehood* and of its political identity within the new Yugoslavia's context was a pleasant surprise even to Croatian nationalists.

New Yugoslavia sought to solve the 'Croatian question' by accepting the main demands of the prewar Croatian political leaders – republicanism and federalism. But, unlike Stjepan Radić and Vladko Maček, the leaders of the interwar HSS, Tito was successful in creating a Croatian republic within the

Yugoslav federation. What Stjepan Radić only dreamt of, Josip Broz success-fully delivered.[20] However, the Yugoslav communists did not think of a republicanism and federalism as their final objectives, but rather as a means by which Marxist ideals of equality and social justice should be promoted and implemented into reality. Republicanism and federalism had to be connected with the deep-seated problem of inequality between classes and nations. Yugoslav, and Croatian, communists claimed that national issues and class issues were interconnected and that they could be resolved only by radical changes. When they came into power, they founded Yugoslavia as a federation, gave it a republican character, and announced radical changes in the class structure in order to end the exploitation of the small, weak and unprotected by the large, powerful and privileged. This promise related not only to the protection of workers in relation to their previous class exploiters, but also the protection of smaller peoples by the larger ones.

Federalism was a compromise solution, which included a high degree of autonomy, even 'internal independence', as well as the preservation of the Yugoslav union. Furthermore, it was a modern concept. Both of the two post-war global superpowers – USA and USSR – were federations. The concept of federalism conformed to the principle of self-determination of peoples as pro-moted by Lenin and Wilson. In 1944 and 1945, Tito very often referred to the promise of self-determination, as stated in the Atlantic Charter, demanding self-determination for all Yugoslav peoples and their co-nationals living in the neighbouring countries.[21] Federalism was not only the only realistic solution in Croatia – it was also the best solution for it. The idea of total state inde-pendence from Yugoslavia was compromised by the prior existence of the Independent State of Croatia. Anyone promoting it, regardless of ideological background, ran the risk of being connected to the *ustaša* ideology. A return to pre-war centralism was also impossible (largely due to Yugoslav Commu-nists' fierce rejection of anything that would ressemble the old Yugoslav Kingdom), and it certainly was unattractive to the majority of Croats.

The division of Europe into two large blocs – the socialist Eastern bloc and the capitalist Western bloc – additionally solidified the existing structure and prevented significant further changes, especially the disintegration of European states. With the 1975 Helsinki Final Act came further stabilization. The Act helped the Yugoslav communists to significantly reduce separatist tendencies, as well as to eliminate irredentist claims to Yugoslav territory. They hoped that this would minimize the possibility of Yugoslavia's disintegration. Changes became possible only when the Cold War ended, and when the memory of the Second World War, including the animosities that persisted based on those memories, began to fade.

In addition to all these internal (ideological) and external (Cold War) realities, there was another reason for relatively successful consolidation of the new system in Croatia. A 'return' to the interwar past did not appeal to Croats. In addition to one obvious reason – the domination of Serb-style and Serb-dominated institutions – there was another: the Croatian Peasant Party

(HSS), which had been a national movement as much as a political party, became divided, confused and eventually marginalized during the Second World War. Some HSS members joined the partisans, some supported the government-in-exile in London (which included HSS ministers), some joined the *ustaša*, while many passively awaited the outcome of the war. This policy marginalized and compromised the HSS. Croatian nationalists never forgave it for the 1939 agreement with the Cvetković government,[22] while Croatian partisans never forgave the party its passivity during the war. With the disappearance of the HSS as a relevant political actor, the KPH (Communist Party of Croatia) filled the political vacuum and emerged as the dominant party in Croatia. Croatia, having been practically a one-party state before the war given the predominance of the HSS over all other parties, re-emerged from the war as a one-party state, within Yugoslavia, and in some respects it remained a one-party state in the early 1990s, when the Croatian Democratic Union (HDZ) dominated politics in the years following the break-up of Yugoslavia. The real or potential presence of the so-called 'national question' suppressed political, and all other, pluralism in Croatian politics of the inter-war period. Now, after the war, the 'successful resolution' of the Croatian national question kept the SKH firmly in the seat of Croatian politics. Political differences and even conflicts did not of course completely dissapear. However, they were all somehow naturally directed towards intra-party disputes: thus, disputes among communists rather than between communists and others. Many joined the SKH not because they believed in communism as ideology, but rather because they supported a particular informal group within the Party, which was either more liberal, or more nationalist, or more centralist than others. Many joined for pure career-driven purposes. The SKH membership thus became relatively pluralistic in their political views – although this pluralism was rather discrete and often visible only to well-informed observers and members of the party. It is not a surprise then that with the end of the regime, the SKH became the 'mother' of all Croatian political parties – which was especially the case with the HDZ.

Considering the legitimacy of the new socialist order in Croatia, it is important to highlight that the leadership of socialist Yugoslavia believed that creating a Yugoslav nation was not only an impossible, but also an undesirable, project. As distinct from pre-war Yugoslavia, new Yugoslavia was not conceived to minimize the significance of the existing nations (ethnic groups), but rather was meant to act as an instrument for their preservation and growth. It could be said that Yugoslavia was conceived as an 'incubator' for the small, previously unrecognized nations – Macedonians and Bosnian Muslims (Bosniaks). Yugoslavia also returned the symbols of statehood to the Montenegrins. The Slovenes, although recognized as one of the three 'tribes' of interwar Yugoslavia (officially called the Kingdom of Serbs, Croats and Slovenes between 1918 and 1929), gained their own parliament and government in socialist Yugoslavia. Some minorities, though not all, also achieved a new political status. Albanians in Kosovo, for example, were granted a provincial parliament and government, and a degree of real political autonomy. Croats and Serbs held the status of the nation-building peoples (or 'constitutive' peoples) recognized in all constitutions and emphasized in the political structure of the country. But even for Serbia the new Yugoslavia brought a return of its own (at least internally recognized) statehood. Unlike in the Kingdom of Serbs, Croats and Slovenes and the Kingdom of Yugoslavia, in which it had no political status, Serbia was in 1945 re-established as a political unit. Serbia too became – for the first time since 1918 – a state. Its statehood was as symbolic as it was in the case of other Yugoslav republics, but it was nevertheless nominally re-established within the Yugoslav federation of six republics.

As far as the authorities of new Yugoslavia were concerned, the 'national question' in general and within this also the 'Croatian question' was thus solved. Paradoxically, at the end of the war, when many Croats expected revenge for the crimes by the authorities of the Independent State of Croatia, some of the key positions in new Yugoslavia were occupied by Croats. For the first time in modern history a Croat, Ivan Ribar, became head of state in the aftermath of the Second World War. The real leader of Yugoslavia was, of course, Tito, also a Croat. This further diminished the resistance towards both Yugoslavia and the new order in Croatia, and served as a stabilizing factor in the reunited Yugoslav state.

One may say that if there was a problem with the Croatian position in Yugoslavia, it appeared when Croatia was either recognized by others as a large republic (relative to others) or when it started perceiving itself as being large, and thus entitled to a privileged status compared to others. In the interwar period, the Croatian problem was that it was 'small' compared to Serbia. In new Yugoslavia, it was when and if it acted as 'big'. As the second largest Yugoslav republic according to political significance, economic structure, size and population number, it was among larger, more developed and 'stronger' republics in Yugoslavia. With respect to linguistic criteria (not insignificant for national identity, especially in countries where the religious element has no important public role as was the case in socialist Yugoslavia), Croats belonged to the dominant group of Serbo-Croat speakers. With Zagreb as the largest industrial centre in the whole country, and featuring important Yugoslav cultural institutions, such as the Yugoslav Lexicographical Institute, the oldest university in the country and the first TV station (RTV Zagreb) Croatia was, in some respects, the 'centre' of Yugoslavia. However, in a country where domination of one republic over others was not encouraged, all of this was not an advantage, but a handicap. The less developed regions viewed Croatia with suspicion, just as they did Serbia. Croatia's leadership had to justify itself frequently to them and also to prove that it did not seek to dominate or exploit the less developed republics and regions – either on its own or jointly with Serbia.[23] This was especially the case with Bosnia-Herzegovina, the leadership of which was more often than not suspicious of their colleagues in the SKH. It was the same case with Slovenia.

Croatia's position in Yugoslavia was thus somewhat ambivalent. On the one hand, in socialist Yugoslavia, Croatia finally saw the achievement of its main objectives (federalism and republicanism). On the other hand, Croatia (almost as much as Serbia) was burdened by suspicion that it sought to dominate Yugoslavia. Smaller republics feared that Croatia might join forces with Serbia in order to establish a complete domination of the federation. Vladimir Bakarić, the leading politician in socialist Croatia, understood the ambivalence and the sensitivity of the Croatian position, and acted very carefully, sometimes even too carefully. Bakarić's Croatia never attempted to take the initiative, but instead took a back seat and observed political developments from the background, leaving the limelight to others. Conscious of the ambivalence of its position, of the legacy of the *ustaša* state, as well as of the deep divisions within Croatian society, Bakarić's Croatia relied as much as possible on Tito, believing that he would best protect Croatian interests in the federation. Of course, Croatia knew, and accepted, that Tito was not a representative of any single republic per se, Croatia included. But, Croatian leaders were fully aware that Tito's life experience was largely shaped by the Croatian political scene, and that thus he was 'one of them' – perhaps even to a larger extent than this was the case with other nations. Support of Tito, however, was largely expressed in ideological terms – as loyalty to the project of Titoist self-management system, which included equality of all nations/ republics in the federation too. To an outside observer thus it looked as if Croatia was the most dogmatic supporter of Marxism and Titoism – while in fact this was also a stubborn defence of Croatian national interests, which were (as communists believed) best protected within the new structure of the Yugoslav federation.

Tito talked cautiously about his national identity. In 1950 he even declined to fill in the questionnaire for newly elected members of the federal parliament as, among other items, it included a question about nationality.[24] He later emphasized that he was above all a Yugoslav, although with Croatian ethnic origins. In a conversation with the delegation of Serbia on 28 October 1970, Tito said that he could hardly accept the nationality box in various candidate lists for elections. 'Nobody can force me to declare myself as a Croat. I am not even a pure Croat – my mother is Slovenian', he said at the time.[25] He was even more explicit in a conversation with Svetozar Vukmanović Tempo, on 6 February 1969: 'Why are they making me be a Croat? I am a Yugoslav'.[26] Such statements, including also statements made publicly, were numerous, although there had been the opposite examples where Tito declared himself (also) as a Croat. However, Croatia felt that the achievement of its two great goals, the defeat of the *ustaša* ideology, the perspective of equality in Yugoslavia, as well as its international reputation, were above all Tito's accomplishments. Since he 'solved the Croatian question', Tito always had a free hand to act in Croatia, even during the controversial events in the period of 1967–71.

Tito also enjoyed a more-or-less genuine popularity in the general population who believed him to be, 'a man of the people', and occasionally even the only advocate of the people against the system which many thought was 'bureaucratized' and unjust.[27] It is hard to tell whether the trust in him was greater in Croatia than in other parts of Yugoslavia, because the other Yugoslav peoples – especially the smaller ones – had reasons also to support him. For example, the Macedonians and the Bosnian Muslims regard Tito's Yugoslavia as their 'golden age', while Kosovo Albanians also experienced an age of progress, despite many difficulties. This, of course, did not mean that there had not been discontent in Croatia (as elsewhere) with Tito's policies.

The Croatian Spring and its aftermath

No other political crisis illustrates this better than the 'Croatian Spring' or related events known as the 'Mass Movement' (*Maspok*), in Croatia. To some observers of Yugoslav politics, the Croatian Spring was perhaps the beginning of the end, when it came to Yugoslavia. However, it is wise to note that the end of Yugoslavia had more than one beginning – among the 'candidates' are also the 1966 purge of Aleksandar Ranković, the 1972 purge of Serbian 'liberals', the 1974 Constitution, the 1981 protests in Kosovo, the 1986 Memorandum of a group of Serbian Academicians, the 1987 *putsch* within the Serbian League of Communists, the 1989 suspension and then the abolition of autonomy for Kosovo – to name but a few. In this chapter I will, however, focus on the Croatian crisis of 1967–71, which was indeed a logical consequence of controversial processes which began with the removal of Yugoslavia's Vice President, Aleksandar Ranković, in 1966. The meaning of this internal *coup* was ambivalent. On the one hand, Yugoslavia embarked on the course of relative liberalization and further decentralization. On the other hand, however, the ousting of a pragmatic-oriented Ranković strengthened those in political leadership – primarily Tito's chief ideologues, Edvard Kardelj – who promoted a more ideologically-focused politics. The defeat of Ranković was thus – on both counts – a potential threat to Tito too. Both liberalization and re-ideologization could (and the later indeed would) reduce his power in the years to come.

Along the same lines, the events in Croatia that unfolded between 1967 and 1971 could not be explained in black and white terms. On the one hand, they were an expression of reformist tendencies, which were, in particular, driven by the victory of the concept of further decentralization (at the 8th Congress of the League of Communists of Yugoslavia in 1964), through economic reform (1965), by the deposition of the Vice President Aleksandar Ranković and the reform of the police apparatus (1966), and by the general opening of the country in the first part of the 1960s. On the other hand, they also brought the nationalists and other anti-communist groups into the public arena, perhaps for the first time in the post-war history. Competition between these groups was primarily confined to intra-SKH conflicts. However, when groups and individuals that did not belong to the SKH joined the debate, the alarm bell rang, primarily among the Croatian Serbs.

These developments alarmed Croatian Serbs, especially those from the partisan generation of veterans who had already objected to the gradual decentralization of Yugoslavia. These fears and the degree of opposition were understandable. Croatian nationalism in the Second World War – which had finished only 25 years earlier – was the root of so much suffering and it was understandable that wartime generations were afraid of its return in any form. The revival of nationalism in Croatia (which soon proved to be the only serious alternative to Tito's programme of socialism), destabilized and divided Croatia politically, ideologically and along ethnic lines. The revival of the 'Croatian question', considered solved in Tito's Yugoslavia, brought into serious question one of the greatest achievements of post-war politics. Unity and peace between the Croatian and Serbian peoples were disturbed not only in parts of Croatia, but also in Bosnia and Herzegovina.[28] The tension became such that both the army and police pressured Tito to intervene. Tito felt especially responsible for the situation in Croatia, not only as a Croat, but also because he had supported from the start demands of the Croatian leadership for further reforms and decentralization.

In the end, Tito's intervention in Croatian politics was limited, but nevertheless forceful. However, in 1972, Tito's action was not without significant support. To many it appeared that it was only through his intervention that the continuing stability was secured, even at the price of limiting democratic freedoms and reformist trends. In those years, it still appeared that political and individual freedoms were not the most desirable political value that a political system should provide or secure. Stability and peace was valued above democracy and human rights. In the areas where the memories of the terror of the relatively recently concluded war were very much alive, stability and peace were valued above all else. In the context of the 'doctrine of limited sovereignty', and under the still fresh impression of the violent ending of the Prague Spring by a Soviet intervention in 1968, it appeared that Tito's intervention in political conflicts was to many a better solution than the possibility of Soviet occupation. Foreign observers, especially some Western diplomats and journalists – as has been discovered in recently published documents from American and British archives – believed that Tito's decisive intervention against Croatian nationalism was not only justified, but also desirable.[29]

This is also confirmed by a relatively quick recovery from the crisis in Croatia itself. In 1972, the SKH membership in fact started to grow, in spite of 741 members withdrawing from the party in the immediate aftermath of the 1971–72 purges.[30] For example, in 1974, 20,444 new members were accepted into the SKH, while 11,001 members voluntarily left, and 1,223 members were excluded from the membership (of which 723 members were removed from the records due to inactivity). As reported at the 5th Session of the Central Committee of the SKH, on 14 May 1975, by Rikard Pompe, the then Secretary of the Statutory Committee of the SKH, in 1974 for the first time the erosion of the SKH membership, which had begun in

1961 and stopped for a brief period in 1968, ended.³¹ However, there had been stagnation in the intellectual sphere, since many authors were scared of the possible consequences of freely expressing criticism of the system. Croatian culture was impoverished by the absence of people like the social critic and writer Vlado Gotovac and a popular singer and political commentator Vice Vukov, while Croatian politics suffered a loss due to the forced retirement of the most prominent member of the younger generation of reformists – Ante Miko Tripalo. But, a new generation of authors, politicians, businessmen and journalists emerged swiftly, using the opportunity offered to them by the political coup of 1971.

The post-1971 Croatian authorities made a special effort to demonstrate that they held Croatian interests dear, and that in numerous aspects the new authorities could be even more successful than the administration which brought Croatia into isolation within Yugoslavia. Almost all of the post-1971 leaders had been part of the reformist 1967–71 leadership, and thus contributed to political reforms, and especially to further decentralization of Yugoslavia in this period. Their differences with pre-1971 leadership (led by Savka Dabčević-Kučar and Miko Tripalo) were over the degree of toleration of anti-communist groups, not over the issues of Croatian position in Yugoslavia. It came as no surprise, thus, that post-1972 Croatia continued to insist on the decentralization of Yugoslavia, while the constitutional amendments (declared before the fall of the *Maspok*) remained unaltered. Moreover, they were extended and codified in new Yugoslav and Croatian Constitutions in 1974. In order to emphasize the Marxist, class-based character of Croatian demands, the new leadership returned to old relying on class rhetoric, even when it meant 'national interests'. The end of exploitation was one of the key Marxist demands. But it also meant, to those who knew how to read between the lines, and in communism this skill was rather useful, the end of exploitation of Croatia by Belgrade. And Belgrade in this context could mean both 'the capital of Serbia' and 'the capital of Yugoslavia' – this was left to the imagination of speakers and their audiences. The new class-based rhetoric again appealed to Tito's ears. He too was becoming critical of what appeared to be an obsession with decentralization without any clear benefit to workers. In 1973 Tito sharpened his Marxist rhetoric by sending an open letter to members of the Yugoslav communist party. Croatia again appeared to be most supportive of this new discourse.

Hence, although some leaders were removed from the public sphere after 1971, Croatian policy defended the position of Croatia within Yugoslavia perhaps even more persistently than before 1971. With Tito's aid – who, from 1973 until his death in 1980 spent more time in Croatia than in any other republic including more time than in Belgrade itself, Croatia managed to convince others to treat the new leadership and the republic with respect and benevolence. Tito was personally engaged in trying to protect the new Croatian leadership when the rest of Yugoslavia started suspecting it of continuing 'nationalist' politics. The new Croatian leadership warned against the emerging trend that would permanently 'suspect' Croatia of nationalism, and insisted that others in Yugoslavia clean their own house before criticizing others. In yet another area Croatian post-1971 politics quickly recovered: in economics. Croatia easily found its way in the new circumstances of devolved, and to a degree, anarchic economic politics. In the aftermath of the 1974 Constitution and 1976 Associated Labour Act, economic decisions were further decentralized, while the interventions of the federal state were reduced to the minimum. In the 1970s, Croatia had the greatest level of investment of all the republics. Strategic facilities were built, especially in the energy sector, while Croatian tourism entered its golden age. As far as infrastructure was concerned, the highway from Zagreb to Karlovac was built, as well as the Zagreb and Rijeka bypass. The largest bridge in Yugoslavia was constructed, connecting the island of Krk to the mainland. Croatia, together with Slovenia, built a nuclear plant Krško, where the plant is based. This strategic investment was the first that was entirely financed by two Yugoslav republics, without involvement of the federal centre. This symbolized a new era – the one in which the republics were to be all but fully sovereign. The participation of the American company Westinghouse in the construction of this facility indicated a significant level of openness of Croatia and Slovenia towards the West, even in such a sensitive branch of industry. A waste-oil thermal power plant was built in Rijeka, and another one in Sisak along with a gas thermal power plant. The energy network around Yugoslavia was under construction, including stations in Ernestinovo and Dugopolje. Construction of Molve I and Molve II provided an alternative to the coal mines in Raša. Rijeka's refinery underwent modernization. The oil pipeline from Omišlje via Sisak to Pančevo was completed. By the mid-1980s the construction of INA Petrokemija on Krk had commenced, and so on.[32] Previously underdeveloped areas were developing, such as Istria, the Dalmatian islands (except the distant ones, Vis and Lastovo, where the Yugoslav Navy maintained its presence). For the first time Croatian companies (for example 'Djuro Djaković' from Slavonski Brod) were given military-industrial contracts. This symbolized that Croatia was now again trusted – and that old suspicions (whether from the Second World War, or more recently: from 'Croatian Spring') were dead and buried. At least an effort was made to convince everybody that this was indeed the case.

In part, those investments were politically motivated – maybe to an even greater extent than in any other areas of Yugoslavia. This was necessary to demonstrate that Croatia was not damaged in Yugoslavia and that the new leadership was capable of developing Croatia to an even greater degree than those who led the republic before 1971 (and included the economics professor Savka Dabčević Kučar). Investments in the less developed areas of Croatia also had a political background, especially in the case of areas with Serb ethnic majority. After Tito's intervention in the Croatian politics, the Serb cultural society 'Prosvjeta' (the leading cultural and social institution of Croatian Serbs) had also been banned (it was re-established only in 1992); nevertheless Croatia wanted to demonstrate that it did not neglect its Serbs, economically or politically. Tourism in the predominantly Serb area of the Plitvice Lakes developed, the TVIK factory was built in Knin, a timber industry was developed in Vrgin Most, while in Vojnić 'Jugoturbina' from Karlovac opened its facilities. Serbs were still over-represented in some state services – especially in the police, customs, and the state apparatus in general – but the reappearance of Croatian nationalism in the late 1960s and early 1970s had awakened their fears and suspicions. It was this fear and suspicion that the new Croatian leadership wished to eliminate. Among Serbs in Croatia the unitarist tendencies were fairly strong – more than those of Serbian nationalism – so many did not understand why the new leadership also insisted upon the criticism of unitarism and centralism which, both constitutionally and in practice, all but disappeared from the Yugoslav political life. Rather, they welcomed claims for re-centralization and for the strengthening of the Yugoslav political and cultural identity (which grew stronger in the general population in the early 1980s, as a form of protest against the decentralizing and chaotic nature of post-1974 politics) as a form of protection against real or imagined separatist tendencies among the non-Serbs. When the crisis developed in the mid-1980s, Croatian Serbs identified decentralization as its main cause, while Croats argued that any re-centralization would go against the spirit of the whole post-1945 politics. These differences, latently present in the politics of socialist Croatia, would explode after the political and constitutional crisis emerged in the 1980s, especially with the change of rhetoric in Belgrade, where, in 1986, Slobodan Milošević came to power.

The paradox of Croatian politics lies in the fact that the golden age of Croatia's political status within Yugoslavia was precisely in the aftermath of the 'Croatian Spring', i.e. in the period which also brought some serious restrictions on intellectual and political freedom and which re-ideologized Croatian politics. During that period (1972–90), the republics and autonomous provinces became more powerful and autonomous from the centre than ever before. The institutions of the federal state continued to preserve important authority in terms of external politics, defence and monetary politics, but even in those areas decision-making came to be strongly influenced by agreements between the republics and the autonomous regions. For the first time, Croatia had a federal secretary for foreign affairs, Josip Vrhovec (1978–82) and its 'international' position seemed stable. The 1975 Osimo Agreement with Italy led to the long-term stability in Istria and the Adriatic, two regions which have always (since the time of creation of the first Yugoslav state in 1918) beeen seen as a potential target of foreign – primarily Italian – intrusion into Yugoslav affairs. Yugoslavia's relations with Austria and Germany (where many Croats worked) improved, while the country was ever more open to the influences of the West. The borders were opened, enabling the entry of a large number of foreign tourists, who mostly visited Croatia. Western cultural influences (such as music, fashion, television programmes, standards of journalism and public communications), increased as well, and technology, and some ideology too (for example: consumerism, feminism and philosophical anarchism), came from the West. Croatia had a significant impact on other areas of decision-making processes in the federation, where its representatives occupied prominent positions.[33]

But, the events of 1971 also left the potential for deeper political divisions, which the new authorities wanted to eliminate or minimize. The mythological interpretation of the 'Croatian Spring' emphasized that almost the entire Croatian people – or at least those who were in Croatia – supported the demands which had been propagated by reformists in the party, as well as by liberals and nationalists outside the party.[34] In reality, only 0.3 per cent of members of the SKH were excluded from the party because of their alleged nationalist activity in the first six months after the fall of the former leadership.

In order to emphasize that the Croatian intelligentsia mostly supported the changes that took place after 1971, the new authorities tried to attract to its side the leading members of the intellectual elite of socialist orientation in Croatia. The role of Miroslav Krleža, the most senior Croatian writer and Tito's political and personal friend since the interwar years, was crucial in this process. Over several decades, Krleža aimed at linking Marxism and internationalism with the more substantial concept of Croatian national identity – with more or less success. In this attempt he had followers in Croatian intellectual circles and he used his influence to pacify any voice of serious discontent within the regime. Krleža's sincere belief was that only with Tito firmly in charge of Yugoslavia was Croatia[35] – and thus he opposed any 'adventurism' whether from the position of left-wing radicalism, Croatian nationalism or democracy. Krleža's influence over Croatian intellectuals was certainly one of the reasons why they seemed relatively passive, especially when compared with their Slovenian and Serbian colleagues in the 1970s and 1980s.[36]

In addition to Krleža's personal influence, the new post-1971 authorities also actively worked on promoting socialist culture in Croatia. Thanks to the persistence of Stipe Šuvar, at the time Croatia's Secretary for Culture and Education (1974–82) and one of the leading *Krležists* in Croatian cultural circles, more cultural and educational facilities were built in the 1970s than ever before. The construction of the new National and University Library, completed in the early 1990s, began during Šuvar's term in office. In 1974, Museum of Croatian Archaeological Monuments was built in Split, and Zadar saw the construction of a Permanent Museum of Church Art in 1976. Talks started about the founding of the Mimara Museum. The Museum finally opened in 1987, after 13 years of negotiations with Ante Topić Mimara, a Croat emigrée arts collector who pointedly donated his collection to 'Croatian people' – not to either Croatia or Yugoslavia. The Mediterranean Games were held in Split in 1979, while in the late 1970s a national sports centre was built at Bjelolasica. During this period, around 700 elementary and high schools were built or renovated.[37] This trend continued until 1990.

The end of Socialism and post-Socialist radicalization of Croatian politics

One should, however, ask also: why then did socialism collapse in Croatia too, where a relatively functional balance between the ideological goals and realistic political solutions had been achieved? Why did the system which had managed to address the difficult question of the Second World War legacy and to move the republic forward come to an end?

Croatia, of course, was not isolated from the events and trends taking place across the entire socialist world or indeed from those that were happening in Yugoslavia itself. Just as all other parts of the former Yugoslavia, Croatia too was hit by the economic crisis[38] and found itself in a new situation in which the balance of international relations had been disturbed. In terms of Croatian politics within Yugoslavia, this was reflected in a more-than-obvious crisis of a fragile (but for long efficient) balance that was achieved among various parts of the Yugoslav jigsaw. The first to disturb it were not Croats, but Kosovan Albanians, and then Serbs and Slovenes. Nevertheless, the *domino effect* made Croatia also unstable. Furthermore, it dramatically increased the general level of uncertainty, anxiety and fear about the future, especially once Tito was no longer there to *protect* – or at least *understand* – Croatian interests.

In addition to the post-Titoist crisis of leadership at the federal level, Croatia also faced its own change of generations in politics, after the death of Krleža in 1981, and its leader for the whole of the post-war period, Vladimir Bakarić, in 1983. In addition, another senior party leader, Mika Špiljak, retired in 1986. At the first opportunity to choose party leaders – which was introduced in 1986 – the Central Committee of the SKH rejected two older candidates (Milka Planinc and Jure Bilić) and for SKH's representatives in the federal party leadership chose two much younger men: Ivica Račan (born 1941) and Stipe Šuvar (1936). This was in line with the election in Slovenia of Milan Kučan (1941) and in Serbia of Slobodan Milošević (born also in 1941) as party leaders. The new generation of leaders had no direct experience of the interwar period or indeed of the Second World War. To them, comparisons were no longer to be made with the past, but with contemporaries who lived elsewhere: in other Yugoslav republics (primarily Serbia and Slovenia) and abroad. The new generation brought with it a new agenda. Furthermore, it was open to more radical changes than its predecessors were. They were relatively inexperienced – especially in issues of federal politics – and impatient. All this, together with problems that already emerged in Kosovo (1981), and due to economic crisis throughout the country, posed a very serious challenge to this new generation of leaders.

In the 1980s, Croatia was affected by the wave of liberalization, although to a lesser extent than neighbouring Slovenia and Serbia. Media were not free in any sense in which the freedom of press is understood by contemporary liberals. However, they were freer than ever before. Their relative freedom was, however, conditioned upon supporting local (regional) or national leaders, when they needed such support. In Croatia too, the press served the interests of the new Croatian elite – but this meant also that it was allowed to criticize 'freely' political leaders in other republics, especially those with whom Croatian leaders were at loggerheads. The Croatian political weekly, *Danas*, launched in February 1982, soon became the main critic of what the Croatian leaders recognized (more or less rightly) as 'centralism', 'unitarism' and 'Serbian nationalism' – especially after 1986, when Milošević came to power in Belgrade. To its readers it looked as if the journalists were brave and independent heroes of the new post-dogmatic era. However, the Party and its loyal organizations (such as the Socialist Alliance of Working People, and the Youth Organization) still preserved and occasionally exercised power to intervene, whenever the media tried to emancipate themselves completely. *Danas* in fact often spoke for the leadership (not least because Štefa Špiljak, the president of its Advisory Board, happened to be the wife of the President of SKH, Mika Špiljak), and thus enabled leaders to remain in the shadow and continue with Bakarić's ultra-prudent policy of Croatian apparent non-involvement. However, with Slovenian and Serbian new policies – both of which were much more straightforward in their demands for changes – the Croatian 'policy of silence' looked increasingly inadequate. As the Serb-Slovene verbal conflicts developed into an open split within the SKJ, some people in Croatia began to notice that Croatia was almost completely absent from fundamental debates on the future of Yugoslavia. It is on this basis that the criticism of the SKH grew in the mid-1980s.

When Slobodan Milošević launched his *antibureaucratic revolution* in 1988,[39] he claimed that he was fully supported by the people, and thus democratically legitimated. Because it was obvious that he could activate hundreds of thousands of his supporters all over Serbia (and also some in other republics), Milošević argued that democratic elections were not necessarily needed. He also claimed that Croatian and Slovenian leaders had lost all support even in their own republics. And indeed, ever since 1988 it looked as if Slovenian anticommunist opposition had been stronger and more popular than the League of Communists. But, the Croatian leaders still believed that their balanced and cautious policy was genuinely supported by the majority. When the LCY practically disintegrated at its 14th (extraordinary) Congress in January 1990, the SKH decided to call immediate elections. The decision was very surprising and not really seriously thought through.[40]

The Croatian political elite made such a decision largely because it was convinced that it would win the first multi-party elections, and that it had nothing to lose. It saw itself as being the most reasonable and thus also the most progressive alternative to what already looked like a dangerous rise of ethnic nationalism in both Serbia and Slovenia. This confidence in returning to power after the elections was also based on hopes that Croats would reward SKH's role in supporting Slovenia – rather than Serbia – at the 14th Party Congress in January 1990. It was because of this conviction that the elite called the elections quickly, and with an electoral law created to maximize the advantage of the (recently renamed) SKH-SDP (Croatian League of Communists – Social Democratic Party). The intention they had in mind was not only to demonstrate that the SKH was indeed supported by the people (now formally turned into an electorate), but also to prevent a similar growth of nationalism in Croatia itself. With Milošević now increasingly interested in instrumentalizing the position of Croatian and Bosnian Serbs to his own benefit, Croatian communist leaders feared that this would inevitably lead to a strengthening of (so far dormant) Croatian nationalism. As Celestin Sardelić, at the time the main SKH-SDP ideologist, explained, while presenting reasons for the introduction of the multiparty system in Croatia, the multiparty system was seen 'as a means of de-hegemonisation, and not the hegemonisation of ethnic community'.[41]

In a speech given at the 26th Session of the Central Committee of the Croatian League of Communists, Sardelić stated that political pluralism, 'emerges as an obstacle to the creation of the unified national programs and national mass movements'.[42] It is necessary to remember that all of this was happening in the context of the disintegration of the League of Communists of Yugoslavia (SKJ), which was caused above all by the conflict between the Slovenian and the Serbian party leaderships. Until the end, the Croatian Party remained loyal to the SKJ and acted as an agent of compromise, not conflict. Only with its disintegration did they abandon the old political system. However, once they moved towards elections, they found themselves in unknown territory, to which they invited all others to compete. It was very courageous indeed to expect that a party which had had full monopoly of power for the last 45 years would win the first democratic elections called after 52 years (the last fully multiparty elections were held in 1938).

However, while Croats indeed wanted a change of government and of the system, there is no evidence that before the 1990 elections they were in favour of leaving Yugoslavia and creating an independent Croatian state. According to a public opinion survey, conducted in December 1989 in two Croatian cities, Zagreb and Osijek (I was head of the survey team of the weekly *Danas*) the majority (77 per cent in Zagreb and 67 per cent in Osijek) of people were in favour of introducing the multi-party system. This includes the majority of the members of the SKH, who sought a new functional basis for the party and political system, particularly after the dramatic events across Eastern Europe.[43]

However, the introduction of the multi-party system did not necessarily equate with a desire to break away from Yugoslavia. In March 1990, immediately prior to the elections, more than 90 per cent of survey participants in Knin and Karlovac, and 79 per cent of respondents in Varaždin, were in favour of Yugoslavia's survival, while only a small number of citizens (7 per cent in Knin, 8 per cent in Karlovac and 18 per cent in Varaždin) believed that the relations in Yugoslavia were disturbed to such a degree that further coexistence was impossible. Although it seemed unlikely that socialist

Yugoslavia could have survived the collapse of the ideology upon which its political structure was based and the rise of ever more aggressive nationalism, this did not mean that its citizens actually wanted Yugoslavia's disintegration. Even nationalist leaders had to take account of this. Not one of them campaigned before the elections on a programme of Croatia's secession from Yugoslavia. In an interview for *Danas*, immediately after the results of the elections had been proclaimed, Franjo Tudjman, leader of the victorious Croatian Democratic Union (HDZ) and soon to be president of Croatia, confirmed this very explicitly: 'To be clear, I am not saying that this is the end of every Yugoslavia. I am only saying that this is the end of Yugoslavism intended as a compulsory brotherhood that one needs to be enslaved to, as well as an end to the preservation of Yugoslavia at any cost'. At the time, Tudjman saw the solution in a confederation, stating that, 'there is no significant difference between what is advocated by the Slovenian politicians and that advocated by the HDZ'. Additionally, he saw the basis of the future system, 'in the coexistence of sovereign nations who would agree regarding what they had in common and how they would organise their lives in the future'.[44]

Franjo Tudjman won the elections by advocating a confederal restructuring of Yugoslavia, not Croatia's independence; a position which was in complete harmony with the prevalent public mood in Croatia. That the confederation was the most desirable option is demonstrated also by a survey conducted and published in *Danas*, immediately prior to the April 1990 elections. According to this survey, conducted in Zagreb, Rijeka and Split, a confederation was the most desirable option for 52 per cent of survey participants in Zagreb, 48 per cent in Rijeka, and 47 per cent in Split. The second most desirable option was not Croatian independence but the preservation of federalism, which was supported by 37 per cent of survey participants in Rijeka, 27 per cent in Split, and 24 per cent in Zagreb. Those in favour of independence amounted to 25 per cent in Zagreb, 26 per cent in Split and 13 per cent in Rijeka. Thus, it is possible to say that even at the moment of the elections, Croatia actually rejected the option of complete state independence, favouring instead another compromise among the Yugoslav republics.

A daring hypothesis could be made, perhaps, that by voting for change, Croatian voters actually wanted the changes which were in harmony with the general trend of decentralization of Yugoslavia, as conducted up until that point. They voted to make a step forward in that direction, instead of voting for a radical break with the recent past. It was Milošević who argued for a (antibureaucratic) revolution, not Croats. It was Serbia – not Croatia – that now wanted the 1974 Constitution completely abolished, with autonomies significantly reduced both for its two provinces (Kosovo and Vojvodina) and all republics – except perhaps Serbia itself. Croats wanted new people and new parties, but not necessarily those people and parties advocating a radical cut with Yugoslavia. In this sense, the HDZ profited from the fact that its four main leaders were former partisans and communists who had become dissidents: Franjo Tudjman, Josip Manolić, Josip Boljkovac and Stjepan Mesić. In addition, its main leader, Tudjman, described himself even in 1990 (at the time of elections) as being a Croatian Marxist and admirer of Tito's life work, whose main political ambition was to preserve and enhance the status that Croatia had obtained (at least nominally) in socialist Yugoslavia, and which he saw being threatened by 'anti-bureaucratic revolution' and 'Great-Serbian tendencies'.[45] It was only later on that radical, pro-*ustaša* politicians such as Gojko Šušak, emerged among the HDZ leadership.

Resistance to radical changes could be seen even more prominently in the case of ethnic Serbs, the majority of whom voted for the SKH-SDP and not for the newly-formed and more radical Serbian Democratic Party (SDS). It was only later on, with further radicalization, that the radical, nationalist fraction of SDS managed first to force out the moderate SDS leader Jovan Rašković, and then to organize mini-coups against all legitimately elected municipal leaders of the SDS who were in favour of the politics of compromise, until it achieved full control of all the municipalities with a Serb majority. Some of them (for example, the mayor of Vrginmost, Dmitar Obradović) were subsequently assassinated by Serb extremists.[46]

The results of the first Croatian parliamentary elections also add to scepticism regarding the claim that Croatia had already in 1990 decided in favour of independence. The HDZ won 42 per cent of the votes, while SKH-SDP won 35 per cent. However, due to the electoral system promoted by the SKH-SDP itself (based on an over-optimistic prediction of victory), the HDZ won the majority of parliamentary seats: 205 of 351. SDP won 107 seats, while the centrist Coalition of People's Accord (led by Dabčević-Kučar and Tripalo, former leaders of the SKH ousted after the Croatian Spring in 1971), which won about 15 per cent of votes, had only 21 seats. However, even among those who voted for the HDZ, only 54 per cent were at the time of elections in favour of leaving Yugoslavia,[47] while the same percentage supported the changing of the borders of the Republic by extending Croatia so as to encompass its 'ethic, natural and historical territories' in Bosnia-Herzegovina, Vojvodina and Montenegro. The data obtained through the public opinion survey, conducted immediately before the 1990 elections, demonstrates that in all likelihood not more than 25 per cent of all Croatian citizens were, at the time of the 1990 elections, in favour of complete independence for Croatia. Unfortunately, the events that followed, both inside and outside Croatia, were to the advantage of this radical minority, which in time began to dictate the state politics. The secessionist groups within the HDZ, helped and financed by the most extreme political émigrés whose return to Croatia was now possible (including some former *ustaše* and their political followers), soon prevailed and did everything to change the public opinion and to convince the public of the necessity of state independence. For further radicalization they needed a war to demonstrate that a compromise was no longer possible. Also, it was necessary that 'the Other' be turned into 'the Enemy' in order to 'prove' the impossibility of even being neighbours with 'the Other'. In creating the war, the radicals easily found 'partners' in Croatia itself, such as among those radical Serbs who blamed socialist Croatia for being a continuation of the NDH. But, even more important was help they had from outside Croatia, above all among the extremist forces in Serbia. By joint efforts, extremists in Zagreb and Belgrade worked on spreading fears and reviving genuine – and fabricating false – memories of injustice, violence and genocide committed by Others against Us. 'At Arms, At Arms, for Our People!' became the main slogan of both Croat and Serb extremists in 1990 and 1991. This was the context in which radical rhetoric and practice on one side fed radicalism on the other. The war then became not only 'inevitable', but worse than that: it became desirable for those forces which had not won the elections but soon became the most powerful groups in the new leadership, due to offering their services as 'Saviours of the Nation'. With them firmly in charge of the whole political, security and media apparatus – which they swiftly purged of all who argued for peace and compromise – they relatively quickly managed to secure support among the general population. When the conflict in Croatia began (in August 1990), and when Slovenia voted in favour of its independence (in December 1990), Croatian public opinion shifted towards supporting secession. This was the end of any Yugoslavia.

Notes

1 An earlier and longer version of this work appeared as 'Hrvatska u socijalističkoj Jugoslaviji', *Reč* (Belgrade), no. 75/21, December 2007, pp. 61–98.

2 See former Croatian President Stjepan Mesić's statement in *Jutarnji list*, 10 December 2009.

3 See Franjo Tudjman's interview for Jakov Sedlar's biographical documentary, available at: http://www.youtube.com/watch?v=wDlSJixGzh4.

4 See T. Dulić's chapter in this volume. See also *Totalitarian Movements and Political Religions*, Volume 7, Number 4, 2006, special issue on the Independent State of Croatia, guest-edited by S. Ramet.

5 See Tito's interview in *Borba*, 7 October 1971.

6 For the politics of HSS in the interwar period, see M. Biondich, *Stjepan Radić, the Croat Peasant Party, and the Politics of Mass Mobilization, 1904–1928* (Toronto: Univesity of Toronto Press, 2000), Lj. Boban, *Maček i politika Hrvatske seljačke stranke, 1928–1941* (Zagreb: Liber, 1974) and D. Djokić, *Elusive Compromise: A history of interwar Yugoslavia*, (London: Hurst, 2007).

7 As Tito warned in September 1941: 'The weakness of the partisan movement in Croatia is that it mainly encompasses the Serbian population in Kordun, in Lika, and so on, but only a small number of Croatian peasants […] It all depends on Croatian people themselves. It depends on whether it would remain passive or engage actively in the battle, shoulder to shoulder with the Serbian people … ', J. B. Tito, *Govori i članci* (Zagreb: Naprijed, 1959), Volume I, pp. 14–15. Tito issued several similar warnings in articles published throughout 1942, ibid, pp. 40, 72.

8 V. Ivetić, 'Srbi u antifašističkoj borbi na područjima NDH, 1941–45. godine', *Vojnoistorijski glasnik*, No. 1, 1995, p. 155.

9 I. and S. Goldstein, 'Srbi i Hrvati u narodnooslobodilačkoj borbi u Hrvatskoj', available at: http://www.cpi.hr/download/links/hr/7243.pdf, accessed on 2 February 2010.

10 V. Ivetić, *op. cit.*, pp. 156 and 158.

11 I. and S. Goldstein, *op. cit.*, p. 264.

12 I. and S. Goldstein, *op. cit.*, pp. 264–65.

13 For this see P. Ballinger, *History in Exile: Memory and Identity at the Borders of the Balkans* (Princeton, Princeton University Press, 2002).

14 Tito, *Govori i članci*, pp. 287–99.

15 In this respect, the policy of new post-1945 authorities was not so different from the one introduced by King Alexander in 1929. He too argued against 'quarrelsome parties' and abolished them. Instead, he favoured a single political organization, the JNS, which he saw as a vehicle towards unity. For this see D. Djokić, *Elusive Compromise* op. cit.

16 The number of Serb members of the SKH was always proportionally greater than the number of members from the general Croatian population, but not to a degree which would have enabled them to play a decisive role in the Party. For example, in 1974, 64.4 per cent of the SKH members were Croats, while 24.7 per cent were Serbs; 6.6 per cent of members declared themselves as Yugoslavs, while other ethnic groups were represented with less than 2 percent. *Informativni Pregled (Official Bulletin of the Central Committee of SKH)*, no.3, 1976.

17 See official notes from Tito's meeting with representatives of the publishing house Forum, Archiv J. B. Tita, Belgrade (Archives of J. B. Tita, hereafter AJBT), KPR II-2/1962, pp. 11–13.

18 See D. Jović, 'Fear of Being Minority as a Cause of the post-Yugoslav Wars', *Balkanologie*, Volume 5, Number 1–2, 2001, pp. 21–37.

19 See analyses of demographic losses of Serbs in Croatia during the Second World War in two studies: V. Žerjavić, *Opsesije i megalomanije oko Bleiburga i Jasenovca. Gubici stanovništva Jugoslavije u Drugom svjetskom ratu* (Zagreb: Globus, 1992) and B. Kočović, *Žrtve drugog svetskog rata u Jugoslaviji* (London: Veritas, 1985).

20 Link between Stjepan Radić and Tito in the sense of political ideas they had, is still very much under-researched. Stjepan Radić was the only person who had more than one street named after him in Zagreb: there is Radićev trg, Radićevo šetalište and Radićeva ulica. All these places were named after him during the Communist period – and remained unchanged after 1989. On a symbolic level this shows his exceptional place in the official discourse of Communist Croatia. This would not have been possible without Tito's approval.

21 See, for example, his speech in Ljubljana, 27 May 1945, *Govori i članci*, I, p. 302.

22 See D. Djokić's chapter in this volume.

23 Numerous examples are to be found in AJBT in Belgrade. Also, Petar Fleković, former prime minister of socialist Croatia, told me about frequent Bosnian-Croatian disagreements during Tito's era in an interview conducted on 23 April 2003 in Zagreb.

24 AJBT, KPRH II-5-A-1/22. In the questionnaire, Tito wrote 'I am not providing data'.

25 AJBT, KPRH II-1/1970, Zapisnik razgovora s delegacijom SR Srbije, 28 October 1970, p. 38.

26 AJBT, KPRH II-1/1969, Zapisnik razgovora sa Svetozarem Vukmanovićem Tempom, 6 February 1969, p. 5.

27 In a critical letter sent to him by (anonymous) inhabitants of the Lika region, at the end of June 1967, they acknowledge him as 'a man of the people' and invite him to come to the people instead of listening to the 'lying politicians'. AJBT, KPRH II-1/1967, Pismo Ličana Titu, p. 4.

28 Supporting this are the numerous letters arriving at the Cabinet of the President of the Republic after 1967, particularly in 1971, in which the citizens from predominantly Serbian regions complained about the current state of inter-ethnic relations.

29 See T. Jakovina, 'Tajni izvještaji CIA-e o Hrvatskoj', *Globus* (Zagreb), 11 July 2007, and Milivoj Djilas, 'Britance oduševila Titova odluka da slomi Hrvatsko proljeće', *Nacional* (Zagreb), 26 February 2002. See also D. Rusinow, *Yugoslavia: Oblique Insights and Observations* (ed.by Gale Stokes), (Pittsburgh: University of Pittsburgh Press, 2009).

30 See 'Izvještaj o stanju u Savezu komunista Hrvatske u odnosu na prodor nacionalizma', Zagreb, May 1972, in *Hrvatsko proljeće: Presuda Partije* (Zagreb: Dom i svijet, 2003), p. 131.

31 Referat Rikarda Pompea na 5. sjednici CK SK Hrvatske, 14. svibnja 1975, *Informativni Pregled (Službeni bilten CK SKH)*, br. 3, June 1975.

32 I would like to thank Petar Fleković, then Chairman of the Republic Executive Council (1978–82) for the brief summary of main investments made in Croatia. Conversation with Fleković, 23 April 2003.

33 Milka Planinc served as the Yugoslav Prime Minister between 1982 and 1986, while in the same period Branko Mamula was the Federal Secretary of National Defence. Among those Croatian representatives in federal bodies holding executive functions were also Dušan Dragosavac (General Secretary and President of the Presidium of the League of Communists of Yugoslavia), Mika Špiljak (President of the Presidency of the Socialist Federal Republic of Yugoslavia), Vladimir Bakarić (Vice-President of the Presidency of the Socialist Federal Republic of Yugoslavia), Josip Vrhovec (Federal Secretary for Foreign Affairs), and later Veljko Kadijević (Federal Secretary of National Defense), Stipe Šuvar (President of the Presidium of the League of Communists of Yugoslavia and Vice-President of the Presidency of the Socialist Federal Republic of Yugoslavia), Budimir Lončar (Federal Secretary for Foreign Affairs), and Ante Marković (President of the Federal Executive Council). Although federal functions in decentralized Yugoslavia became somewhat less important than earlier, this list indicates that Croatia was an equal and important political factor in Yugoslavia in the period after 1971 (and especially in the period after Tito).

34 The fact that the protagonists of Croatian Spring did not win many votes in the 1990 elections illustrated that this was just a myth. The Coalition of People's Agreement, led by Savka Dabčević Kučar and Miko Tripalo, won only 15 per cent of votes. Dabčević Kučar won only 6 per cent of the votes as a 1992 presidential candidate. Another prominent member of the Croatian Spring was Dražen Budiša, who lost presidential elections twice – in 1992 he won 21.9 per cent (he lost to Tudjman), while in 2000 he won 27.8 per cent in the first round, and 44 per cent in the second round of the presidential elections (losing to Stjepan Mesić).

35 For this see S. Lasić, *Krleža: kronologija života i rada* (Zagreb: Grafički zavod Hrvatske, 1982) and his *Krležologija* in six volumes (Zagreb: Globus, 1993).

36 For this see J. Dragović-Soso, *'Saviours of the Nation': Serbia's Intellectual Opposition and the Revival of Nationalism*, (London: Hurst, 2002).

37 For this information I am grateful to Stipe Šuvar. Conversation with Šuvar, Zagreb, 19 March 2003.

38 In fact, Croatia was one of the Yugoslav republics that were hit hardest by economic crises in the early 1980s, which was largely due to its high rate of investment. Some of these investments were politically motivated – to present the post-1971 leadership as economic developers and modernizers. See D. Jović, *Yugoslavia: A State That Withered Away* (West Lafayette, IN: Purdue University Press, 2009).

39 For this see N. Vladisavljević, *Serbia's Antibureaucratic Revolution: Milošević, the fall of Communism and Nationalist mobilization* (Basingstoke: Palgrave Macmillan, 2008) and his chapter in this volume.

40 See D. Hudelist, *Banket u Hrvatskoj: Prilozi povijesti hrvatskog višestranačja, 1989–1990* (Zagreb: Globus, 1999).

41 *Start* (Zagreb), 22 July 1989.

42 Ibid.

43 *Danas* (Zagreb), 26 December 1989.

44 *Danas*, 1 May 1990.

45 Tudjman's interview was originally published in *Polet* in two parts, on 27 October and 10 November 1989, thus six months before the first elections. The interview is available in M. Baletić (ed.), *Ljudi iz 1971. Prekinuta šutnja* (Zagreb: Vjesnik, 1990).

46 For this see N. Barić, 'Dmitar Obradović – prilog poznavanju jedne ljudske sudbine', research paper available at: http://www.cpi.hr/download/links/hr/7338.pdf. Accessed 14 February 2010.

47 *Danas*, 10 April 1990.

8 The Break-up of Yugoslavia

The role of popular politics

Nebojša Vladisavljević

The break-up of Yugoslavia was a complex affair. The main feature of late socialist Yugoslavia was its sheer convolution, involving a highly diverse multinational society, radically decentralized power-sharing federalism, as well as ideologically rooted and elaborate authoritarian institutions. In this context, many factors helped undermine its stability towards the end of the 1980s, such as the economic crisis; leadership succession; elite conflicts; attempts at economic, political and constitutional reforms; the rise of nationalism among the intellectuals and wider populace; memories of past nationalist conflict and of extreme large-scale violence; and the end of the Cold War and the collapse of communism across Eastern Europe and the Soviet Union – to mention only the most obvious. Scholars of Yugoslavia have widely and insightfully discussed this complexity of the state and society, and intricate and fast unfolding political developments in the 1980s, especially at the elite level, as well as their impact on the break-up of Yugoslavia.[1] What is largely missing in this literature, however, is the study of popular politics and its political consequences, not least the unintended ones.

This chapter takes such a perspective – from below – and explores the protest of various, often dissimilar and unconnected non-elite groups and their interaction with elites, especially with the authorities at various levels of the highly complex party-state, as well as their role in the fall of Yugoslavia. It discusses the origins, forms and dynamics of key episodes of grass-roots mobilization in the second half of the 1980s and focuses on the impact of popular politics on the regime and state. The study of popular politics and its consequences in late socialist Yugoslavia is all the more important considering that ordinary people across Eastern Europe played an important role in political struggles that surrounded the fall of communism, at times in massive demonstrations that broke the back of the old regime, which was widely acknowledged in scholarly and popular writing.

Indeed, the levels of mobilization of ordinary people across Yugoslavia in the late 1980s exceeded considerably popular involvement in politics in most states of Eastern Europe and the Soviet Union. Large numbers of participants, a great variety of groups involved and of their protest strategies, wide geographical sweep of popular protests and often dramatic consequences, including the resignation of scores of high officials, even regional governments, were the key features of this mobilization. This chapter argues that without exploring popular politics and its political implications, and especially its unintended consequences, one can hardly explain the break-up of the Yugoslav federation.[2]

Yugoslavia in the 1980s

The political conflicts and constitutional and party reforms of the late 1960s and early 1970s left a legacy of unusually decentralized institutions, which strongly shaped political developments in the 1980s. After the Second World War, the communists had remodelled Yugoslavia as a Soviet-style federation, on the basis of collective rights and the territorial autonomy of its newly proclaimed constituent nations – Serbs, Croats, Slovenes, Macedonians, Montenegrins and, later, Muslims – and insisted on the 'brotherhood and unity' of the nations and national minorities. The federation was initially of a nominal or façade type due to the supremacy of the highly centralized party organization, though the central control was relaxed in the 1950s and early 1960s. In contrast, the constitutional reform of the late 1960s and early 1970s involved radical federalization and the locus of sovereignty shifted decisively from the centre to the republics and Serbia's autonomous provinces. The federal units gained jurisdiction over important political, economic and cultural issues as well as full control over cadre appointments in central organs. The formulation of policy at the centre now required the consensus of regional representatives and the federal organs lost control even over the execution of federal policy, that is, the implementation of agreements between federal units.

Moreover, party reforms, which took place simultaneously, turned a highly centralized structure of the League of the Communists of Yugoslavia (LCY), run by the Executive Committee and powerful party secretaries, into a radically federalized organization and thus strongly contributed to the empowerment of federal units. Under the slogan 'de-étatization', self-management – initially conceived as workers' participation in the management of enterprises and the autonomy of those enterprises from the state – was transformed into a comprehensive and elaborate system. In industry, it started at the 'shop' level; the small proto-organizations would associate on a contractual basis to form an enterprise and workers participated in decision making throughout. In social services, 'producers' and 'consumers' established contractual relations through enterprises and local communities. Political institutions were also redesigned to form an elaborate, interconnected and pyramidal system of indirect functional, territorial and political representation.

Towards the end of Tito's rule, this legacy of radically decentralized institutions was officially considered as essential to the country's political stability, economic growth and to broad popular involvement in the political and economic life of the authoritarian regime. Indeed, the political instability of the late 1960s and early 1970s seemed long gone, economic development proceeded apace and the international prestige of Yugoslavia continued to grow. However, within only a few years Yugoslavia found itself at the centre of growing political and economic crises. The highly decentralized institutional structure failed to increase effective participation of ordinary people in the making of key economic and political decisions and the costs of fragmentation in the economy, and the unproductive use of resources were massive. The country's political institutions, especially at the federal level, had relied too much in their day-to-day operation on Tito and the older generation politicians, and leadership succession and a sharp economic downturn revealed that the institutions were now turning increasingly dysfunctional.

Tito died in 1980. While the transfer of power to the collective state Presidency of Yugoslavia unfolded smoothly, the long-term implications of his exit for the country's political stability were considerable. Tito was widely seen as a unifier of the multi-national state, the regime founder and protector of Yugoslavia's independence during the Cold War, and also controlled key levers of power and served as an ultimate arbiter in political affairs. In contrast to the Soviet Union in which the death of old general secretaries in the first half of the 1980s triggered political and economic reforms, Yugoslavia remained without a clear successor to Tito and with a deadlock at the federal level. The deadlock had already occurred at the centre over economic issues since the republics and autonomous provinces often did not share economic interests and since all held veto power over federal policy. Ultimately, the central organs that retained unity would help reach the consensus over key issues. After the death of Tito, which undermined the unity, it became virtually impossible to reach agreement between federal units.[3]

The change of political generations further undermined political stability. Tito's old guard – the pre-war communists and war veterans who still held key offices in the state and party organs – largely went into retirement in the first half of the 1980s. Edvard Kardelj, a chief party ideologue, and Vladimir Bakarić died in 1979 and 1983, respectively. Miloš Minić retired in 1982 and Petar Stambolić, Lazar Koliševski, Cvijetin Mijatović, Fadil Hoxha and Stevan Doronjski followed suit two years later. Members of the post-war generations now took over key levers of power. As a result, close personal bonds among regional representatives at the centre, which had played an important role in preserving political stability since the radical federalization of the late 1960s and early 1970s, faded away. The younger generation politicians had very different formative experiences, values and skills from the elders, which strongly shaped relations within the political establishment and between the party-state and society. Being well educated and with extensive experience in business, administration or local politics, they were more interested in economic reform, greater openness within and outside the party and the relaxation of repression.

Thus, one consequence of leadership succession was the relaxation of restrictions in, and a gradual pluralization of, Yugoslavia's socialist authoritarianism. There was a pragmatic relaxation of repressive practices, but its scale varied considerably among the republics. Belgrade and Ljubljana were the focus of activity of dissident intellectuals since Slovenia's and Serbia's high officials held a somewhat less repressive attitude towards society than their counterparts in other republics. The pluralization of political life unfolded partly through increasing involvement of non-political and professional associations and partly through growing conflict in the political establishment, both within and between the republics and autonomous provinces. High officials increasingly tolerated cultural and political dissent and formed informal alliances with protest groups and dissident intellectuals in the second half of the 1980s. Having in mind Yugoslavia's legacy of the liberation war and indigenous revolution, the main consequence of this political liberalization by default was the blurring of boundaries between the political class and society.

The signs of economic crisis had appeared in the late 1970s in the wake of the investment drive, financed by massive foreign borrowing. High rates of economic growth fell sharply and foreign debt reached $18 billion by 1980. Unemployment and inflation increased considerably, while living standards fell by one-quarter between 1979 and 1985 and by one-third by 1988. The government introduced rationing for petrol, electricity, sugar and flour.[4] While rationing had been common in nearly all states of the Soviet bloc, the citizens of Yugoslavia had become used to a higher standard of living. The response of the leadership to the economic crisis was timid and ultimately ineffective. Most high officials defended key features of the self-management system despite ample evidence about its devastating impact on the economy. The debate on economic reform triggered an ideological conflict between conservatives and economic reformers, but also between the advocates of the stronger centre and the supporters of further decentralization. Indeed, the economic crisis revealed previously hidden regional grievances and disparities. These conflicts now reinforced the deadlock at the federal level and gradually ended up widely debated in the local press, thus raising popular passions. In short, political change that started after Tito's death undermined the stability of the authoritarian regime and left the loosening Yugoslav federation amidst mounting economic crisis and political conflict.

Early stages of popular politics

In the mid-1980s Yugoslavia provided a fertile ground for grass-roots mobilization thanks to its highly decentralized political structure and the political change. Regardless of the nature and intensity of grievances they hold, ordinary people generally feel powerless to confront authorities, political parties, other organizations and interest groups. This is because they find themselves outside the political process and without information, funds, organizational resources and access to media. Political change however may reduce this disparity in power between ordinary people and elites and thus provide a motive for the former to engage in protest. Generally speaking, decentralized states and those that are moderately inclusive towards popular challenges open more space to social movements by providing various channels through which they can operate and influence the political process.[5]

Throughout the post-war period, the prevailing party's strategy towards challenges to its authority was normally exclusive and repressive, especially towards ideological dissidence. Due to the party's communist ideology and its historically shaped sensitivity to the national question, the expression of grievances of industrial workers and grass roots groups with ethnonational demands potentially involved less risk than that of others.[6] Still, there was little popular protest in the last decade of Tito's rule. His immense authority and elite unity effectively discouraged potential protest groups. Conversely, growing political instability after Tito's death, the change of political generations, growing elite conflict, and partial political liberalization, increased the salience of a highly decentralized political structure and opened up space for popular mobilization.

The grass-roots protest of Kosovo Serbs

The grievances of Kosovo Serbs originated from the post-1966 shift in the politics of ethnonational inequality and were compounded by their rapid demographic decline, caused by a much higher rate of population growth of Albanians and by steady out-migration of Serbs from the province.[7] The exacerbation of Albanian-Serb antagonisms in the nineteenth century had set the stage for this pattern of politics. While winners and losers changed over time, the hegemonic position of either one or the other group remained an important feature of political life in Kosovo. From the perspective of the disadvantaged group, the only way to escape a subordinate position was political action, which over the history meant wars and uprisings, parliamentary initiatives and party building, struggles within the Communist Party of Yugoslavia (CPY, renamed League of Communists of Yugoslavia (LCY) in 1952) and popular protest. Kosovo Serbs now faced inequalities in terms of the use of language, access to jobs in the huge state-controlled part of the economy, allocation of public housing and especially inadequate protection of their rights and property by the courts and law enforcement agencies. They rarely voiced their grievances in the 1970s because Kosovo's leadership prevented any attempts to contest the official position on the Albanian-Serb relations. These grievances thus resulted in the growing politicization of Kosovo Serbs but not in open popular protest.

The changing political context strongly shaped the timing, forms and dynamics of the mobilization of Kosovo Serbs. The 1981 Kosovo Albanian demonstrations triggered fears among high officials in the federation and republics of the rise of a major separatist movement. The LCY therefore initiated a re-evaluation of its policy on Kosovo. Kosovo's leadership was purged of a number of officials, blamed for condoning Albanian nationalism and irredentism and for artificially separating the province from Serbia and

Yugoslavia, and the role of the security apparatus in the region increased considerably. Kosovo's officials came under the much closer scrutiny of the federal party and state organs, and Albanian–Serb relations within Kosovo ceased to be in their exclusive domain. High officials now increasingly acknowledged the inequalities facing the non-Albanian population and the prevention of out-migration of Serbs and the tackling of their concerns now became a part of the party's policy.

These developments raised the expectations of Kosovo Serbs and opened up space for various groups to lobby high officials outside of the autonomous province and to initiate debates about their concerns in official organizations at the local level. The slow response of the authorities to growing complaints shifted the efforts of some of the debaters to non-institutional action and to the building up of local protest networks. Between 1985 and 1987, Kosovo Serb activists initiated a number of petitions targeted at high officials of Yugoslavia and Serbia and staged numerous protests and protest marches, principally in Kosovo, but also in the country's capital, Belgrade. The most influential protest events included the February 1986 visit of a large group of Kosovo Serbs to the Federal Assembly, the June 1986 protest march, framed as the 'collective emigration' of Kosovo Serbs, and the April 1987 Kosovo Polje protest over the visit of Slobodan Milošević, Serbia's new party leader, and Azem Vllasi, the most influential Kosovo Albanian high official. The main consequence was the rise of a broad social movement among Kosovo Serbs.[8]

The Serb protesters believed that the local Kosovo officials deliberately obstructed protection of the rights of Serbs and thus demanded their resignations and threatened them with further protests. As divisions within and among officials of the federation, Serbia and Kosovo grew, the activists' demands gradually evolved towards constitutional issues. During the radical decentralization of Yugoslavia in the late 1960s and early 1970s, Vojvodina and Kosovo – hitherto little more than Serbia's administrative regions – acquired a status similar to that of the republics. As a result, Serbia's highly decentralized structure sharply contrasted to the unitary character of the other republics and adversely affected its standing in the federation. The protesters now asserted that if the province's officials were unable to guarantee protection of the rights and property of Serbs then Kosovo should be brought back under full jurisdiction of Serbia's authorities. The support of Belgrade-based dissident intellectuals and Milošević helped publicize the cause of Kosovo Serb activists, but mattered little in the creation and consolidation of the local protest networks, not least because the grass-roots mobilization predated the rise to power of Milošević. While activists engaged in contacts with a range of influential people and opted for specific protest strategies with an eye to the broader political context, they remained an autonomous political factor.

The high officials of Yugoslavia, Serbia and Kosovo tolerated this mobilization since, unlike Kosovo Albanian protesters in 1981 who aimed for the change of the constitutional status of Kosovo, Kosovo Serbs demanded initially little more than the implementation of the existing party's policy, which was much less likely to trigger repression. Also, this was a small-scale mobilization, with a limited potential for expansion, in contrast to the 1981 protests. High officials were mainly concerned about the potential implications of the mobilization for political stability at the centre, since the protesters' demands were potentially highly resonant with Serbs outside Kosovo. Moreover, the grass-roots composition of the growing social movement also mattered, as well as the activists' moderate protest strategies, especially their readiness to work within the official organizations.

Protests of industrial workers

There were few protests by the working class in the early 1980s, despite the onset of the economic crisis and sharply falling living standards. The workers' growing discontent initially appeared in the form of a sizeable increase in absenteeism and sick leave.[9] The rise in the number of strikes, a more visible and dramatic form of protest, occurred between 1985 and 1987. In 1987 there were 1,685 registered strikes, while 4.3 per cent of all workers were involved in contrast to less than 1 per cent earlier. The protests now lasted longer than a day on average and, significantly, the number of strikes in large state enterprises, with more than 500 workers, increased considerably. Roughly half of the strikers came from heavy industries and mining, but strikes in other sectors of the economy, as well as in health services and education, became increasingly frequent. In 1988 the number of strikes and strikers further increased, especially in large enterprises, and strikes became longer. In the early 1980s, the number of strikes was higher in Slovenia and Croatia, the most economically developed parts of the country, but differences in the level of strike activity between the workers of Yugoslavia's republics largely disappeared by 1987–88.[10]

The single most important strike during the whole post-war period in socialist Yugoslavia unfolded for over a month in Labin, a mine on the Istrian peninsula of north-west Croatia, in April and May 1987. That the strike lasted so long demonstrated both the determination and strength of the Labin miners and growing restraint on the side of high officials in dealing with industrial action.[11] In November steel workers marched along the streets of Skopje and held a demonstration outside the Assembly of Macedonia. Although their wages remained above their republic's average wage, the workers protested against a recent drop in wage levels. Their comrades from other large factories based in and around Skopje joined the protest, bringing the crowd to over 8,000 people. They chanted slogans against the 'red bourgeoisie' and demanded the resignation of Macedonia's government. In December nearly 4,500 metalworkers from Ljubljana organized a similar protest outside the Assembly of Slovenia. Those involved later claimed the Skopje protest encouraged them to proceed with theirs.[12]

Another wave of strikes across Yugoslavia, along with several dramatic and widely reported protest marches and demonstrations of miners and industrial workers in the capital and regional centres, followed the May 1988 austerity measures of the federal government, principally a pay freeze. Workers' demands remained focused on higher wages and subsidies for their failing companies, but were now cast before the whole of Yugoslavia's public. The targets of protests also shifted from local to high officials, mainly the federal government. Miners organized several large and well-publicized strikes, at times accompanied with long protest marches to the capital or other regional administrative centres (e.g., mines in Živinice, Breza, Kreka, Kakanj and Lipnica-Bosnia; Magura-Kosovo; Soko-central Serbia). On 17 June 3,000 metalworkers from *Zmaj*, Belgrade's tractor manufacturer, marched along the streets of the capital and then held a demonstration outside the Federal Assembly building, chanting slogans 'Thieves', 'Out', 'We want bread'.

Three weeks later 5,000 workers from Borovo, a large Croatia's shoe manufacturer, left for Belgrade in buses and trucks covered with pictures of Tito and flags of the state and the LCY, and protested outside the Federal Assembly. Since high officials did not address the demonstration, workers pushed aside the small police cordon and broke into the Federal Assembly building. The police did not use force and workers withdrew peacefully from the Assembly. They ended the protest after their demands had been accepted, just like in the case of the *Zmaj* workers' protest.[13] Only ten days later 1,500 workers from Agrokomerc, a large agricultural company from northwest Bosnia, the centre of a huge embezzlement scandal that had shaken the political class in Bosnia-Hercegovina a year before, held another protest in the capital.

The working class occupied a strategic ideological position in communist states because the party formally ruled in its name. The LCY promoted the cult of labour and claimed to have further empowered the working population through self-management, or the direct involvement of workers in the management of their enterprises and social services. The rising wave of protests by the working class thus undermined the very foundation upon which the political class legitimated its rule, leaving its authority open to other challenges. The strikes and demonstrations attracted wide media attention and the images of defiance of the authorities spread widely across the country. The Belgrade and other protests from May to July 1988 therefore revealed that industrial and socio-economic struggles had now turned into a political conflict.

Why did high officials not suppress the protests? After all, the strikes and demonstrations at times went beyond the boundaries of officially permitted dissent. Firstly, the miners, who occupied a strategic position in the working class, led the early stage of mobilization. For years after the war the miners were officially considered a symbol of Yugoslavia's industrialization drive and found themselves at the centre of the party's promotion of the cult of labour. Against this ideological and historical background, the suppression of the miners' protests was highly unlikely. Secondly, the gradual relaxation of political controls over society also mattered. Earlier, company managers or party-state officials had followed up on strikes by searching for 'inspirators'; this practice had nearly disappeared by 1988.[14] Thirdly, workers did their best to demonstrate their loyalty to the party-state. The symbolism that heavily permeated their protests said it all: the workers displayed prominently the pictures of Tito and the flags of Yugoslavia and the LCY; at times they ended their protests in the capital by visiting Tito's grave. Unlike their Polish comrades, the workers saw the regime and state as essentially legitimate and showed discontent only with specific policies and party-state officials.

The summer 1988 mobilization and its political consequences

In the summer of 1988 the social movement of Kosovo Serbs staged several large protests – now also in Vojvodina, central Serbia and Montenegro – with increasingly radical demands and protest strategies. They initiated protests in Vojvodina because the predominantly Serb leadership of Vojvodina was the main opponent of constitutional reform that would reduce the autonomy of Serbia's autonomous provinces, which became one of the movement's key demands. Kosovo's leadership, which had been under increasing pressure from the federal organs since 1981, quietly supported this policy. The movement's leaders also thought that the demand by Montenegro's high officials – who otherwise supported the constitutional reform in Serbia – that they call off protests in Vojvodina and Kosovo sharply contrasted the broad popular support they enjoyed in Montenegro. In the end, they organized large protests in Novi Sad and Pančevo in July, and in Nova Pazova, Titograd, Kolašin and Titov Vrbas in August. The protests revealed broad popular support for the protesters' cause as well as discontent with high officials of Vojvodina and Montenegro. While Kosovo Serb activists brought their own crowds of several hundred to the protests, the vast majority of participants were local people.

The summer protests of industrial workers and Kosovo Serbs set the stage for the expansion of popular politics. Although the mobilization increasingly undermined political stability, high officials did not issue orders for the use of force against protesters. Multiple long-standing cleavages in the political class over constitutional reform in Yugoslavia and Serbia, the Kosovo problem, economic reform and political liberalization prevented the emergence of consensus over popular protests. Many younger politicians also felt that repression would be incompatible with the values of their generation. In turn, the summer protest campaign had important implications for the internal dynamics of the party-state. The protests of the industrial workers, along with growing discontent with high officials among the general public and party members alike – already observed by pollsters[15] – triggered a revolt in the lower ranks of the party-state, which started at the May 1988 Conference of the LCY, and left high officials increasingly vulnerable.

The LCY Conference, or the small party Congress, accepted proposals for radical economic reforms, the dismantling of the party's monopoly in the cadre policy and a transparent multi-candidate selection procedure for high offices, and left six months for their implementation. It was publicly announced that the failure to meet the deadline was to trigger an early party Congress and the replacement of all members of the federal party Presidency and a sizeable proportion of the Central Committee of the LCY.[16] The July and August protest campaign of Kosovo Serbs and their allies then turned long-standing cleavages in the higher echelons of the party-state into a political conflict on the public stage. The popular protests and elite conflict gradually undermined Vojvodina's high officials and further empowered their rivals from Serbia's leadership, and further obstructed decision making in the federation.[17]

The summer protest campaign and growing conflict in the political class in turn aided further mobilization. The protests produced activist networks across Vojvodina, central Serbia and Montenegro and protest strategies that other protest groups, similar or unrelated, could freely borrow and employ while pursuing their own goals. The rallies held in late August demonstrated that challenger groups had become an important political force, which made the decision-making centres behind them – such as the informal Kosovo Polje group of movement's leaders, the Committee of Kosovo Serb activists and various leaders of the industrial workers – desirable allies for ambitious political actors, such as parts of the political establishment and dissident intellectuals. The summer mobilization ultimately destroyed a long standing image of a unified and dignified political establishment, which had long held back popular protest.

The anti-bureaucratic revolution

In the months between September 1988 and March 1989 there were high levels of mobilization in Serbia and Montenegro, which is a rare phenomenon under authoritarianism. Public meetings, large street rallies, strikes, marches and demonstrations abounded, with a few hunger strikes, and even violence by the end of March. The only exception is December when there were no major non-institutional events. In early September Kosovo Serb activists arranged their first rally in central Serbia and their last one in Vojvodina. The rally in Smederevo, a city with a high concentration of Kosovo Serb emigrants, was their largest thus far, with 60,000 participants, while the rally in Kovin, just across the Danube, involved a crowd of 10,000. Simultaneously, local activists in Vojvodina organized rallies in Sombor and Crvenka, which revealed the accelerating rate of parallel local mobilization.

In Vojvodina, protesters recruited among various supporters of Kosovo Serb activists, such as earlier Serb migrants from Kosovo, members of their extended families, and post-war settlers from Montenegro and Bosnia-Hercegovina and their descendants, who found the themes of protest highly resonant with their memories of conflict and the response of Vojvodina's leadership plain wrong. Also, all sorts of people discontented with the province's high officials, especially their opponents – disgruntled local officials, managers of state-controlled enterprises and trade unionists – became involved, as did all those who wanted to see constitutional reform in Serbia. The stalemate between the high officials of Vojvodina and their non-elite opponents ultimately broke down in the second half of September, with large protests in Sremska Mitrovica and Novi Sad, when the province's leadership already felt helpless in the face of growing mobilization.[18]

In Montenegro, the Kosovo Serb movement enjoyed a strong popular support, while most of the republic's high officials were increasingly unpopular, not least because of a sharply deteriorating economy and falling living standards. Despite a strong disapproval by the small republic's leadership, local officials organized rallies in Nikšić, with 50,000 participants, and Cetinje, with 30,000, under the auspices of the Socialist Alliance of the Working People on 18 September. Another rally of 30,000 participants, occurred in Andrijevica a week later, at which point the leadership lost political control.[19] Simultaneously, Kosovo Serb activists triggered mobilization across Kosovo and their demands turned more radical.

In contrast, parallel developments in central Serbia involved a large measure of top-down mobilization. High officials of Serbia authorized local authorities and managers of large state enterprises to provide broad logistical support for the rallies and encouraged popular participation through comprehensive and sympathetic media coverage of the events. These rallies featured first rate stage and amplifying equipment, industrially produced banners and at times even organized transport and lunch-packages for the participants. The largest such rally occurred in Belgrade on 19 November, labelled the 'rally of brotherhood and unity', and involved roughly 700,000 participants. The rally of solidarity, which started as an innovative protest strategy of grass-roots groups in an inclusive but weakening authoritarian regime, gradually turned into a staged performance by Serbia's consolidated political establishment.

The position of Serbia's leadership on constitutional reform benefited from mobilization because it weakened its key opponents, principally Vojvodina's high officials. Milošević had shown his populist leanings before. He had long stressed the parts of the Titoist legacy which celebrated the role of ordinary people in the war of liberation and of the working class and self-management, while glossing over other parts of this legacy, such as the radically decentralized structure of the party and state. Milošević tended to pose as the protector of ordinary people and the image of the people's politician was very helpful at a time when high officials grew unpopular. Top-down mobilization therefore dominated developments in central Serbia. Still, Kosovo Serb activists played an important role even there, which is revealed in the geographical distribution of the rallies. The rallies before 22 September were held almost exclusively in towns and cities less than 100 kilometres away from Kosovo, where sensitivity to the Kosovo problem was greater than in other parts of central Serbia and where the activists could bring their own crowds.

Large demonstrations, which undermined Yugoslavia's political class, started in early October. On 4 October 5,000 workers of the large industrial works from Rakovica, on the outskirts of Belgrade, organized a protest outside the Federal Assembly building. They called for the federal government to resign and demanded a 60 per cent pay rise. The workers booed the Speaker of the Assembly, a federal cabinet minister and a top trade union official who tried to address the protest, and insisted that Milošević should speak to them instead. In the end, Milošević turned up and delivered a short populist speech, supporting the demands from the protest and assuring the workers that Serbia's leadership would take their demands seriously. The following morning, another group of workers from Rakovica staged a demonstration outside the Federal Assembly and broke into the building, refusing to leave until Milošević arrived and repeated his pledges from the previous day.[20]

Simultaneously, large demonstrations broke out in Novi Sad, with the sole demand that the high officials of Vojvodina resign. Although the widely reported Belgrade demonstrations had encouraged popular mobilization elsewhere, the Novi Sad protest originated from the discontent of Vojvodina's population with their leadership and from the conflict between the latter and local officials from Bačka Palanka, a town in southwest Vojvodina. When the province's party Presidency invoked the anti-faction rule against the local officials who openly demanded their resignations, several thousand workers from Bačka Palanka set off on a protest march to Novi Sad. The protesters, strengthened by thousands of workers from the large state enterprises of Novi Sad, booed Milovan Šogorov, Vojvodina's party leader, who tried to speak to the workers, and then surrounded the Province Committee building. By late evening there were 50,000 participants. Vojvodina's leaders appealed to the party Presidency and state Presidency of Yugoslavia to halt demonstrations without success.[21] On the following day, the crowd grew to roughly 100,000 and Vojvodina's high officials resigned. The event later came to be called, somewhat ironically, the Yoghurt Revolution because protesters repeatedly threw packs of yoghurt at the Province Committee building.

On 7 October, large demonstrations of industrial workers, students and citizens erupted in Titograd, the administrative centre of Montenegro. Excited by the well-reported demonstrations in Belgrade and Novi Sad of the previous days, around 2,000 workers of *Radoje Dakić*, the largest enterprise in Titograd, and 100 students from the University of Titograd turned up outside the buildings of the Assembly and state Presidency of Montenegro. The protesters demanded a pay rise, the resignations of several high officials of Montenegro, a new economic policy, an inquiry into rumoured embezzlements by high officials, and the reduction of a heavy burden on the economy. The crowd jeered and heckled Montenegro's prime minister and warned that they would continue with their protest until their demands had been resolved. By evening there were around 25,000 participants in the square. In the early morning of 8 October, Montenegro's leadership declared a state of emergency and the police forces cleared up the square. Later that day, security forces used tear gas to prevent 300 workers from the *Nikšić Steelworks* from coming to Titograd and forced them back to Nikšić. Throughout the week there was a substantial presence of security forces on the streets of Titograd and other larger towns, and protests repeatedly broke out in Titograd, Nikšić and Ivangrad.

Although the demonstration effect of the Belgrade and Novi Sad protests mattered, the Titograd and other demonstrations in the small republic originated principally from local sources. Montenegro was ripe for an eruption of popular discontent in the second half of 1988. The state of Montenegro's economy was worse even than that of most other republics of Yugoslavia. Large state enterprises were literally nearing collapse, with recent layoffs and many industrial workers receiving only a minimal wage. Although organized over a different matter, the August and September rallies provided an opportunity for the expression of deep-seated popular discontent that originated from various, mainly socio-economic sources. The suppression of the October demonstrations then turned against the leadership even those who had earlier remained indifferent, and triggered elite conflict within the small republic.

In the end, large demonstrations in Titograd on 10 and 11 January 1989 sealed the fate of Montenegro's leadership. Around 1,000 workers of Radoje Dakić organized a demonstration in the city centre, demanding that the high officials resign. Students and many others joined the demonstration and the crowd swelled to 10,000. Despite freezing weather, thousands of workers from large state enterprises and citizens from all parts of Montenegro joined the demonstration throughout the day and evening. The number of participants rose to over 60,000. On the following day Montenegro was brought to a halt – effectively, though not officially, there was a general strike. After prolonged deliberation, the high officials resigned.[22] At the time, there were nearly 100,000 protesters on the streets of Titograd, which in a republic with a population of only 600,000 was an unprecedented demonstration of popular discontent with its leadership.

Popular politics and nationalist conflict

The antibureaucratic revolution was a complex phenomenon. There was a considerable regional and temporal variation regarding the relative importance of the role of elite and non-elite actors in the events and of the dominant themes of popular protests. The main agents behind the spread of mobilization were non-state and non-elite actors, including Kosovo Serb activists and their allies, the industrial workers and individuals from institutions in Vojvodina, Montenegro and central Serbia. Without doubt, mobilization benefited from logistical support from Serbia's party-state officials, whose role was crucial in central Serbia, indirect and limited in Vojvodina and sporadic in Montenegro. The prevailing themes of mobilization also shifted between the constitutional status of the autonomous provinces of Vojvodina and Kosovo, Serb-Albanian relations, socio-economic issues, industrial relations, the accountability of high officials and popular participation in politics. The mobilization wave culminated with the rise of the highly resonant antibureaucratic theme, which had widely been used in socialist Yugoslavia, both in the official discourse and at the grass roots. While featuring nationalist demands and symbolism, the antibureaucratic revolution was simultaneously a social movement with an important socio-economic focus and one aimed at the extension of political participation and the accountability of political elites, just like the social movements that developed throughout Eastern Europe on the eve of the fall of communism.[23]

Massive mobilization and the far-reaching political consequences of the antibureaucratic revolution raised fears among Kosovo Albanians. Not least because it became clear that the support in some republics for the opposition of Kosovo's high officials to the reduction of the autonomy of Serbia's autonomous provinces was fading away. The principal reaction came from the grass roots in the form of the protest march by 2,000 miners from Stari Trg which in turn triggered large demonstrations in Pristina between 17 and 21 November. Since the authorities preferred to ignore the protesters' legitimate demands and repeated displays of loyalty to the Yugoslav state and communist regime, 1,300 miners from Stari Trg started a dramatic hunger strike on 20 February 1989 and thus set off another wave of protests, including a general strike. The federal state Presidency in response declared a state of emergency in Kosovo. The events triggered wider confrontation between Serbia and Slovenia on both the elite and mass levels, the real source of which was their conflicting views about constitutional reform in Yugoslavia. The Ljubljana meeting of support for the Kosovo Albanian protests sparked off massive rallies in Belgrade, Novi Sad and Titograd, which involved hundreds of thousands. The wave of popular politics finally ended in state repression in late March, following violent exchanges between Yugoslav security forces and groups of Kosovo Albanian protesters.[24]

The dominance of exclusionary and confrontational nationalist themes in late February and March 1989 signalled that the attitudes of political actors, high officials and non-elite groups alike, had changed considerably. This shift only partly originated from the nationalist strategies of the various actors and was principally an unintended consequence of the high levels of mobilization and spiralling of various conflicts in a highly decentralized, authoritarian multi-national state, which found itself in the middle of severe economic crisis and rapid political liberalization. Popular politics brought to light old and triggered new conflicts across the polity and society, including industrial and socio-economic conflicts, struggles over popular participation in politics, the accountability of high officials, and relations between Yugoslavia's republics and nations. The resulting widespread conflict, at a time when political institutions appeared increasingly dysfunctional and the power structure was changing rapidly, became the vehicle which transformed all of these struggles into exclusionary conflict, which now reflected the main underlying structural divisions in Yugoslavia between its republics and nations.

Popular politics underscored and augmented earlier conflicts within the political class and altered the power relations between political elites in the republics and autonomous provinces, thereby altering their strategic choices. As stakes in the conflict grew, earlier elite divisions – between different political generations, over economic reforms and political liberalization – and more recent ones, such as between high officials and lower-ranking officials, local officials and company managers became less important. Key high officials in the republics now openly extended exclusive nationalist appeals to their national constituencies. Since the major re-distribution of power among the republics' elites now unfolded on the public stage, these events also resulted in shifts in attitudes of the general public. The growing prospect of the constitutional restructuring of the Yugoslav federation, perceived as threatening to the interests of some republics and their constituent nations, overshadowed other, previously important political concerns. As a result, the high officials' nationalist appeals resonated well among their national constituencies.

Popular politics also facilitated the radicalization of most political actors by bringing conflicts over constitutional reform and Kosovo onto the public stage. Earlier, heated conflicts over these issues remained largely confined within the political establishment and among professional observers, which made negotiated policy solutions possible. Now, the republics' leaders were not ready to offer any concessions to high officials from other republics because their constituencies might consider these to be a sign of weakness. Popular support had become a major power resource in the course of the wave of mobilization surrounding the antibureaucratic revolution. Thus, growing efforts of regional leaders to gain the support of their national constituencies ended up in nationalist outbidding, even among moderate high officials and those without nationalist credentials.

Another consequence of the widespread conflict in the polity and society was that individuals felt increasing pressure to choose between competing political loyalties, which had previously co-existed largely in harmony with one another. Conflicts over constitutional reform and that between Serbia and Slovenia among elites and the masses, as well as the uncertainty that followed from high levels of mobilization, pushed individuals to adopt more exclusive political identities. Earlier, separate national identities and the umbrella Yugoslav identity had been considered fully compatible. The majority felt at ease considering themselves both Serb and Yugoslav, Croat and Yugoslav, Slovene and Yugoslav, and less so, Albanian and Yugoslav. Now, the supranational Yugoslav identity was rapidly losing ground to more exclusive national identities. Thus, the conflicts became decisively and exclusively nationalist only towards the end of this wave of popular politics.

Conclusion

The rise and spreading out of popular politics in the second half of the 1980s was hardly the only factor behind the nationalist conflicts that led to the break-up of the Yugoslav federation. The fall of communism was bound to make the survival of Yugoslavia difficult, with popular mobilization or without it. All communist multi-national federations collapsed in the early 1990s and Yugoslavia – in contrast to the Soviet Union and Czechoslovakia – was a radically decentralized state in which political and economic life was structured largely along the borders of its six republics and Serbia's two autonomous provinces. However, the break-up of Yugoslavia was by no means inevitable. In the 1980s opinion polls registered very low levels of rejection of members of other nations[25] and high party-state officials did not seem to be aiming at the break-up of Yugoslavia.

The contribution of popular politics to the break-up of the state was that it produced high levels of conflict of all varieties in a highly diverse multi-national society at a time when political institutions turned increasingly dysfunctional and the old power structure was rapidly disintegrating. This in turn led to the change of attitudes among elites and the population from broad support for continued existence of Yugoslavia to growing conviction that it fell short of satisfying the interests of particular republics and nations. As a result, the break-up of the state, previously considered virtually inconceivable by the vast majority of its citizens, gradually came to appear as a distinct possibility.

This is not to say that some actors, such as dissident intellectuals, had no role whatsoever to play in the spread of nationalism. Some had long before articulated various nationalist arguments that high party-state officials would subsequently take over. Still, their impact on the Yugoslav politics was not significant before the autumn of 1988, and the popular appeal of their nationalist demands and claims grew only with the outburst of elite conflict and conflicts between high officials and the masses. The wave of popular politics served as the instrument which turned various socio-economic and political – nationalist and non-nationalist – struggles into nationalist conflicts, and which transformed inclusive nationalist themes into exclusionary ones. The critical actors that brought about the break-up of Yugoslavia were themselves transformed by the spread of nationalism, just like in the Soviet Union.[26] What follows is that the claim that Slobodan Milošević and Milan Kučan, the communist leaders of Serbia and Slovenia, respectively, had long secretly drafted plans to radically re-design Yugoslavia or engineer its collapse, or had gone for exclusive nationalist strategies only to remain in power at a time of major political change, is misleading. The high officials in fact gradually embraced nationalist strategies under the pressure of the spiralling conflicts, which had been initiated or augmented during the wave of popular politics. Failure of leadership was however obvious. Instead of responding effectively to growing economic and political crises, most high officials in Yugoslavia engaged initially in petty conflicts and subsequently in nationalist outbidding.

Notes

1 For reviews of the literature on the fall of Yugoslavia see D. Jović, *Yugoslavia: A State that Withered Away* (West Lafayette: Purdue University Press, 2009), pp. 13–46; J. Dragović-Soso,

'Why Did Yugoslavia Disintegrate? An Overview of Contending Explanations', in L. J. Cohen and J. Dragović-Soso (eds), *State Collapse in South-Eastern Europe: New Perspectives on Yugoslavia's Disintegration* (West Lafayette: Purdue University Press, 2008); and S.P. Ramet, *Thinking about Yugoslavia: Scholarly Debates about the Yugoslav Breakup and the Wars in Bosnia and Kosovo* (Cambridge: Cambridge University Press, 2005).

2 For a detailed analysis of the antibureaucratic revolution and related protest campaigns and their political consequences, including the fall of communism and the rise of new authoritarianism, see N. Vladisavljević, *Serbia's Antibureaucratic Revolution: Milošević, the Fall of Communism and Nationalist Mobilization* (Basingstoke: Palgrave Macmillan, 2008).

3 S. L. Burg, 'Elite Conflict in Post-Tito Yugoslavia', *Soviet Studies*, vol. 38, no. 2, 1986, p. 180.

4 M. Korošić, *Jugoslavenska kriza* (Zagreb: Naprijed, 1988); S.L. Woodward, *Balkan Tragedy: Chaos and Dissolution after the Cold War* (Washington, D.C.: Brookings Institution, 1995).

5 See S. Tarrow, *Power in Movement: Social Movements and Contentious Politics* (Cambridge: Cambridge University Press, 1998); and H. Kitschelt, 'Political Opportunity Structures and Political Protest: Anti-Nuclear Movements in Four Democracies', *British Journal of Political Science* vol. 16, no. 1 (1986), pp. 57–85.

6 For details about popular protest in socialist Yugoslavia before the 1980s see Vladisavljević, *Serbia's Antibureaucratic Revolution*, chapter 1.

7 For details see Vladisavljević, *Serbia's Antibureaucratic Revolution*, chapter 3.

8 N. Vladisavljević, 'Grass Roots Groups, Milošević or Dissident Intellectuals? A Controversy over the Origins and Dynamics of the Mobilization of Kosovo Serbs in the 1980s', *Nationalities Papers*, vol. 32, no. 4, 2004, pp. 781–96, N. Vladisavljević, 'Nationalism, Social Movement Theory and the Grass Roots Movement of Kosovo Serbs, 1985–88', *Europe-Asia Studies*, vol. 54, no. 5, 2002, pp. 771–90.

9 Korošić, *Jugoslavenska kriza*, p.63.

10 S. Fočo, *Štrajk između iluzije i zbilje* (Belgrade: Radnička štampa, 1989), L. Mohar, 'Štrajk i nemoć radnika: pokušaj sinteze rezultata istraživanja o štrajkovima', *Sociološki pregled*, vol. 21, no. 3, 1987, pp. 7–34; D. Sekulić, 'Štrajk ili obustava rada – jedan sociološki pristup', *Kulturni radnik*, vol. 40, no. 6, 1987, pp. 23–33.

11 Z. Simić, 'Skica za monografiju o štrajku rudara u Labinu', *Sociološki pregled*, vol. 21, no. 3, 1987, pp. 47–58; T. Kuzmanić, 'Prvi dan Labinskog štrajka – 8.4.1987', *Sociološki pregled*, vol. 21, no. 3, 1987, pp. 59–68; T. Kuzmanić, 'Samorepresivnost: primjer labinskog štrajka 1987', *Kulturni radnik*, vol. 40, no. 6, 1987, pp. 34–49.

12 *Danas*, 24 November 1987, p. 17; 15 December 1987, pp. 22–23.

13 *Borba*, 7 July 1988, pp. 1, 4; *Danas*, 12 July 1988, pp. 7–8.

14 Fočo, *Štrajk između iluzije i zbilje*, pp. 91–92.

15 For details see V. Goati, *Politička anatomija jugoslovenskog društva* (Zagreb: Naprijed), pp. 31, 81–82.

16 *Danas*, 7 June 1988, pp. 7–11; *NIN*, 5 June 1988, pp. 7–12.

17 For details see Vladisavljević, *Serbia's Antibureaucratic Revolution*, chapter 4.

18 Boško Krunić, a member of the federal party Presidency and formerly its President, and a leading member of the province's party Presidency who wanted to remain anonymous, interviews with the author, 28 August 2000 and 18 July 2001.

19 A leading member of Montenegro's state Presidency who wanted to remain anonymous, interview with the author, 20 July 2001.

20 For details about the events see *Borba*, 5 October 1988, pp. 1, 3; 6 October 1988, p. 5; *Danas*, 11 October 1988, pp. 22–23; *NIN*, 9 October 1988, pp. 11–12.

21 Telegram to the party Presidencies and state Presidencies of Yugoslavia and Serbia was read out at the session of Serbia's party Presidency on the following morning. See excerpts from the session's transcript in *Borba*, 7 October 1988, pp. 2–4, 5.

22 *Borba*, 11 January 1989, pp. 1, 3; 12 January 1989, pp. 1, 3–4.

23 For details see Vladisavljević, *Serbia's Antibureaucratic Revolution*, chapter 5.

24 For details see ibid., chapter 6.

25 B. Kuzmanović, 'Socijalna distanca prema pojedinim nacijama (etnička distanca)', in M. Lazić, D. Mrkšić, S. Vujović, B. Kuzmanović, S. Gredelj, S. Cvejić, and V. Vuletić (eds), *Razaranje društva: Jugoslovensko društvo u krizi 90-tih* (Belgrade: Filip Višnjić, 1994), pp. 225–44.
26 For events in the Soviet Union see M.R. Beissinger, *Nationalist Mobilization and the Collapse of the Soviet State* (Cambridge: Cambridge University Press, 2002).

9 Popular Mobilization in the 1990s

Nationalism, democracy and the slow decline of the Milošević regime

Florian Bieber

On 4 October 1988, several thousand workers met in front of the Federal Assembly in Belgrade demanding better economic opportunities and the resignation of the Federal government and trade union leaders.[1] After federal officials failed to calm the crowds, they called for Slobodan Milošević, the chair of the League of Communists of Serbia. Addressing the demonstrators, he assured the workers of his support, promised reforms in the context of the struggle against bureaucracy and the division of the nation.[2] Later an observer would note that 'the protestors came as workers, and went home as Serbs'.[3]

Nearly 12 years to the day later, on 20 September 2000, some 1,000,000 Serbs participated in the final rally of the Yugoslav presidential elections by the Democratic Opposition of Serbia (DOS). In his speech, Vojislav Koštunica, the DOS candidate, emphasized the need for peace and quiet after ten years of war and unrest:

> I am absolutely sure that we [are] tired of all those stormy and tempestuous events. What we need is ... peace amongst ourselves. We need calm. We need a kind of life in which excitements would be confined primarily to the personal plane – let the public, political life be monotonous, even boring if you like. In a nutshell, what we need is a normal and civilized state.[4]

So, did the participants come as Serbs and leave as citizens?

Between the late 1980s and 2000, citizens of Serbia had gone to the streets to protest against the government dozens of times. The original wave of public protests of 1988–89 was supported and in part choreographed by the Milošević regime and directed against the leadership in Vojvodina, Kosovo and Montenegro as well as other opponents. After a short lull around the first elections of December 1990, the second wave of protests by the democratic and national opposition against the Milošević regime began in March 1991. The war in Bosnia brought about another hiatus in protests, although smaller demonstrations against the war and the regime still took place. Following on from this, the third wave of protests began in late 1996 after the government falsified local election results. Thereafter, the final phase of protests began after the end of the Kosovo war, in June 1999. This was supported by the protest movement *Otpor* (Resistance), and culminated in the street protests that triggered the resignation of Slobodan Milošević on 5 October 2000.[5] Mobilization and counter-mobilization had therefore determined political and social life for more than a decade and protests were a greater provider of political legitimacy than many elections.

This chapter will discuss the interrelationship between nationalism and the ability to mobilize a broad social movement against the semi-authoritarian Milošević regime. The key question it will seek to answer is why, despite repeated efforts, the mass mobilization against the regime was successful in autumn 2000 and not earlier. In addition to a number of other factors, the role of nationalism and ethnopolitical mobilization is key in explaining the timing and nature of this delayed democratic revolution. The study of social movements in Serbia will, in conclusion, allow for some observations in understanding the broader role of ethnonationalism in late democratization processes, as they have occurred in the post-Communist countries during the past decade.[6] Serbia experienced multiple cycles of mobilization. These cycles are characterized by the mobilization through early risers, followed by the diffusion to a broader range of social groups. In particular, early mobilization can have a demonstration effect and set the agenda for broader political discourse, thus securing a significance beyond the numbers of protestors themselves.[7] The themes over which mobilization took place were nationalism, democracy and dissatisfaction with elites in power, however, as the introductory accounts already suggest, these are not separate and neat processes; democracy and nationalisms are interwoven in the way they have informed social movements in Serbia and how they delayed the democratization of the country by over a decade.

Mobilization and nationalism

The first major social movement in late Yugoslav Serbia first emerged, as discussed in the previous chapter by Nebojša Vladisavljević, among Kosovo Serbs against the Kosovo authorities. As this movement gathered support in Serbia, this social movement was directed against parts of the late socialist elite, especially in Montenegro and the Serbian provinces of Vojvodina and Kosovo. As such it formed the backdrop to the consolidation of the Milošević regime in its disputes with competing parts of the socialist regime. These protests were thus both revolutionary in demanding the overthrow of parts of the elite, as well as supportive of other parts of the Socialist elite.

This instance of social mobilization has often been dismissed for its manipulation by the regime.[8] This instrumentalization and orchestration notwithstanding, the intensity of the protests, as well as the numbers of demonstrators present, signified a degree of social mobilization which should not be easily dismissed. The protests have been given different names, most drawing on motifs of some mythical awakening of the nation. Some have termed it the 'third uprising', in reference to two uprisings against Ottoman rule in the early nineteenth century.[9] Equating Ottoman rule and Communism thus became a common theme in nationalist mythology. The protests have also been called the 'happening of the people' (*događanje naroda*).[10] This term emphasizes the supposed unity of the nation and the supposedly spontaneous character of the protests.[11]

The origins of these *mitinzi* (literally, meetings) lay with the protests organized by Kosovo Serbs since 1985 against the authorities in Kosovo. The Kosovo Serb solidarity meetings were planned by several committees of Kosovo Serbs, some of whom had migrated to Serbia itself.[12] The groups brought together disgruntled former party members and other activists linked to the League of Communists of Serbia through some formerly prominent party members.[13] Originally critical towards state and party, this link allowed these organizations to achieve major successes, especially once Milošević aligned himself and the party with the cause. As Vladisavljević has convincingly argued, the social movement initiated by the Kosovo Serb groups was not just a pawn of Milošević but had its own agenda and goals, which first coincided with the forms of mobilization sought after by Milošević.[14] However, once the mobilization was facilitated by the Serbian League of Communists and republican structures, it was increasingly co-opted, not just in terms of the organization, but also in terms of its goals and duration.

One of the Kosovo Serb leaders later on noted that 'nationalism would not have had a chance, had it not received support from something as powerful as the state.'[15] There was little doubt that the protests were increasingly directed and organized by the state, including media support and the participation of party, army and police.[16] Accordingly, the dissident Milovan Djilas called the protest 'partially organized spontaneity.'[17] The protests ceased to be about Kosovo only, but became more about an inner-party conflict. The use of extra-institutional means in inner-party power struggles broke with a long tradition which had party battles being fought out behind mostly closed doors. As a Vojvodina party functionary noted at the time, 'In the history of our party, we never had such a dramatic conflict on an open stage.'[18]

The popular mobilization not only shifted the stage from support within party structures to support on the street, it also resulted in a shift away from the arguments which would have swayed party members. Unsurprisingly, communist ideology only played a secondary role in the message of the protests. Primarily, as the organizing committees had intended, the protests sought to draw attention to the emigration of Serbs and Montenegrins from Kosovo. As the goals and messages extended beyond Kosovo, the themes brought up in the meetings became eclectic, invoking economic hardships as well as the Serbian Orthodox Church. The transformation of economic into national demands occurred not only during the protest mentioned in the introduction, but also at many other protests.[19]

As the protests became controlled by the regime, they directed themselves against the party leadership in Kosovo and Vojvodina, as well as in Montenegro and against other opposition within the party. They nevertheless remained eclectic. They did not present a unified picture of what it meant to be Serb. Religious icons, American flags, portraits of Milošević and communist slogans appeared next to each other.[20] The key theme of the protests was that they supposedly reflected the will of the people. This was echoed in slogans during the protests, such as 'the people are the best judge' or 'the people are speaking, listen to it.'[21] As supposed representative of the people, the protests can be regarded as an example of fake direct democracy, allowing for the regime to further delay more genuine democratization.[22]

The first of these mass protests began in Vojvodina in July 1988 against the provincial leadership. This was considered an easier target than the leadership in Kosovo, as it enjoyed less popular support.[23] Nevertheless, the first rally drew few people. Throughout the summer, however, the number of participants grew. During some 59 demonstrations over the course of the summer and autumn of 1988, tens of thousands participated in demonstrations across the province, including in small towns with tiny populations.[24]

This wave of protests concluded with a large rally at Ušće, at the confluence of the Danube and Sava River in Belgrade on 17 November 1988. By this stage, the organization of the demonstrations had come under complete control of the party: 'They became listeners, and the gathering became a political spectacle ... Through that ritual political transformation of the people from a political subject to a political object and instrument has been finished. All the strings were definitely in the hands of the organizers.'[25] Apart from a few further protests in 1989, and the large commemoration held to mark the 600th anniversary of the Kosovo battle, on 28 June 1989, the mass mobilization had been completed.

Slobodan Milošević became the central figure in the protests, placing himself at the helm of a protest movement that had the potential to sweep away the party leadership – as had happened in neighbouring countries. As such Milošević had two roles in 1988: he was both an intra-party counter-revolutionary and a revolutionary of the streets and squares of Serbia.

With the regime's consolidation of power, mass mobilization had not only outlived its usefulness, but gradually emerged as a genuine threat. With the development of multi-party politics in late 1989 and early 1990, the League of Communists, renamed Socialist Party of Serbia in mid-1990, could no longer claim to be the only representative of the nation. In fact, a fierce competition emerged over who represented the nation. The ability to bring together an eclectic combination of world views – from dogmatic supporters of Tito's partisans and Yugoslav unity to followers of the right-wing nationalist *četnik* movement – would only be temporarily successful. During the coming decade different interpretations of what it meant to be a Serb and what Serbia should look like would dominate public discourse. Ironically, the inability to create a coherent national movement in Serbia also played to the advantage of the Socialist Party in its success in thwarting any coherent opposition national movement.

Demobilizing ethnonationalism

The protests in Serbia during the 1990s had a two-fold significance. First, the protests were an expression of social mobilization, even if in most protests the participants hardly constituted a large or representative part of the population. Nevertheless, the motives of the protests did reflect social moods and in turn shaped them. Furthermore, if we understand nationalism not in terms of being a given, but as being created and requiring reaffirmation, social movements hold a central place in affirming the existence of a nation – or even of ignoring the nation as the primary frame of reference.[26] Thus, the question arises how these 'events' of the 1990s on the streets of Belgrade and other Serbian cities can be reconciled with the state effort of reaffirming Serbian 'groupness' on the battlefields of Croatia, Bosnia-Herzegovina and Kosovo.

Secondly, the Milošević regime rested not only on the legitimacy of elections and the control of institutions, but also claimed some extra-institutional popular legitimacy. In particular, this legitimacy derived from the support and use of the protests of Kosovo Serbs in the late 1980s, which made the government appear popular even before the first elections.[27]

During the pre-democratic phase, circumventing traditional institutions allowed Milošević to marginalize political opponents within the League of Communists of Serbia, which were unable or unwilling to similarly mobilize public support. After the introduction of a multiparty system, the Milošević regime claimed to represent the population and carefully sought to maintain formal democratic legitimacy through elections. However, it also drew on alternative tools to re-affirm apparent consent by the population. One example was the use of referenda, such as the one to legitimize the new constitution in 1990. Ever since the early 1990s, this form of 'plebiscitary Ceasarism'[28] was unable to generate support. Even the referendum in 1998 against foreign intervention in Kosovo, which was supported by an overwhelming majority of the electorate, was unable to play a strong mobilizing function for the government. Shortly afterwards, the regime accepted international mediation in the conflict.

First protests

The first protests against the Milošević regime began only a few months after the end of the mass mobilization of 1988–89. On 13 June 1990, some 50,000 citizens took to the streets, thus marking the beginning of a decade of anti-government protests.[29] The first large-scale protests took place in March 1991 and signalled the transition to a pluralist society a few months after the first multi-party elections, in December 1990. The inability of the opposition to win the elections, or even gather a serious share of the vote, marked the need for extra-institutional mobilization to challenge the authorities. From then on, elections and protests were linked, and only when the protests could draw legitimacy from elections in 2000 did they fully succeed.

As the 1990 elections confirmed the Socialist Party in power, no measures were undertaken to democratize or pluralize the institutions. Thus, the thrust of the first major protests was against state television, which had been, and remained, a key pillar of the regime. The protests, called for by Vuk Drašković, the then main opposition leader, and later carried on by students, succeeded in triggering the resignation of the head of state TV, but not in the liberalization of the station itself (he was replaced by another regime figure). Meanwhile, Milošević used the demonstrations to push for the use of the army in internal conflicts and for the state presidency to declare a state of emergency. Drašković had campaigned on a more nationalist political platform, and the regime media accused him and his followers of endangering Serbs and being traitors – two reoccurring motives in the characterization of the opposition. The support Serb leaders from Croatia and Bosnia extended towards the regime appeared to confirm the government's assertion, but also led to a temporary cooling of relations between the opposition in Serbia and these nationalist Croatian and Bosnian Serb leaders.[30]

This first attempt at democratizing Serbia failed due to both the willingness of the regime to use force to end any threat against it and the use of nationalism by the regime to discredit the opposition. In addition, the calls for Miloševic's resignation, made by students, lacked clear legitimacy as Milošević had just been elected with overwhelming support to the presidency.

Similar demands were made during the 1992 student protests, which began as sanctions were imposed on Serbia following the start of the war in Bosnia. Students demanded a new government of national unity, a constitutional assembly and other measures to overcome the political crisis.[31] While coinciding with the Bosnia war, the war itself was mostly irrelevant during the protests. Nationalism was only expressed in terms of party preferences, which benefited more patriotic political leaders. As the possible head of national unity government, Vojislav Koštunica received the most support among students.[32] Moreover, the student population participating in the protests was far from being unified, either in terms of their view of national identity or the importance they attributed to it.[33] During this phase, the opposition parties struggled to present a coherent alternative to the regime. In particular, in 1993 and 1994, following the decision of the Democratic Party to reject peace agreements that Milošević appeared to accept, parts of the opposition seemed more radical than the regime. In fact, one of the features of the regime was to always present itself as 'moderate'; with more nationalist parties (such as the Serbian Radical Party) playing the role of the bogeyman from which the Socialist Party would save the country. The supposedly moderate position of the ruling party helped not only gain domestic electoral support,[34] but also secured international backing, especially in the period between the wars in Bosnia and Kosovo.

The protests of 1996–97: dress rehearsal or 'don't mention the war'

The greatest challenge to the Milošević regime emerged barely a year after the end of the war in Bosnia. This time, the duration of the protests and the number of participants exceed all previous demonstrations. Throughout the winter, opposition parties and students protested, largely separately, against the attempts by the government to falsify the November 1996 local election results. For the first time, protests were not limited to Belgrade and larger cities, in particular in Vojvodina, but took place throughout Serbia in towns where the opposition victory had been challenged by electoral fraud. These lasted until the recognition of the results of the opposition coalition *Zajedno* (Together) and the resignation of the rector of the Belgrade University in February and March 1997.[35] However, the apparent victory proved to be Pyrrhic. The university did not become more liberal. In fact, it became more restrictive with the introduction of a new university law in 1998. Meanwhile, the *Zajedno* coalition broke apart and parts of the opposition cooperated with the regime at the local level.[36]

Nationalism did not play a major role in the protests. In fact, pacifist protesters joined supporters from more nationalist parties. A study of attitudes of students participating in the protests suggest that the responses reflect broader social tendencies, which include the increased importance of national identity.[37] More importantly, the protests sought to end the isolation of the country, which resulted from both the policies of the Milošević regime and the internationally imposed sanctions. Whereas the symbols signified a reconnection with the world, there was little apparent opposition to the wars in Croatia and Bosnia-Herzegovina.[38] Nevertheless, the anti-collectivist attitude of the protest and the ironic use of national myths, such as the slogan '*Samo šetnja Srbina spasava*' ('Only a walk will save the Serbs', in reference to the national saying that 'Only unity will save Serbs'),[39] signified a clear distance between the content of the protests and their approach towards authority and the 'nation' than the vision promoted by nationalist groups and the state.

The protests highlighted the existence of two Serbias; a country divided between those supporting the authorities and those critical of the regime and collectivist ideologies. However, even the second, democratic Serbia was far from unified. As the cultural anthropologist Ivan Čolović notes: 'Not mentioning Kosovo or the war highlights as well how this part of Serbian society which demands an enlightened, democratic and European Serbia remains uncertain and divided in regard to these questions.'[40] The protests were thus unable to resolve the profound tensions that shaped opposition politics in Serbia. Instead, the larger social context in which the protests took place, left 'national questions' unaddressed.

Otpor: resistance instead of protests

The failure of the previous protests brought about the formation of the *Otpor* movement, which has been rightly credited with a key role in bringing down the Milošević regime and has been copied in a number of popular revolutions since (such as in Georgia and Ukraine). *Otpor* learnt the lessons of previous protests and emerged as a response to the draconian university law of 1998. The divisions among the opposition parties and their attempts to co-opt student leaders, and the failure of mass demonstrations, led to the formation of the movement, which was less hierarchical than other opposition structures. Although it started in 1998, *Otpor* only became fully active after the end of the Kosovo war.[41] Through creative mockery of the regime, including in small towns and cities across Serbia, by summer 2000 *Otpor* mustered some 30–40,000 activists in Serbia, organized through 120 local organizations and 50 offices.[42]

The movement had two primary aims: the resignation of Slobodan Milošević and the democratization of the country. For this purpose, it sought to force the opposition parties into a greater degree of unity than at previous elections.

However, *Otpor* also faced the national question. Its nine-point programme included calls for human rights, decentralization, minority rights and cooperation with the International Criminal Tribunal for the Former Yugoslavia at The Hague.[43] The call for the democratization of Kosovo and the highest possible degree of autonomy was the most controversial point and was more heavily debated than all other points among the *Otpor* leadership.[44] The degree of divergence over this question reflected the diverse background of *Otpor* members. While many came from the anti-war movement, others associated themselves more with the more nationalist opposition parties. These differences within the organization found their reflection also in other *Otpor* documents that mix nationalist references to St Sava (the thirteenth century founder of the Serbian Church) with orientalist visions of rejecting 'Asian models' for 'European roots' and liberal values of democratization.[45] This eclecticism, although with different goals, is thus reminiscent of the divergent backgrounds and world views of Milošević's supporters during the earlier mentioned nationalist mobilization in the late 1980s. The variety of political positions embodied in *Otpor*, as with the earlier mobilization in favour of Milošević, are indicative of the narrow goal of the particular social movement, which allows for such competing political viewpoints to converge.

Although the regime sought to paint *Otpor* as traitors, as it had done with earlier opposition and student movements, these efforts ultimately failed. Several anonymous poster campaigns, apparently sponsored by the government, showed the US Secretary of State Madeline Albright in an *Otpor* T-shirt with the clenched fist of the organization filled with dollars. A second series called *Otpor* 'Medlin [Serbian spelling of Madeline] Jugend' – a reference to *Hitler Jugend* and Madeline Albright – and portrayed *Otpor* using the imagery of Nazi propaganda. Similarly, state media referred to members of *Otpor* as 'quislings' and '*Šiptari*', a pejorative term for Albanians.[46] While such accusations might have fallen on fruitful ground during earlier protests, these attacks actually helped legitimize *Otpor* as it confirmed its role as the primary opposition force to the regime.[47]

Protesting for state and nation

Pro-government and nationalist protests remained the odd exception among the protests of the 1990s. One rare example was the 1997 protest of Belgrade students against the Rugova-Milošević agreement, which foresaw the re-establishment of Albanian teaching at the University of Prishtina (but was never implemented).[48] The main government attempt to mobilize its supporters occurred during the 1996–97 protests, when the regime organized a counter-demonstration that brought together protestors from all over Serbia. Despite considerable efforts, the number of participants nevertheless remained below expectations, varying between 40,000 and 100,000, depending on the estimate, or less than half of participants of the student and opposition protests the same day. The government protest, under the motto 'Serbia shall not be ruled by foreign hands', failed to undermine the street legitimacy of the opposition and also marked the end of the government attempting to mobilize its supporters, with the exception of pre-election rallies.[49] Void of content and praising the regime, the protests also failed to offer a substantive alternative to the opposition.[50] The government protest highlighted a general difficulty of any regime, be it authoritarian or democratic: it is difficult to mobilize citizens to demonstrate *for* a government. Even the attempt here to organize the demonstration *against* the opposition was unable to draw sufficient support.

A more successful episode of nationalist mobilization took place not against the opposition, but against NATO at the beginning of the war over Kosovo. Unlike the previous counter-demonstration which aligned itself closely with the regime, the protests against NATO lacked such a clear pro-government orientation. Organized in part by the state, but drawing on genuine frustration and supported by public figures, the protests appeared to briefly reconstitute the ability of the regime to mobilize mass support. The events included no conventional protests, but rather concerts and vigils on bridges and squares across Serbia. The symbol of the protests was the target sign, which embodied the self-perceived status of Serbia and the Serb population as victims. Unsurprisingly there was no mention of the suffering of Kosovo Albanians during the wartime protests, as critical voices were silenced. In much of the public discourse, the only acceptable victims were Serbs.[51] Ironically, there are a number of similarities between the anti-government protests of 1996–97 and the anti-NATO mobilization in 1999. Whereas the early protests symbolized to some degree the helplessness towards the regime, the protests now embodied a similar helplessness towards NATO. As in 1996–97, humour and mocking the opponent became the main source of expression.[52] This nationalist mobilization, however, was not long-lasting; occurring only for the duration of the bombardment. As the sociologist Zagorka Golubović details:

> Then there is the homogenisation of the population, which the regime succeeded in achieving during the NATO attack under the slogan 'The

Fatherland is threatened'; a renewed Serbian nationalism and, once again, the instrumentalisation of ethnic mobilisation in the name of 'patriotism', abused by the regime in order to maintain power. The attack also revived the populist movements, but soon after the war stopped, the situation changed profoundly: the regime's policy was increasingly blamed for the crisis and the wars – thus various protests and manifestations of civil disobedience have been occurring in the second part of 1999 in Belgrade and across Serbia.[53]

This short-termed mobilization was unable to provide for a more permanent re-legitimization of the government, or even of the war. Even during the conflict, small-scale protests began against government and the war, in particular in smaller towns of central Serbia and among families of recruits, which posed a potentially serious challenge to the Milošević regime.

Nation and social movements

During more than a decade of regular street protests and social mobilization after the semi-staged protests in 1988–89, there were a few moments when nationalism moved centre stage. Nevertheless, as discussed above, it would be false to thus dismiss the significance of nationalism in understanding the success and/or failure of social movements in Serbia. As Jack Snyder has argued, the onset of democratization provides for opportunities to nationalist entrepreneurs to derail the democratization process and pursue illiberal policies instead.[54] However, this approach does not help explain how in a nationalist environment, such as Serbia, democratic movements still succeeded. Here, we need to note that Serbia was certainly no exception; Slovakia and Croatia underwent a democratic transition shortly before Serbia in 1998 and 2000, respectively, both from an ethnonationalist rule which sought to bolster their support through nationalist mobilization.

Running counter to conventional arguments about the relationship between nationalism and democracy, Mark Beissinger has recently argued that there can be a positive relationship between ethnonational mobilization and democratization, that is the ability of nationalism to mobilize a large number of people for a democratic project.[55] The evidence in Serbia certainly would not suggest such a positive relationship. However, it emphasizes the need to understand the interrelationship as complex and multilayered. Simply suggesting that nationalist mobilization prevents democratic mobilization, or vice versa, does not explain how and when each of these movements develop their greatest impetus and why and when regimes succeed or fail in undermining pressure for democratization. In order to understand this relationship, one can argue that we need to consider four factors:

Demobilization

First of all, as Chip Gagnon and Eric Gordy have discussed in their studies of the impact of the war on Serbian society, ethnonationalism and war were hardly popular. Their primary purpose was to demobilize and destroy alternatives to the regime.[56] War was possibly the most powerful demobilizer for social movements in Serbia; with the exception of the student protests and the '*Vidovdan* assembly' protests in June and July 1992, all large anti-government protests took place during peace-time.[57] Wars demobilize for many reasons. Besides providing governments with the tools to clamp down more radically on opposition than in peace time, the use of select drafting of opposition supporters (or leaders) has been practiced in Serbia. Furthermore, the media, the regime and indeed even the opposition never tired of invoking the need for national unity, especially during war time, which in turn can easily be construed as the need to prevent social mobilization against government. The rise of social unrest in central Serbia during the NATO bombardment in 1999 highlights, however, that even war does not put an absolute stop to social mobilization.

Degrees of national legitimacy

Secondly, Serbia under Milošević was an 'ethnic semi-democracy'.[58] As such, it attributed different degrees of legitimacy to political parties. Minority parties were thus largely excluded from the mainstream political debates. The importance of national issues in political discourse also meant that opposition parties were often either unwilling or fearful to cooperate with minority parties against the regime. As a result, the opposition was unable to draw on their electoral support, thus missing out on the voting potential of minorities. It was only in 2000 that minority parties were brought into the main opposition coalition, DOS, and other minority parties began to support the opposition.

Democratic vs. national competition

Thirdly, the early 1990s were marked by competition between political parties over the meaning of nation and national interests. In fact, what appeared to be democratic competition was in fact national competition. Ironically, electoral results and surveys suggested that nationalism was not, for the most part, the political platform with substantial popular support. Instead, the stand taken by parties on the national question, rather than on other political issues, shaped public discourse. The importance of the national question as the defining question in the political system thus prevented a competition over alternative political ideas, which could have provided an opening for democratic opposition parties.

Unfinished nation in an unfinished state

Fourthly, Serbia existed in a constant *de facto* state of emergency throughout the 1990s. The territorial shape of the country, as well as its institutional arrangement, remained unclear and purposefully ambivalent. The unfinished nature of the state and the incomplete transformation into a nation state allowed for the suspension of issues-based political discourse with great ease and its replacement with status questions. In brief, the uncertainty created space for ethnonationalist discourse in an environment where other issues would otherwise command greater public interest. This uncertainty persisted after the fall of the Milošević regime; first with the unclear relations towards Montenegro, but since its independence, in 2006, through the dispute over the status of Kosovo.

As a result of these four factors, moments of ethnonationalist mobilization and/or war provided for a nearly insurmountable obstacle for a democratic revolution. Political alternatives during phases of nationalist mobilization focus on national, not democratic alternatives and generally benefit the incumbent. As a result, all major social movements against the regime in 1990s took place in times of reduced ethnonationalist mobilization. The question remains, when does the salience of ethnonationalism decline and open space for democratic mobilization? As the protests in 1996–97 and 2000 suggest, immediate post-war periods appear to lend themselves most to such a transition.

Conclusion

The decline of ethnonationalism was a key prerequisite for the fall of the Milošević regime and the emergence of a social movement strong enough to topple it. However, this factor is merely one of many requirements for the end of this particular type of regime. The end of semi-democratic regimes, such as the Milošević one, requires a particular set of circumstances. The fact that the regime, as is the case with most post-communist hybrid regimes, held elections at regular intervals provided for an opportunity to end it. However, as the decade long protests movement showed, elections need to be won by the opposition, even if the results are falsified by the regime afterwards. With the exception of the local elections in 1996, the opposition had been unable to win elections, or even come close enough to the regime parties to challenge their legitimacy.

A phenomenon of the Milošević regime, which it shared with other similar governments, was its increasing authoritarianism. A steady fall in popularity and democratic legitimacy was compensated with authoritarian policies, which in turn reduce its democratic legitimacy.[59] It could be argued that the Serbian regime in the 1990s was a classic hybrid, as it both 'wanted' to be authoritarian and to use repressive measures to hold on to power, but at the same time claimed to be democratic. This balance continuously tilted towards greater authoritarianism during the 1990s.

The key motivator against the government, however, as had been the case in Croatia and Georgia, for example, was not so much the regime's authoritarianism, but its corruption. In fact, neither nationalism nor dictatorship discredited the Milošević regime as much as economic mismanagement and poverty.[60]

To return to the question posed at the beginning of the chapter: did the participants in the mass protests in September and October 2000 leave as Serbs or as citizens? Or perhaps both? As the Milošević regime did not fall due to its aggressive use of nationalism, the ideology it used and instrumentalized did not become as discredited as the regime itself. In fact, in the speech in which he promised a 'boring' Serbia, which was cited at the beginning, Koštunica highlighted the unjust border dividing Bosnia and Serbia and called the Kumanovo agreement, which Milošević signed to allow for the establishment of a protectorate in Kosovo, a 'capitulation'.[61] As has become clear in recent years in Serbia, coming to terms with the legacy of the Milošević regime's use of extreme nationalism to wage war is a process which is at least as difficult as deposing the regime itself.

Notes

1 The chapter draws on Chapter 8 of my book *Nationalismus in Serbien vom Tode Titos bis zum Ende der Milošević Era* [Nationalism in Serbia from the Death of Tito to the End of the Milošević Era], (Vienna: Lit Verlag, 2005). I would like to thank Cornell University for the opportunity to discuss the paper in the seminar 'Social Movements and Regime Change in Latin America and Post–communist Eurasia: Comparative and Historical Perspectives' in September 2006.

2 V. Vujačić, *Communism and Nationalism in Russia and Serbia*, unpublished PhD dissertation, University of California, Berkeley 1995, pp. 339–41. In a speech to regional functionaries of the League of Communists, Milošević similiarly linked institutional change in Serbia to economic reform. See S. Milošević, *Les Années Décisives* (Lausanne: L'Age d'Homme, 1990), pp. 227–29.

3 Jagoš Djuretić, quoted from S. Djukić, *Izmedju slave i anateme. Politička biografija Slobodana Miloševića* (Belgrade, Filip Višnjić, 1994), p. 106. Ivan Čolović describes in detail how this transformation took place during the 1988 protests in *Bordell der Krieger. Folklore, Krieg und Politik* (Osnabrück: Fibre Verlag, 1994), pp. 138–42.

4 'Speech by Vojislav Koštunica at the DOS Last Pre-election Convention', DSS Press Service, 20 September 2000.

5 On the phases of protest, see M. Milošević, *Politički vodič kroz Srbiju 2000* (Belgrade: Medija centar, 2000), pp. 58–59 and 'Srbija na ulici' *Reporter*, special issue, April 2000.

6 See M. Beissinger, 'Structure and Example in Modular Political Phenomena: The Diffusion of the Bulldozer/Rose/Orange/Tulip Revolutions', *Perspectives on Politics* 5 (2), 2007, pp. 259–76.

7 S. Tarrow, *Power in Movement. Social Movements and Contentious Politics*, 2nd ed. (Cambridge: Cambridge University Press, 1999), pp. 144–45.

8 On this see M. Pavlović et al., 'Kosovo under Autonomy, 1974–90', in C. Ingrao and T. A. Emmert (eds), *Confronting the Yugoslav Controversies* (Washington, D.C.: West Lafayette, Ind., 2009), p. 75.

9 *The Economist*, 17 September 1988; *The Times*, 12 September 1988.

10 The term was coined by the writer Milovan Vitezović, 'Jogurt i druga oštra pića', *Srbija na ulici*, *Reporter*, special issue, April 2000.

11 See I. Djurić, *Glossaire de l'espace yougoslave* (Paris: L'Esprit des Péninsules, 1999), pp. 20–22.
12 J. Reuter, 'Die jüngste Entwicklung in Kosovo', *Südosteuropa* 38 (6), 1990, p. 334.
13 N. Popov, 'Le populisme serbe (suite)', *Les Temps Modernes* 43 (547), 1994, p. 41.
14 N. Vladisavljević, *Serbia's Antibureaucratic Revolution: Milošević, the Fall of Communism, and Nationalist Mobilisation* (London: Palgrave, 2008). See also his contribution to this volume.
15 *Vreme*, 4 July 1994.
16 *Vreme*, 10 February 1992.
17 Quoted from D. Selbourne, *Death of the Dark Hero: Eastern Europe 1987–1990* (London: Cape, 1991), p. 109.
18 *Frankfurter Rundschau*, 12 August 1988.
19 B. Magaš, *The Destruction of Yugoslavia: Tracking the Break-Up, 1980–92* (London and New York: Verso, 1993), pp. 170–71.
20 Ironically, a similar symbolic eclecticism could be found during the funeral of Slobodan Milošević in March 2006, minus the American flag.
21 Čolović, op. cit., p. 14.
22 S. Naumović, 'Instrumentalised Tradition: Traditionalist Rhetoric, Nationalism and Political Transition in Serbia, 1987–90', in M. Jovanović, K. Kaser, and S. Naumović (eds), *Between the Archives and the Field: A Dialogue on Historical Anthropology of the Balkans* (Belgrade and Graz: Udruženje za društvenu istoriju and University of Graz, 1999), p. 200.
23 *Frankfurter Rundschau*, 1 August 1988.
24 Djukić, op. cit., pp. 104–5.
25 Naumović, op. cit., pp. 201–2.
26 As Rogers Brubaker has argued, the creation of groups, in this case ethnic groups, is an 'event' rather than a given and constant reality. R. Brubaker, *Ethnicity without Groups* (Cambridge, MA: Harvard University Press, 2004), p. 12.
27 S. Antonić, 'Vlada Slobodana Miloševića: Pokušaj tipološkog određenja', *Srpska politička misao*, 1, 1995, pp. 96–97.
28 M. Milošević, *Die Parteienlandschaft Serbiens* (Berlin: Berlin Verlag Arno Spitz, 2000); M. Djurković, *Diktatura, nacija, globalizacija* (Belgrade: Institut za evropske studije, 2002), pp. 55–56.
29 Vujačić, op. cit., p. 430.
30 Relations between the Serb Democratic Party in Bosnia and Croatia and the opposition in Serbia varied over time, while Vojislav Koštunica maintained good relations throughout, Vuk Drašković held close contacts which weakened as his party moved away from endorsing the war in Bosnia and Herzegovina. On the other hand Zoran Djindjić only formed closer links with the Bosnian Serb leadership after their increasing tensions with Milošević in 1994/5.
31 B. Šušak, 'Die Alternative zum Krieg', in T. Bremer, N. Popov and H-G. Stobbe (eds), *Serbiens Weg in den Krieg* (Berlin: Berlin Verlag, 1998), pp. 414 15.
32 D. Popadić, 'Stranačka opredeljenja studenata', in B. Kuzmanović (ed.), *Studentski protest 1992* (Belgrade: Plato, 1993), p. 123.
33 B. Kuzmanović, 'Stavovi i mišljenja učesnika studentskog protesta '92 o nekim društvenim i političkim pitanjima', in ibid., pp. 104–10.
34 This is discussed in detail in regard to the 1990–92 elections in Z. Dj. Slavujević, 'Borba za vlast u Srbiji kroz prizmu izbornih kampanja', in V. Goati, Z. Dj. Slavujević and O. Pribićević, *Izborne borbe u Jugoslaviji (1990–1992)* (Belgrade: Radnička štampa, Institut društvenih nauka), 1993, pp. 81–85.
35 M. Bogdanović, Lj. Milovanović and M. Shrestha, 'Chronology of Protest', in M. Lazić (ed.), *Protest in Belgrade* (Budapest: CEU Press, 1999), pp. 211–30.
36 See the reflection on the protests by participants in Č. Antić (ed.), *Decenija. 1996–2006* (Belgrade: Evoluta, 2006).
37 B. Kuzmanović, 'Value Orientations and Political Attitudes of Participants in the 1996–97 Student Protest', in M. Lazić (ed.), op. cit., p. 143.
38 D. Radosavljević (ed.), *Šetnja u mestu. Gradjanski protest u Srbiji* (Belgrade: B92, 1997); E. Petronijević, 'Streets of Protest: Space, Action, and Actors of Protest 96/97 in Belgrade',

in D. Dornisch, P. Elvin and R. Kania (eds), *Post–Communist Transformations. A New Generation of Perspectives* (Warsaw: Ifis Publishers, 1998), pp. 95–117.
39 The protests were often referred to as 'walks'. Quoted from I. Čolović, *Politika simbola. Ogledi o političkoj antropologiji* (Belgrade: Samizdat B92, 1997), p. 286.
40 I. Čolović, '"Serbien ist Erwacht. Macht Kaffee!" Zur Symbolik der Proteste in Serbien', *Transit*, 13, 1997, p. 120.
41 M. Vasović, 'Belgrade Students Lead Resistance to Bad Government', *IWPR Balkan Crisis Report*, 28 September 1999.
42 S. Homen, Interview with author, Belgrade, 21 July 2000; M. Jovanović, Interview with author, Belgrade, 25 July 2000.
43 *Otpor, Declaration on the future of Serbia*, 25 August 1999. Mime-Version: 1.0.
44 M. Jovanović, Interview with author, Belgrade, 25 July 2000.
45 V. Marković, '"Druga Srbija" u diskrepanciji', *Diskrepancija*, 2 (3), 2001, pp. 21–22.
46 *Vreme*, 29 July 2000.
47 M. Jovanović, Interview with author, Belgrade, 25 July 2000.
48 M. Brudar, *Nada, obmana, slom. Politički život Srba na Kosovu i Metohiji (1987–1999)* (Belgrade: Nova srpska politička misao, 2003), p. 129.
49 *Vreme*, 30 December 1996; *Naša borba*, 7 January 1997.
50 I. Spasić and Dj. Pavićević, 'Simbolization and Collective Identity in Civic Protest', *Sociologija* 39 (1) 1997, p. 88.
51 *Frankfurter Allgemeine Zeitung*, 20 April 1999. Some prominent intellectuals in Serbia criticized both the government policy in Kosovo, as well as NATO bombardment, but their ability to impact public debates during the war was severely limited. See the petition 'Let civility prevail', 16 April 1999, available at: http://www.civilsocietyinternational.org/ ece/yugoslav/kosovo/civility.htm.
52 S. Jansen, 'Discursive Practices of Resistance: Two Waves of Protest in Serbia', *Intergraph* 1 (2), 2000, http://www.intergraphjournal.com/enhanced/vol1issue2/resistance/stef1.htm.
53 Z. Golubović, 'Belgrade in the Beginning of 2000', *Intergraph* 1 (2) 2000, http://www. intergraphjournal.com/enhanced/vol1issue2/belgrade/golubovic/golubovicarticle.htm.
54 J. L. Snyder, *From Voting to Violence: Democratization and Nationalist Conflict* (New York: Norton, 2000), pp. 54–56.
55 M. R. Beissinger, 'A New Look at Ethnicity and Democratization', *Journal of Democracy*, vol. 19, no. 3, 2008, p. 95.
56 V. P. Gagnon, Jr, *The Myth of Ethnic War: Serbia and Croatia in the 1990s* (Ithaca: Cornell University Press, 2004); E. Gordy, *The Culture of Power in Serbia: Nationalism and the Destruction of Alternatives* (University Park, PA: Pennsylvania State University Press, 1999).
57 I. Torov, 'The Resistance in Serbia', in J. Udovički and J. Ridgeway (eds), *Burn this House: The Making and Unmaking of Yugoslavia* (Durham, NC and London: Duke University Press, 1997), pp. 257–62.
58 F. Bieber, 'Serbia in the 1990s: The Case of an Ethnic Semi-Democracy', in S. Smooha and P. Järve (eds), *The Fate of Ethnic Democracy in Post-Communist Europe* (Budapest: LGI Press, 2004), pp. 167–90.
59 Another key factor had been the ability of civil society to mobilize citizens and challenge the regime effectively. See F. Bieber, 'The Serbian Opposition and Civil Society: Roots of the Delayed Transition in Serbia', *International Journal of Politics, Culture, and Society*, vol. 17, no. 1, 2003, pp. 73–90.
60 For example polls of the National Democratic Institute, a US government funded organization promoting democratization active in Serbia, before the elections in 2000 indicate that citizens identify poverty and social problems as the biggest concern. Similar priorities are indicated through a number of questions, including expectations of the candidates. For example, only 2 per cent noted Kosovo as priority for the new government. NDI, 'Serbia Tracking Poll, Fourth Wave', 20 September 2000.
61 DSS Press Service, 20 September 2000.

10 The 'Final' Yugoslav Issue

The evolution of international thinking on Kosovo, 1998–2005

James Ker-Lindsay

When Kosovo declared independence, in February 2008, it was quickly recognized by the United States and by most of the European Union.[1] However, just ten years earlier, these states had taken a very different view on the question of statehood for the province. In 1998, when the conflict first came to international attention, the prevailing opinion of the international community was that Kosovo did not merit independence alongside the republics of former Yugoslavia. Indeed, in the media it was often referred to as a 'separatist conflict'.[2] To this extent, efforts to resolve the situation were centred on providing the province with some form of meaningful self-government. Indeed, even after the NATO intervention, in 1999, which brought to an end Belgrade's direct rule over Kosovo, and instituted UN administration, some form of autonomy remained the preferred outcome for Kosovo. And yet, by late-2005, when the decision was taken to start status talks, it was clear that a change of opinion had already taken place. Instead of self-government, the mainstream view appeared to be that independence was the only viable option for the province.

This chapter examines how and why this transformation occurred. It traces the development of the Kosovo issue up until the start of status talks, showing that the move from autonomy to independence was a direct result of growing instability caused by the lack of a formal and finalised status, and the realization that any attempt to push for the retention of Serb sovereignty over the province would lead to further fighting. In other words, the argument that Kosovo required independence was not based on any change in attitudes towards the resolution of ethnic conflict, a wider acceptance of the principle of self-determination,[3] or a change in the underlying principles of international law.[4] Instead, and as will be shown, the decision to support independence in the case of Kosovo was based on the need to formulate an exit strategy in response to growing instability on the ground.

The origins of the conflict

While Serbs and Kosovo Albanians will often point to ancient claims to the territory, the modern roots of the conflict can be traced back to the First

Balkan War, in 1912.[5] Following the defeat of the Ottoman forces, and despite opposition from its largely Albanian inhabitants, Kosovo was divided between the Kingdoms of Serbia and Montenegro. Thereafter, in 1918, Kosovo became part of the new Kingdom of Serbs, Croats and Slovenes – renamed Yugoslavia in 1929. The creation of the Federal People's Republic of Yugoslavia at the end of the Second World War saw the area reincorporated into Serbia, this time as an autonomous region called Kosovo and Metohija (Kosmet for short), a process that also saw the demarcation of Kosovo's present-day boundaries.

While this marked an explicit recognition of its special status, the decision did not go far enough for Kosovo's Albanians. Over the coming years they gradually began to demand that they be recognized as a nation within Yugoslavia, and for Kosovo to become the seventh Yugoslav republic – alongside Bosnia and Herzegovina, Croatia, Macedonia, Montenegro, Serbia and Slovenia. Such a move, which would have separated them from Serbia, but not from Yugoslavia, was not accepted by Marshal Tito, the Yugoslav leader, and the Socialist government. According to the official Yugoslav ideology, only the South Slavs could qualify for their own republic, and be recognized as a nation within Yugoslavia. This status could not be awarded to peoples within Yugoslavia considered to have an external homeland or belonging to transnational stateless groups, such as the Ruthenians, Jews and Roma. In the case of Kosovo, the existence of an independent Albania precluded recognition as a nation. Instead, the Kosovo Albanians were recognized as a 'nationality' alongside, amongst others, Hungarians, Slovaks and Italians.[6]

Although this subordinate status was effectively reconfirmed in 1963, in the latter half of the 1960s the Kosovo Albanians began to gain an increased standing in the federation, experiencing, 'an overall national, political, economical and cultural revival and development.'[7] This was most clearly symbolized by the founding of Pristina University, which lectured in both Albanian and Serbo-Croat. However, rather than dampen national sentiments, this in fact led to demonstrations, in 1968, calling for Kosovo to be recognized as a republic. While this did not occur, in 1974 Kosovo was upgraded from an autonomous region to an autonomous province of Serbia; thereby gaining equality with Vojvodina, in the north of Serbia, which had been awarded this status in 1946.[8] It now came to enjoy almost all the rights and privileges granted to a republic, including its own constitution, assembly and seat on the federal council. Crucially, though, it was still denied the right of secession – a privilege theoretically enjoyed by republics.[9] Thus pressure for the province to be upgraded to a republic continued to grow. In 1981, a series of student riots highlighted the strength of feeling over the issue. Meanwhile, as many Serbs started leaving the province amidst growing anti-Serbian prejudice, the question of Kosovo also became increasingly politicized in Serbia. In 1985, a number of Serbian intellectuals prepared a memorandum in which, amongst other things, they argued that the Serbs of Kosovo were facing 'genocide' at the hands of the Albanian majority and called on Serbia to reassert its authority over the province. This 'threat' to the Kosovo Serbs provided an ideal issue for Slobodan Milošević, a rising official within the ruling Communist Party, to enhance his political career. In 1989, having assumed the Serbian Presidency, he effectively removed the province's autonomy, instituting direct rule from Belgrade.

The collapse of Yugoslavia transformed the debate in Kosovo. Following the examples set by Slovenia and Croatia, the Kosovo Albanians now focused their campaign on formal statehood, holding a referendum on independence and electing Ibrahim Rugova, a firm adherent of non-violent resistance to Serb rule, as their unofficial president, in May 1992. Meanwhile, fearful that the bloody war in Bosnia could proliferate to Kosovo, the United States warned Milošević that any attempt by Belgrade to react with force to developments in the province would meet with air strikes – a threat that was subsequently repeated the following year by the new Clinton administration.[10] At the same time, however, the Kosovo Albanian claim for independence went unrecognized by the international community. In 1992, the Badinter Arbitration Commission, a body set up by the European Union to consider the legal issues arising from the dissolution of Yugoslavia, concluded that the six formal republics of Yugoslavia were states emerging from the collapse of the federation, and thus could be recognized.[11] Crucially, though, Kosovo was not mentioned. Therefore, despite its former standing as a unit within federal Yugoslavia, and the fact that it had enjoyed almost all the rights of a republic, Kosovo was nevertheless denied international recognition.

Although there was little desire within the international community to recognize Kosovo as an independent state, the start of peace talks in Dayton aimed at ending the civil war in Bosnia was seen by many in Kosovo as an opportunity for their own claims to be addressed. But it was not to be. Although some in the US Administration wished to raise the issue, the need to keep Milošević – who insisted that Kosovo was an internal matter for Serbia – engaged in the overall process meant that it was kept off the agenda.[12]

The Kosovo conflict, 1998–99

The decision severely undermined Rugova's credibility. After following a policy of passive resistance, many now felt that the only way to secure independence was to fight for it. In February 1996, the Kosovo Liberation Army (KLA) launched its first attack against a Serbian police patrol. Over the next couple of years the movement gradually intensified its operations and by early 1998 the KLA had become increasingly bold in its attacks and now appeared to be in control of parts of the province. Importantly, though, the weight of opinion appeared to be on Serbia's side. Speaking in Pristina, Robert Gelbard, the US special envoy for the Balkans, famously described the KLA as a terrorist organization.[13] In response to this apparent 'green light', Serbian security forces launched several operations against presumed KLA strongholds, which resulted in significant civilian casualties.[14] This marked a turning point in the conflict. Meeting at the start of March, the Contact Group – a political body made up of Britain, France, Germany, Italy, Russia and the United States – demanded that formal negotiations now begin between Belgrade and the Kosovo Albanian leadership. Soon afterwards, the UN Security Council passed Resolution 1160. Condemning Serbia's 'excessive force' against civilians and the 'acts of terrorism' by the KLA, the resolution made it clear that the talks should be based on autonomy and meaningful self administration.[15]

Responding to this, Washington initiated a peace process between the two sides. At the same time, Russia, fearful that NATO would intervene if the fighting did not stop, put pressure on Milošević, who promised to scale back Serb activities in the province and agreed to the establishment of the 50-strong Kosovo Diplomatic Observer Mission.[16] But the lull in fighting did not last long. In August, following a further series of KLA attacks, Serb forces launched yet another counter-offensive. By September, the violence was escalating quickly. In response, the Security Council passed another resolution. Again condemning Belgrade's 'excessive and indiscriminate' force, the resolution proposed the establishment of an observer mission to oversee a ceasefire in the province.[17] It also repeated the call for a solution based on autonomy, a position confirmed by Madeleine Albright, the US Secretary of State. As she stated at the time, 'We have made it clear to Milošević and Kosovars that we do not support independence for Kosovo, that we want Serbia out of Kosovo, not Kosovo out of Serbia.'[18]

This in turn acted as a spur for the KLA. Unhappy with the continued international support for autonomy as a model for a solution, it continued its attacks in the hope that this would provoke a heavy handed Serbian response, which in turn would force Western leaders to act decisively on behalf of the Kosovo Albanians.[19] Milošević duly obliged. Mistakenly believing that NATO would not act, or that Russia would prevent an attack, he ordered the continuation of counter-insurgency operations. However, in January 1999, Western patience finally ran out when the bodies of 45 Albanians were discovered in the hamlet of Račak. Following a meeting of the Contact Group, the various sides, including the KLA, were summoned to a peace conference at a chateau in the French town of Rambouillet, on the outskirts of Paris.[20] Emulating the coercive form of diplomacy that had brought an end to the conflict in Bosnia, the parties were told that they had two weeks to agree to the details of the peace plan developed by Hill, or else face the consequences.[21]

Despite this stern warning, the initial discussions proved fruitless. In response, therefore, international mediators unveiled a finalised set of proposals, which, amongst other things, included provision for a major conference on the future of Kosovo, to be held three years later, which would 'determine a mechanism for a final settlement for Kosovo, on the basis of the will of the people, opinions of relevant authorities, each party's efforts regarding the implementation of the Accords, and the Helsinki Final Act, and to undertake a comprehensive assessment of the implementation of this Agreement and to consider proposals by any Party for additional measures.'[22] However, while the Kosovo Albanian delegation reluctantly agreed to accept the terms of the proposal, Milošević rejected the document. Although willing to accept the main plan, especially as it reaffirmed Yugoslav sovereignty over Kosovo, he opposed the annexes to the agreement giving NATO forces access to all of Yugoslavia.[23]

Just days later, and following a final attempt to reach an agreement, NATO launched Operation Allied Force, a bombing campaign targeting a range of strategic targets in Serbia, including bridges and refineries, and Yugoslav forces operating in Kosovo. At this point, a major humanitarian crisis erupted. Responding to the NATO attack, Milošević ordered Serb forces to step up their operations against the Kosovo Albanian population. In the weeks that followed, approximately 850,000 people were either forcibly expelled or fled the province, taking refuge in neighbouring Albania and Macedonia.

Meanwhile, on 9 May, at a meeting in Germany, the leaders of the G8 initialled a seven point set of principles for the settlement of the Kosovo issue. Significantly, this once again proposed a solution that supported some form of autonomy, noting that the end of hostilities would lead to, 'a political process towards the establishment of an interim political framework agreement providing for a substantial self-government for Kosovo, taking full account of the Rambouillet accords and the principles of sovereignty and territorial integrity of the Federal Republic of Yugoslavia and the other countries of the region'.[24] This provided Moscow, which had thus far been sidelined altogether, with the political cover it needed to help bring the air campaign to an end. At the start of June, Victor Chernomyrdin, the envoy of the Russian Federation, accompanied Martti Ahtisaari, the president of Finland, who was representing the European Union, to Belgrade where they presented Milošević with a finalized set of principles.[25] Informed that they were non-negotiable, and with reports that Moscow was now willing to accept an imposed solution if Serbia did not comply,[26] Milošević had no choice but to accept the terms. The next day the decision was ratified by the Yugoslav parliament. Six days later, another agreement confirmed the withdrawal of all Yugoslav forces from the province and the deployment of a UN civil mission and a security force – the Kosovo Protection Force (KFOR) – under NATO control.[27]

Kosovo under international administration

On 10 June, the United Nations Security Council passed Resolution 1244 (1999). This formally brought the province under international control, authorizing the creation of the United Nations Interim Administration Mission in Kosovo (UNMIK). But even at this point, autonomy remained on the table as the preferred solution. Under paragraph 10 of the resolution, UNMIK was tasked with creating the conditions, 'under which the people of Kosovo can enjoy substantial autonomy within the Federal Republic of Yugoslavia, and which will provide transitional administration while establishing and overseeing the development of provisional democratic self-governing institutions to ensure conditions for a peaceful and normal life for all inhabitants of Kosovo'. This in turn would pave the way, according to paragraph 11, for 'a final settlement'.

While the exact nature of the 'final settlement', and the timeline for reaching an agreement, were not stated, even at this stage, there were those who believed that a decision should have been taken to grant Kosovo independence at this point.[28] However, even after the bombing campaign, and the large scale revenge attacks waged by Kosovo Albanians against the Serbian inhabitants of the province in the aftermath of the establishment of the UN administration, international officials still saw the possibility of reaching a deal based on some form of autonomy once the situation in the province had settled down.[29] However, as far as the Kosovo Albanians were concerned, there was no going back on their demands for statehood. Having managed to secure NATO intervention to support their armed campaign against Serbia, they accepted that a limited period of time as an international protectorate was little more than a necessary prelude to independence. As one leading political figure stated, the Kosovo Albanian leadership 'understood that Serbia cannot just get out, and the process of independence for Kosovo cannot be initiated without the presence of NATO, the EU, and the OSCE. A Western protectorate, and later independence through a referendum, is the national strategy of the Albanians of Kosova.'[30]

Although some within the US State Department may also have believed, or hoped, that statehood was 'clearly on the way',[31] events now appeared to swing the other way. In October 2000, Milošević was forced from power by an alliance of democratic opposition parties.[32] At the same time, UNMIK officials stressed that the unveiling of a Constitutional Framework, in May 2001, which established the Provisional Institutions of Self-Government (PISG),[33] did not cede control over areas that might in any way be seen to take away the sovereign rights of Belgrade.[34] As Hans Haekkerup, the Special Representative of the UN Secretary General (SRSG) and head of UNMIK, explained, Kosovo officially remained an integral part of the Federal Republic of Yugoslavia, as set down in Resolution 1244.[35] This view appeared to be further confirmed when Haekkerup signed an agreement with Nebojša Čović, the moderate deputy prime minister of Serbia, which not only established a more formal process of consultation between UNMIK, the PISG and Belgrade, but also confirmed that UNMIK would not take any steps towards resolving Kosovo's final status.[36] Not unexpectedly, the Kosovo Albanian leadership were 'outraged' by the document.[37]

The impression that Kosovo's path towards statehood was now on the backburner only grew after 11 September 2001. As US attention became focused on the Middle East, in Europe there was a marked reluctance to deal with the status question as this could destabilize Serbia's democratic transformation. Independence was simply not on the agenda.[38] This message was reinforced in May 2002, when the Kosovo Assembly passed a resolution annulling a controversial border agreement that had been between Yugoslavia and Macedonia – despite calls from the EU and UN not to do so. Although the new SRSG, Michael Steiner, had been a strong advocate of NATO intervention in 1999, and was known to favour 'conditional independence',[39] he could not let such an obvious challenge to Resolution 1244 stand. He therefore annulled the resolution and banned Kosovo Albanian officials from attending a number of international meetings.[40]

The incident not only created a serious rift between the UN and the Kosovo Albanians,[41] it also signalled the degree to which, after three years of international administration, pressure for a status decision was now increasing sharply. In an attempt to lessen the growing tensions, the new SRSG, Michael Steiner, unveiled what would become known as the 'Standards before Status' policy.[42] Under this scheme progress would need to be made in eight key areas – such as the establishment of democratic institutions and the enforcement of the rule of law – before the province could conceivably start to think about its final status.[43] Although the policy was applauded internationally, it did little to ease the calls for a status decision from the Kosovo Albanian leadership. Indeed, in Pristina, there was talk of holding a referendum as a prelude to a unilateral declaration of independence.[44] With concern growing about the implications of an indefinite delay, in November 2003, the Contact Group announced that a review of the standards would take place in mid-2005. If 'sufficient' progress had been made, a process to determine the final status of Kosovo could then begin.[45] The announcement was welcomed by the Security Council.[46]

The move towards status talks, and independence

Despite this important move, less than six months later Kosovo suffered its worst outbreak of fighting since 1999. On 16 March 2004, three Albanian boys drowned in the Ibar. Although there was no evidence to support the story, within hours the media, including RTK, the national broadcaster, were reporting that they had been chased into the river by dogs belonging to Kosovo Serbs. It could not have come at a worse time. That same day a series of demonstrations were taking place to protest about the indictment of a number of KLA leaders for suspected war crimes committed in 1999. Thus the anger directed towards the UN was magnified and directed towards the Serbs as well. Despite the best efforts of KFOR to contain the violence, it rapidly spread across the province. This was aided in part by the ambivalence of local leaders. Rugova, who had forged his reputation on passive resistance, refused to condemn the violence.[47]

The impact of the riots was enormous. By the time the fighting was contained, on 19 March, it was estimated that almost 51,000 people had taken part in at least 33 separate incidents across the province. As a result, 19 people had been killed, 8 Serbs and 11 Albanians, and over 1,000 injured. Over 550 homes had been burned, along with 27 monasteries and churches.

This had left approximately 4,100 people displaced. This number included not just Kosovo Serbs, but also members of the other minorities, including the Roma.[48] Naturally, the riots had an immensely negative effect on inter-communal relations. Whatever trust that may have been developing between Serbs and Albanians was severely undermined. The incidents also led to a breakdown in contacts between Belgrade and Pristina. In the aftermath of the violence, the technical talks between the Kosovo PISG and the Serbian Government stopped.

However, the riots also marked a catastrophic blow to the standing of UNMIK and KFOR. For a start, after five years of work, they highlighted just how little headway had been made towards ethnic reconciliation between Serbs and Albanians. It also had a profound impact on the relationship the two bodies had with both communities. The Kosovo Serbs, and the other minorities, had lost whatever trust they had in the UN to protect them.[49] Meanwhile, reports of peacekeepers failing to prevent attacks, or fleeing in the face of violence, coupled with reports that the Kosovo Police Service had participated in incidents, had fatally undermined the authority of the UN in the eyes of the Kosovo Albanians. As a report by Human Rights Watch noted several months later, 'The international community has lost tremendous ground in Kosovo as a result of the March violence: ethnic Albanian extremists now know that they can effectively challenge the international security structures, having demolished the notion of KFOR and UNMIK invincibility.'[50] Matters were not helped by the fact that many of those involved in the attacks were never brought to justice or were given unduly light sentences.[51]

The realization that the international community in Kosovo was unable to stop the fighting transformed the whole debate over status. It was now understood that the question of Kosovo's future could not be put off indefinitely. A decision would be needed sooner rather than later. It also made it all but certain that statehood would be the final outcome. As two senior officials from UNMIK later observed, 'Violence had once again advanced the independence agenda as nothing else in the previous five years had.'[52]

This was seemingly proven just months later when Kai Eide, a senior Norwegian diplomat, delivered a political assessment of the situation in Kosovo to the UN Secretary-General.[53] Noting the growing levels of frustration and dissatisfaction, in part caused by a 60–70 per cent unemployment rate, Eide emphasized that it was now necessary to take a longer perspective on Kosovo's future status. To this end, and despite the fact that the UN had unveiled a compressive 117-page Standards Implementation Plan just two weeks after the riots,[54] the standards before status policy needed to be replaced by a 'priority based standards policy'. Rather than insist on improvements across the board as a pre-requisite for status talks, an 'unrealistic and unachievable goal', attention should instead be focused on Kosovo's most urgent needs, including those areas relating to a future status process. Likewise, he concluded that UNMIK was no longer the appropriate body to run Kosovo's affairs. Instead, and assuming that any eventual status decision would see

Pristina run its own affairs, it was now time for the European Union to take greater responsibility in the province.[55] As two former UNMIK officials later explained, the riots had 'produced a paradigm shift that some might describe as accepting reality and others as giving up.'[56]

By now any thoughts of autonomy appeared to have disappeared altogether. It was quite clear that the Kosovo Albanians would not accept anything short of full statehood. This was seen by their reaction to Belgrade's proposals for extensive self rule, presented in mid-2004, which was based on the principle of 'more than autonomy, but less than independence'.[57] As one leader explained, Kosovo had been given autonomy under the 1974 Yugoslav Constitution, but this had later been rescinded. It would not happen again. 'Independence is the only solution for Kosovo'.[58] More to the point, the proposals received short shrift from the international community. Although there had been no more serious incidents of violence since the riots the previous year, the threat of further attacks was ever present. More worryingly, there was an increasing fear that in the future the violence might now be directed towards UNMIK and KFOR. Whereas once the Serbs had been viewed as the occupying power, many Kosovo Albanians, such as 'Self-Determination' (*Vetëvendosje*), a pro-independence protest movement, were now starting to view the international presence as a form of colonial occupation. Indeed, by the summer of 2004 the widespread view in Kosovo was that the international administration was no longer opening the way to independence, but was now an obstacle to that goal.[59] This was graphically highlighted in March 2005 when Ramush Haradinaj was forced to step down as prime minister following his indictment on war crimes charges by the ICTY,[60] which in turn led to several bomb attacks on UNMIK property. Meanwhile, patience was running out in Washington. With pressing concerns elsewhere, such as Iraq and Afghanistan, the United States, which had long been keen to drawdown its presence in the Balkans and hand over to the European Union, was now growing increasingly impatient with the situation.[61] The problem, however, was that while the European Union was willing to take a greater role in Kosovo,[62] without a clear status any EU presence ran the risk of being seen as little more than a replacement for UNMIK, with all the dangers that this would entail. Given that autonomy was out of the question, independence now became the only way out.

It therefore came as little surprise when, on 23 May, Annan announced in his latest report on Kosovo that he had decided to appoint a special envoy to conduct a full review of the progress made towards the implementation of the standards.[63] After receiving the endorsement to the Security Council for the review, Annan again turned to Eide to carry out the task. Although Annan was quick to point out that the outcome of the review was not a foregone conclusion, few believed this. The prospect of violence if a negative report was produced meant that most observers believed that the start of formal status talks was now almost certain.[64] And so it was the case. On 4 October, Eide presented his review to the Secretary-General. Even though progress towards the implementation of standards had been 'uneven', he nevertheless recommended the start of status talks, and noted that the time had come for the EU, in particular, to take a lead role in Kosovo.[65] Annan immediately welcomed the report's findings. Sending the report to the President of the Security Council, he fully endorsed the call for status talks.[66] However, despite the fact that Belgrade was surprised and disappointed by the recommendations,[67] London and Washington were adamant that the prevailing situation was no longer sustainable. It was time to decide Kosovo's final status.[68]

By now, few were in any doubt that this meant statehood. As Janez Drnovšek, the Slovenian president, noted, it was not just the entire international community that knew that Kosovo would become independent, Serbia's politicians did too.[69] Speaking in Pristina a few weeks before the UN sponsored talks began, John Sawers, the political director of the British Foreign and Commonwealth Office, openly stated that independence was the likely outcome of the process,[70] a view repeated soon afterwards by Jack Straw, the British Foreign Secretary, who stated that independence was 'almost inevitable'.[71] Indeed, even Russia was felt – incorrectly, as it turned out – to have come to the conclusion that independence was now the only option. For example, the demands put in place by the Contact Group – including Russia – that any solution must be acceptable to the people of Kosovo, was seen to be a coded reference to statehood. Indeed, the UN team appointed to manage the status talks, which was led by Martti Ahtisaari, understood this to mean that independence was now regarded as the only viable option. To this end, the status process was not about discussing status options, such as autonomy. Instead, it was about creating the structures for a Kosovo state.[72]

Conclusion

Although statehood eventually came to be seen as the only viable outcome for Kosovo, it represented a marked shift in thinking from the original view taken of the conflict. Until 1999, and despite the events in Yugoslavia, Kosovo was seen by the international community as little different from the wide range of ethnic and separatist conflicts elsewhere in the world. The Badinter Arbitration Committee – a commission formed in 1991 by the European Union under the chairmanship of Robert Badinter, the president of the French Constitutional Court, to consider the legal implications of the break up of Yugoslavia – clearly stated that while the right of secession was open to the republics, it was not applicable to minority communities within the republics. In the case of Kosovo, the report made no recommendation for recognition alongside the republics.[73] Thus, by default, the position of the Kosovo Albanians was regarded as analogous to the Serbs of Croatia and Bosnia, and by extension to other minority communities throughout the republics. In these cases, the Committee ruled that right of self-determination was not conceived as a right to statehood, 'instead, self-determination in this context was reduced in content to human and minority rights, and to autonomous structures of governance in areas where Serb constituted a local majority.'[74] As a result of these decisions, when Kosovo came to prominence at the end of the 1990s, the UN Security Council therefore resolved that any settlement must recognize Yugoslavia's territorial integrity, in accordance with the UN Charter and the Helsinki Final Act, and should therefore be focused on some form of 'enhanced status', 'which would include a substantially greater degree of autonomy and meaningful self-administration.'[75]

Significantly, even after the NATO intervention, and despite calls for a quick resolution of the status question, it appeared as though some form of self-rule remained the optimum and most desired outcome in the minds of most international officials. While many US officials were quite clearly ardent supporters of independence even before the intervention, they did not represent mainstream international thinking. Instead, the hope was that once the initial trauma of the events of that year had subsided there might be a possibility for some form of reconciliation and political solution based on extensive autonomy. As one official pointed out, as the efforts to keep Serbia and Montenegro united showed, there was simply no wish to create further states in the Balkans.[76] However, it gradually became clear that the decision to intervene in Kosovo, and subsequently establish an international administration, necessarily changed the parameters of a settlement – in reality, if not in principle. As far as the Kosovo Albanians were concerned, the NATO intervention had taken place for their benefit and represented a further step towards independence. While they were willing to accept a limited period of international rule, there was no question that this would be a transitory phase leading to statehood sooner rather than later. Moreover, any suggestions of autonomy were completely rejected by the Kosovo Albanian leadership. In view of this, and given rising frustrations in the province, and the danger that this could lead to violence directed towards international administrators and peacekeepers, it was seen as imperative to resolve the status issue, and do so in a manner acceptable to the majority of Kosovo's inhabitants.[77] Thus, despite the recognition of Serbia's sovereignty over Kosovo recognized under Resolution 1244, and the previous efforts to find a solution based on self-rule, there appeared to be little choice but to shift support towards independence. In other words, those countries that had originally supported humanitarian intervention – perhaps without fully realizing at the time the complexity, and general brutality, of the conflict they were facing in Kosovo[78] – had no choice but to support independence in order to extricate themselves from the situation before they too became seen as some form of neo-colonial occupier.

In this sense, the decision to support statehood was not about recognizing the unique case created by the break up of Yugoslavia or the fighting of 1998–99, as was later claimed. Had that been the case, the best option would have been to pursue independence in 1995, at the time of Dayton, or in 1999, as has been widely suggested.[79] At that time, when Milošević was still in power, the political costs would have been lower, and the justification greater. Instead, the shift in favour of statehood came about in response to the unstable situation that had arisen following the decision to intervene, and the establishment of international administration, both of which were seen by Kosovo Albanians as a clear indication of Western support for their statehood. Moreover, with the realization that UNMIK had essentially failed in its task of building a functioning multi-ethnic democracy in Kosovo it now became obvious, as pointed out by Eide, that the task of managing Kosovo would fall on the European Union. However, given the political climate in Kosovo, the EU would not be able to take on this role, which would certainly require a more robust approach towards state building than that taken by UNMIK, unless the Kosovo Albanian population believed that they were independent. For all these reasons, and despite the earlier decision to support autonomy, as status talks began independence had come to be widely regarded as the only viable option for Kosovo – or so it seemed.

Notes

1 By the start of June 2008, just 42 of the 192 members of the United Nations had recognized Kosovo. In addition to the US and most of the EU, Kosovo was also recognized by other leading economic democracies, including Japan, Canada and South Korea. Please note that this chapter originally appeared in the *Journal of Balkan and Near Eastern Studies*, vol. 11, no. 2, June 2009. It is reprinted here with kind permission.

2 Throughout this period, the conflict was often referred to as a separatist conflict in the international media. For example, 'Kosovo peace efforts continue', *BBC News*, 10 May 1998; 'EU tightens sanctions on Serbia over Kosovo', *CNN*, 8 June 1998; 'Conflict in the Balkans: The Tactics', *New York Times*, 12 June 1998; 'Conflict in the Balkans: The Separatists', *New York Times*, 29 March 1999.

3 As one British official told the author, the word 'self-determination' was being avoided at all costs. Kosovo was not a case of self-determination. It was a unique case devolving from the dissolution of Yugoslavia in the 1990s. However, speaking on the margins of a UN Security Council debate in December 2007, Sir John Sawers, the British permanent representative at the UN, stated the following: 'You have the principle of territorial integrity. You also have the principle of self-determination. There are times when those principles are in tension with one another, and the principle of territorial integrity is qualified by the principle of self-determination.' 'Media Stakeout: Informal comments to the Media by the Permanent Representative of the United Kingdom, Ambassador Sir John Sawers KCMG, on the situation in Kosovo and other matters', Webcast, *UN Website*, 19 December 2007.

4 This chapter will not examine the legality or otherwise of the decision to support independence. For a review of this issue see the debate between Alice Lacourt, a legal advisor at the Foreign and Commonwealth Office, and Dr Ralph Wilde, Reader in Law, UCL. 'Kosovo: International Law and Recognition', A Summary of the Chatham House International Law Discussion Group meeting held on 22 April 2008.

5 For a background history of Kosovo, see N. Malcolm, *Kosovo: A Short History*, 2nd ed. (London, Pan Books, 2002); M. Vickers, *Between Serb and Albanian: A History of Kosovo* (New York: Columbia University Press, 1998); and T. Judah, *Kosovo: War and Revenge* (New Haven: Yale University Press, 2002).

6 It is perhaps easier to think of these 'nationalities' as national minorities, although this term was never used in Socialist Yugoslavia.

7 R. Marmullaku, 'Albanians in Yugoslavia: A Personal Essay', in D. Djokić (ed.), *Yugoslavism: Histories of a Failed Idea, 1918–1992* (London: Hurst, 2003), p. 307. For an overview of the position of the Kosovo Albanians see, H. Poulton, 'Macedonians and Albanians as Yugoslavs', in the same volume.

8 Significantly, and as a further concession to the Kosovo Albanians, the term 'Metohija' was dropped from the official name of the province. This term, which roughly translates as 'Land of the Monasteries' in Serbian, and refers to the Western part of the province, was widely resented by Kosovo Albanians as a throwback to Medieval Serbia. Under the Constitution, Serbia continues to refer officially to the province as 'Kosovo and Metohija', often shortened to 'Kosmet'. 'Constitution of the Republic of Serbia', 30 November 2006.

9 In reality, it was rather unclear as to where the right really lay: with the republics or with the nations. The question was thus left open to interpretation.

10 R. Caplan, 'International Diplomacy and the Crisis in Kosovo', *International Affairs*, vol. 74, no. 4, 1998, p.753.

11 The opinions of the Commission can be found as appendices to Alain Pellet, 'Appendix: Opinions No. 1, 2 and 3 of the Arbitration Committee of the International Conference on Yugoslavia', *European Journal of International Law*, vol. 3, no. 1, 1992.

12 W. Clark, *Waging Modern War* (New York: Public Affairs, 2001), p. 65.

13 'The KLA – terrorists or freedom fighters?', *BBC News*, 28 June 1998.

14 'The KLA – terrorists or freedom fighters?', *BBC News*, 28 June 1998.

15 'Statement on Kosovo adopted by the members of the Contact Group, meeting in London on 9 March 1998', S/1998/223; and 'Statement on Kosovo issued by members of the Contact Group in Bonn on 25 March 1998', *UN Security Council Document*, S/1998/272. UN Security Council Resolution 1160(1998), 28 March 1998.

16 O. Levtin, 'Inside Moscow's Kosovo Muddle', *Survival*, vol. 42, no. 1, Summer 2000, p. 130. T. Youngs, 'Kosovo: The Diplomatic and Military Options', *House of Commons Research Paper 98/93*, 27 October 1998, p. 11.

17 UN Security Council Resolution 1199 (1998), 23 September 1998. The Kosovo Verification Mission (KVM) was formed under the auspices of the Organization for Security and Cooperation in Europe (OSCE). Agreement on the OSCE Kosovo Verification Missions signed in Belgrade, on 16 October 1998, by the Chairman-in-Office of the OSCE and the Foreign Minister of the Federal Republic of Yugoslavia (CIO.GAL/65/98/Corr.1).

18 'In Balkans Again, Promises, Promises', *New York Times*, 14 October 1998.

19 As one KLA leader stated, 'all solutions but independence are not acceptable to the K.L.A.', 'In Balkans Again, Promises, Promises', *New York Times*, 14 October 1998. 'The KLA brought NATO to Kosova: An Interview with Hashim Thaqi', in William Joseph Buckley (editor), *Kosovo: Contending Voices on Balkan Intervention* (Cambridge: Eerdmans, 2000), p. 287.

20 For an account of the Rambouillet talks see A.J. Bellamy, 'Lessons Unlearned: Why Coercive Diplomacy Failed at Rambouillet', *International Peacekeeping*, vol. 7, no. 2, Summer 2000, pp. 95–114; and, M. Weller, 'The Rambouillet Conference on Kosovo', *International Affairs*, vol. 75, no. 2, April 1999.

21 'Statement to the Press by NATO Secretary General, Javier Solana', 30 January 1999.

22 'Interim Agreement for Peace and Self-Government in Kosovo, February 23 1999', Chapter 8, Article 3.

23 Judah, *Kosovo*, p. 220. As noted, Milošević believed that NATO forces could be used either to detach Kosovo from Serbia, or to depose him.

24 Annexe 1, UN Security Council Resolution 1244 (1999), 10 June 1999.

25 Annexe 2, UN Security Council Resolution 1244 (1999), 10 June 1999.

26 'Moscow Set To Back UN Resolution on Kosovo', *International Herald Tribune*, 3 June 1999.

27 'Military Technical Agreement between the International Security Force (KFOR) and the Governments of Federal Republic of Yugoslavia and the Republic of Serbia', 9 June 1999.

28 Paddy Ashdown, comments made during an interview on *Sky News*, 9 December 2007. Capitalizing on Serbia's defeat, and Russia's weakness, Western decision makers would almost certainly have been in a stronger position to impose this type of settlement. Although it may not have been entirely easy to engineer given that Russia would still have been able to block a Security Council resolution recognizing the move, it would certainly

have been far easier to explain and justify than a decision to do so taken a number of years later. Indeed, by failing to act at that time, NATO created a troubling paradox neatly summed up by Sir Ivor Roberts, the former British Ambassador to Yugoslavia, 'It is hard to explain to Serbs why, when Milošević was still in power, a settlement was imposed which left Kosovo legally and formally part of Serbia. But having overthrown Milošević and lived according to the rules of the international community for the last seven years, the Serbs now face being punished by losing nearly 20 per cent of their territory.' Ivor Roberts, 'Partition is the best answer to the Kosovo question', *The Independent*, 5 December 2007. The same point was also made by Tadić at the UN Security Council meeting following the declaration of independence. 5839th Meeting of the Security Council, *UN Security Council Document*, S/PV/5839, 18 February 2008.

29 British official, comments to the author, December 2007.

30 B. Shala, 'Because Kosovars are Western, There Can be No Homeland without a State', in W.J. Buckley (editor), *Kosovo: Contending Voices on Balkan Interventions* (Cambridge: Eerdmans, 2000), p. 187.

31 'Report: U.S. officials expect Kosovo independence', *CNN*, 24 September 1999. John Bolton, who had served as the US permanent representative to the UN throughout 2006, noted on several occasions the deep rooted anti-Serbian attitudes within the State Department and argued that the United States should not recognize a unilateral declaration of independence. John Bolton, interview with Voice of America, October 2007. See also, 'SAD za nezavisno Kosovo' [USA for an Independent Kosovo], *BBC Serbian Service*, 11 May 2007.

32 Despite this, the Kosovo Albanian leaders made it clear that nothing had changed. As far as they were concerned, the new administration in Belgrade was little different from the previous regime. 'Reaction in Kosovo to Koštunica's Victory', *International Crisis Group*, 10 October 2000, p. 2.

33 Constitutional Framework for Provisional Self-Government, UNMIK/REG/2001/9, 15 May 2001.

34 Constitutional Framework for Provisional Self-Government, UNMIK/REG/2001/9, 15 May 2001. The range of competencies covered were listed as: (a) Economic and financial policy; (b) Fiscal and budgetary issues; (c) Administrative and operational customs activities; (d) Domestic and foreign trade, industry and investments; (e) Education, science and technology; (f) Youth and sport; (g) Culture; (h) Health; (i) Environmental protection; (j) Labour and social welfare; (k) Family, gender and minors; (l) Transport, post, telecommunications and information technologies; (m) Public administration services; (n) Agriculture, forestry and rural development; (o) Statistics; (p) Spatial planning; (q) Tourism; (r) Good governance, human rights and equal opportunity; and (s) Non-resident affairs.

35 'Haekkerup believes that Kosovo is still within the FRY', *UNMIK Press Summary*, 2 August 2001.

36 'UNMIK-FRY Common Document', 5 November 2001.

37 'Kosovo's unconventional new chief', *BBC News*, 14 February 2002. I. King and W. Mason, *Peace at Any Price: How the World Failed Kosovo* (London: Hurst, 2006), pp. 122–23.

38 T. Gallagher, *The Balkans in the New Millennium: In the Shadow of War and Peace* (London: Routledge, 2005), p.154. It was stated to the author by a senior British official who had worked on Kosovo that in 2002–3 there had still been no shift towards independence in British thinking. London's position, and that of the other European members of the Contact Group, was that various options were considered open. British official, comments to the author, October 2008.

39 'Kosovo's unconventional new chief', *BBC News*, 14 February 2002; King and Mason, *Peace at Any Price: How the World Failed Kosovo*, p. 175.

40 'Kosovo: Mixed Feelings at Steiner Exit', *Institute for War and Peace Reporting*, 6 June 2003.

41 'UN vetoes Kosovo border resolution', *BBC News*, 23 May 2002.

42 Congressional Research Service, 'Kosovo's Future Status Policy and U.S. Policy', *CRS Report for Congress*, January 27, 2005, p. 2.

43 The basic standards had in fact been initially presented by Steiner to the Security Council in April 2002. However at this stage, they were explicitly linked to a final status.

44 In response, Zoran Djindjić, the Serbian prime minister, who had been sounding an moderate tone on Kosovo up until this point, such as by accepting the PISG and supporting efforts to reintegrate Kosovo Serbs, suggested that if this happened the Serbian community in Bosnia could follow suit. This was followed by calls for Serbian troops to re-enter the province and for the convening of a conference to discuss Kosovo's final status by June, at the latest. Rather than a new, hard-line policy, the statements instead seem to have been directed to the domestic audience in advance of early elections. Indeed, many expected him to continue to follow a moderate line after the polls, perhaps by pursuing some form of partition – an idea that appeared to be gaining ground internationally. 'Djindjić Launches Battle for Kosovo', *Institute for War and Peace Reporting*, 10 February 2003. However, any moves in this direction were effectively halted when, on 12 March, Djindjić was assassinated. Apart from the devastating effect his death had on Serbian politics, it transformed the course of discussions over the future of Kosovo. Neither of his successors as prime minister, Zoran Živković and Vojislav Koštunica, could, or would, take such a moderate view on the future of the province – although Živković later advocated the partition of Kosovo as the 'least worse' solution. 'Partition is fate of Kosovo', *Reuters*, 7 November 2004.

45 'State's Grossman, UN's Holkeri Discuss Kosovo Strategy', *USINFO*, 7 November 2003.

46 'Security Council Presidential Statement, Expresses Support for "Standards for Kosovo", Welcome Launch of Review Mechanism', Press Release, *UN Security Council Document*, SC/7951, 12 December 2003. The exact requirements were set out in, 'Standards for Kosovo', *UNMIK*, 10 December 2003.

47 A full account of the events can be found in, 'Failure to Protect: Anti-Minority Violence in Kosovo, March 2004', *Human Rights Watch*, vol. 16, no. 6(D), July 2004.

48 'Failure to Protect: Anti-Minority Violence in Kosovo, March 2004', *Human Rights Watch*, vol. 16, no. 6(D), July 2004, p. 7.

49 'Failure to Protect: Anti-Minority Violence in Kosovo, March 2004', Human Rights Watch, vol. 16, no. 6(D), July 2004, p. 3; Report of the Secretary-General on the United Nations Interim Administration Mission in Kosovo, *UN Security Council Document*, S/2005/335, 23 May 2006, paragraph 10. Out of the 4100 that had been forced to flee from their homes, a year later over 1600 had yet to return to their rebuilt houses, an operation conducted by the UN. This was on top of the tens of thousands that the UN noted had already been displaced since 1999.

50 'Failure to Protect: Anti-Minority Violence in Kosovo, March 2004', *Human Rights Watch*, vol. 16, no. 6(D), July 2004, p. 3.

51 'The Response of the Justice System to the March 2004 Riots', Report, *Organisation for Security and Cooperation in Europe*, December 2005, p. 4.

52 King and Mason, *Peace at Any Price*, p. 191.

53 'The Situation in Kosovo: Report to the Secretary-General of the United Nations', Brussels, 15 July 2004.

54 Kosovo Standards Implementation Plan, *UNMIK*, 31 March 2004.

55 Kai Eide, 'Kosovo: the way forward', *NATO Review*, Winter 2004.

56 King and Mason, *Peace at Any Price*, p. 189.

57 'Plan for the political solution to the situation in Kosovo and Metohija', Government of Serbia, 2004. In essence, it proposed that the ethnic Albanians, who were openly recognized as the majority in the province, be granted an extremely high level of self rule and called for the Kosovo Serbs and the province's other communities to be granted a high degree of self-governance – in other words, as the document explained, they should be given a degree of, 'autonomy within autonomy'.

58 'Kosovo: Independence or the Broadest Autonomy?', *RFE/RL Reports*, vol. 7, no. 12, May 2005.

59 'Even in Eager Kosovo, Nation-Building Stalls', *Christian Science Monitor*, 22 September 2004. 'Kosovo Loses Patience with UN as Economy Flags', *New Scotsman*, March 29, 2005.

60 'Haradinaj et al.: Initial Indictment', *International Criminal Tribunal for the Former Yugoslavia*, Case No. IT-04-84-I, 24 February 2005.

61 This was suggested by Donald Rumsfeld, the US Defense Secretary, in a news conference in June 2006. 'Secretary Rumsfeld News Conference at the Meeting of NATO Defense Ministers, Brussels, Belgium'. U.S. Department of Defense, Office of the Assistant Secretary of Defense (Public Affairs), News Transcript, 9 June 2005. This was not a new position. As early as 2001, Donald Rumsfeld had wanted to withdraw US forces from peacekeeping in the Balkans. 'Rumsfeld seeks exit from Bosnia', *The Guardian*, 19 May 2001.

62 'A European Future for Kosovo', Com (2005) 156, *European Commission*, Brussels, 20 April 2005.

63 Report of the Secretary-General on the United Nations Interim Administration Mission in Kosovo, *UN Security Council Document*, S/2005/335, 23 May 2005.

64 Congressional Research Service, 'Kosovo's Future Status Policy and U.S. Policy', *CRS Report for Congress*, January 27, 2005, p. 4.

65 The full text of the report can be found as an annexe to a letter sent by the UN Secretary General to the Security Council President. 'Letter dated 7 October 2005 from the Secretary-General addressed to the President of the Security Council', *UN Security Council Document*, S/2005/635, 7 October 2006.

66 'Letter dated 7 October 2005 from the Secretary-General addressed to the President of the Security Council', *UN Security Council Document*, S/2005/635, 7 October 2005. The UN Secretary-General was careful not to prejudge the outcome of the process, simply noting that, 'the question of autonomy and independence has been raised, and we have to talk to Belgrade and Pristina'. 'Kosovo set for "breakaway" talks', *BBC News*, 7 October 2006.

67 'Kosovo set for "breakaway" talks', *BBC News*, 7 October 2006.

68 'Kosovo set for "breakaway" talks', *BBC News*, 7 October 2006. 'Launch of Process to Decide Kosovo's Final Status: Statement by RT Hon Douglas Alexander MP', *Foreign and Commonwealth Office*, London, 8 October 2005.

69 'International community knows "Kosovo will become independent" – Slovene leader', *STA News Agency*, 27 October 2005.

70 'Kosovo can win independence, says British diplomat', *Reuters*, 6 February 2006. This said, a few days later, Sawers gave an interview to B92 in which he appeared to backtrack slightly, noting that independence was an 'option'. 'Independence is an option', *B92*, 31 January 2006.

71 'New Kosovo PM wants independence', *BBC News*, 10 March 2006.

72 This has been explicitly stated by both Martti Ahtisaari and his deputy, Albert Rohan. Martti Ahtisaari, 'Kosovan Questions: National, Regional, International', Roundtable held at the School of Slavonic and East European Studies, *University College London*, 9 September 2008; Albert Rohan, 'International Conflict Resolution: The Case of Kosovo', Public Lecture, *University of Kent*, 19 October 2007. For an analysis of the Ahtisaari process see M. Weller, 'The Vienna Negotiations on the Final Status of Kosovo', *International Affairs*, vol. 84, no. 4, July 2008.

73 B.S. Brown, 'Human Rights, Sovereignty, and the Final Status of Kosovo', *Chicago-Kent Law Review*, vol. 80, 2005, p. 239.

74 Weller, 'The Rambouillet Conference on Kosovo', p.214. The full second opinion of the Committee can be found as an appendix to Pellet, 'The Opinions of the Badinter Arbitration Committee'.

75 UN Security Council Resolution 1160(1999), 31 March 1998.

76 Senior British diplomat working on the Balkans, comments at a closed discussion, September 2008.

77 As Sir John Sawers, the British representative at the UN stated, 'The international community cannot be party to a settlement that is opposed by over 90 per cent of a territory's population. Apart from anything else, it would be contrary to our overriding priority of upholding peace and security'. 'Serbia denounces Kosovo move at UN', *Financial Times*, 18 February 2008.

78 As two former UNMIK officials explained, the international community 'failed to understand that the Kosovo conflict of the late nineties ... was only the latest chapter in a long-running competition between two peoples for control of territory. The international community realised too late that its alliance with the Albanian militants was somewhat arbitrary. Both opposed Serb atrocities, but while the international community was against the atrocities, the guerrillas were against the Serbs. Most Albanians who took up arms to challenge Serbian oppression did not object to one ethnic group bullying all the others; they just wanted to be the one on top', King and Mason, *Peace at Any Price*, pp. 243–44.

79 See a range of examples, 'UN envoy on Kosovo's status says "independence is the only option"', *UN News Centre*, 26 March 2007; 'U.S. Envoy Discusses Kosovo Independence Declaration', *PBS*, 18 February 2008; 'Joint EU reaction on Kosovo's declaration of independence – Doris Pack MEP', Press Release, *EPP-ED Group in the European Parliament*, 20 February 2008; 'Harper defends Kosovo recognition as unique case', *CBC*, 19 March 2008; 'The U.S. and Russia at Odds Over Kosovo', *VOA News*, 25 February 2008; 'Joy in Kosovo, Anger in Serbia', *Time*, 17 February 2008.

11 Coming to Terms with the Past

Transitional justice and reconciliation
in the post-Yugoslav lands

Jasna Dragović-Soso and Eric Gordy

Since the establishment of the International Criminal Tribunal for the Former Yugoslavia (ICTY) in 1993, and especially since the changes of regime in Serbia and Croatia in 2000, a complex and controversial story has developed around the variety of measures that have been generated to produce accounts and promote understandings of the past, identify violations of humanitarian law and penalize their perpetrators, and satisfy international demands for accountability. These initiatives have operated in fits and starts, often in response to conditionality imposed from outside, sometimes in bad faith and frequently in half measures or through processes that remain incomplete. However, what is being asked of the former Yugoslav states is a process which, in its depth and speed, has no close parallel in history. They are expected to participate in both domestic and international criminal proceedings that use an eclectic mixture of procedures and practices and to produce gestures of penance which embody a genuine transformation in popular consciousness – all this without destroying political and legal institutions nor permitting them to remain as they were when their states were complicit in deeds that they now have to punish. Considering that these states have experienced neither a decisive military defeat nor a complete political transformation, the fact that transitional justice initiatives have occurred on a meaningful scale at all is in itself noteworthy.[1]

The states of the former Yugoslavia have functioned as laboratories of transitional justice. Here we have seen the first effort at an international tribunal, the first regional system of special prosecutors and special courts for violations of international humanitarian law; the first invocation of 'confronting the past' as a principle of conditionality; and the first efforts in the civil sector to develop cooperative approaches to reconciliation. If the founding of ICTY is taken as marking the beginning of these processes, it is now possible to evaluate 16 years of experience – to see what efforts have been sustained and which have been abandoned, to assess the contributions of ongoing processes, and to consider the obstacles that have impeded the development of some proposed initiatives, particularly national and local 'truth-seeking' projects.

Judicial processes

Judicial institutions of different types have heard cases involving violations of international and humanitarian law in the wars of the 1990s. The best known of the initiatives to try such cases has been the ICTY or the 'Hague Tribunal'.[2] ICTY was established by UN Security Resolution 827 in 1993, began its first hearings in November 1994 and issued its final original indictments in May 2004. Its completion strategy envisions that all trials be completed in 2010 and all appeals in 2011.[3]

In all Yugoslav successor states domestic prosecutors and courts have also brought and heard a number of international humanitarian law cases, while ICTY has devolved several of these cases to national courts; they will constitute the primary venue for such cases after ICTY closes. Cases before domestic courts might be evaluated in terms of the conduct and credibility of the trials, though it may also be important to consider them in terms of their role in the development of local institutional capacities, and in terms of their function in generating cooperative relationships between legal institutions across borders.

Finally, in a small number of instances former Yugoslav states have brought disputes for resolution before the International Court of Justice (ICJ) in The Hague. In each of these cases there have been (or promise to be) legal rulings that are likely to have implications for the development of international law related to the crime of genocide.

ICTY

As of mid-2009 the ICTY prosecutor has issued 161 indictments, which have resulted in 58 convictions, 20 guilty pleas, 13 referrals to domestic jurisdictions, and 10 acquittals. Charges were withdrawn in 31 cases and 44 indictees are awaiting trial. Two indictees remain at large.[4]

Some of the most closely followed cases at ICTY have also been among the most controversial. Of the top-level government leaders who have been tried, former Serbian president Milan Milutinović was acquitted on the grounds that he did not exercise command, former Kosovo prime minister Ramush Haradinaj was acquitted amid suspicions of extensive tampering, and former Serbian and Yugoslav president Slobodan Milošević died in custody before his trial was completed. High-ranking military commanders have been convicted, including Rasim Delić (Bosniak), Dragoljub Ojdanić and Nebojša Pavković (both formerly of the Yugoslav Army). Sefer Halilović (Bosniak) was acquitted, and Janko Bobetko (Croat) never faced trial. Cases such as those against Bosniak paramilitary commander Naser Orić and Croatian army general Ante Gotovina have raised questions regarding the systematic character of crimes committed against the civilian population and the threshold of evidence required to demonstrate the existence of command responsibility. And of course recurrent controversies over the delivery of indictees for trial have led to periodic reexamination of the relationship between the states of the region and the European Union.

The questions about ICTY that are asked most frequently, however, and that demand answers most urgently, are not questions of fact. They involve answers to the question of how the indictments, convictions, acquittals and other details just enumerated correspond (or fail to correspond) to the requirements of justice.

The Tribunal's official publicity[5] lists the following as 'some of the Tribunal's achievements': holding leaders accountable, bringing justice to victims, giving victims a voice, establishing the facts, developing international law, and strengthening the rule of law. These achievements are mostly real. There is indeed substantial ground for doubt that political, military and para-military leaders would ever have been brought to account without ICTY, or that victims would have had the opportunity to see their evidence considered or in some cases to confront the perpetrators in court. The evidence presented in the Tribunal's open session already constitutes an invaluable documentary record, and in the event that evidence gathered by the Tribunal but not introduced in open session becomes available, it could serve as an extraordinary resource for detailed documentation of the wartime events.

ICTY's Trial Chamber has set major precedents in many of its rulings. Beginning with the Čelebići prison camp case,[6] the ICTY developed a new body of jurisprudence on command responsibility, establishing that civilians as well as military officers could be held responsible if they actually exercised command, and bringing into criminal law the distinction between a *de jure* and a *de facto* commander. Among the consequences of this ruling is an enhanced ability to apply international law to civil wars and to incidents involving paramilitary formations.

Along with the International Criminal Tribunal for Rwanda (ICTR), ICTY has produced jurisprudence that has made a major contribution, including gender-based crimes, including rape and sexual violence, as violations of the Hague and Geneva Conventions and as elements of the crimes of genocide and torture.

While ICTY and ICTR have produced the first international jurisprudence on genocide since the passage of the Genocide Convention in 1948, ICTY's approach to genocide has been decidedly minimalistic. Only the mass killing of males from Srebrenica in 1995 has been defined as genocide, although prosecutors have sought to apply the charge more broadly. Only one individual has been convicted of genocide – Radislav Krstić, commander of the Drina Corps of the Army of Republika Srpska – though his conviction was altered on appeal to a conviction for aiding and abetting genocide. Additional jurisprudence on Srebrenica is anticipated from cases in which judgment has yet to be rendered, including the 'Srebrenica Seven' case and the prosecution of Radovan Karadžić. The Karadžić indictment could expand the ICTY's definition of genocide as it seeks to include the killings and expulsions of civilians in 1992 as acts of genocide.[7]

Finally, the greatest significance of some ICTY cases may derive from the fact that they reached trial at all. The prosecutions of heads of state from the region produced mixed results at best: Milošević died before his trial could be completed, while in the cases of both Alija Izetbegović and Franjo Tuđman there were only general statements after their deaths that they would have been charged if they had survived. Other heads of state brought before ICTY were mostly clients whose command was not at all times completely autonomous (like Babić and Karadžić). Nonetheless the fact that some heads of state were tried at all represents a major defeat for the doctrine of sovereign immunity, according to which political leaders could not be held accountable for their actions under international law.[8]

ICTY has also attracted criticism for some perceived shortcomings: 1) uneasy relationships between the Tribunal and the publics in the region, 2) difficulties in the conduct of trials and the treatment of evidence, and 3) political consequences of the Tribunal's activity and the effects of ICTY-related conditionality in the region.

Among the domestic publics of the former Yugoslavia, there is some resentment that the institution is both externally imposed and operates outside the countries whose citizens it tries. It therefore lacks some of the legitimacy that domestic legal institutions allegedly enjoy. The distant location of the Tribunal is compounded by the fact that no natives of the region act as judges, prosecutors or registry officials. People from the region can appear before the Tribunal only as an indictee, a defence attorney, or a witness. Nor has outreach been a priority of ICTY: its 'Outreach' office was founded only in 1999 and its activity has been largely confined to providing information to journalists and members of the legal profession rather than communicating with the public in a more unmediated fashion. Both knowledge about ICTY and measures of trust in it have been consistently low throughout the region.

The disputed legitimacy of the Tribunal has led to situations in which established courtroom procedure has been followed with great difficulty. An important precedent was set by Milošević at the beginning of his trial, when he refused to recognize the court and led his own defence. This probably had the consequence of strengthening the case against him, as he would inadvertently introduce evidence to which the prosecutors had not had access before, but it also enabled the defendant to use the proceedings to give public speeches, engage in irrelevant exchange with witnesses, and provoke extended delays. Vojislav Šešelj, whose trial is ongoing at the time of writing, has filled much of the Tribunal's time with similar but more antic behaviour, most of it directed toward the media.

A more fundamental problem has involved ICTY's inability to protect witnesses. The prosecution of Ramush Haradinaj failed in part due to intimidation of witnesses.[9] Partly because of ICTY's limited capacity to protect witnesses and control the activity in its trial chambers, there have been trials of tremendous length conducted with great delay. Milošević waited nearly a year for his trial to commence after his arrest in 2001, and it was still incomplete at the time of his death in 2006; Šešelj was taken into Tribunal custody in February 2003 and his trial began in November 2007.

ICTY has been criticized for its effect on politics in the region. Many observers argue that the conditionality of 'cooperation with ICTY' for issues such as EU accession and access to financial assistance has emptied the justice processes of meaning. Rather than confronting the past, states are expected to meet the far more minimal requirement of delivering individuals to the Hague for trial. Sometimes this has led to cynical observations that accused criminals have less difficulty travelling to EU countries like the Netherlands than ordinary visa applicants. In some cases, verdicts or sentences have led to controversy, raising the suggestion that while trials may establish a documentary record they do not necessarily lead to reconciliation – but rather by replaying conflicts encourage their revival.

Among ICTY's successes are the very strong impulse it gave to domestic legal institutions to build up their own capacity to process humanitarian law cases and the construction of a documentary record of the conduct of the armed conflicts in the region. Some of the failures of ICTY may seem greater than they are at least in part because the expectations attached to it were very high, particularly in relation to the enormity of the task and the narrow range of resources available to accomplish it. In some ways the flaws of ICTY have contributed to the evolution of transitional justice initiatives. Subsequent tribunals – such as the ones established for East Timor and Sierra Leone – were designed to correct the most apparent defects in the design of ICTY, particularly with regard to their location in their jurisdictions, their inclusion of people from the region in prosecution and judicial roles, and the separation of the process of preparing a documentary record from the process of trying suspects.

Domestic trials

One strong factor motivating the founding of ICTY was the failure of domestic courts to take on cases themselves. After a poor general start during the wars, the states of the region are building capacity to take on humanitarian law cases.

In Serbia, crimes committed domestically were ignored together with ones committed in neighbouring conflict areas. Ostoja Šibinčić, who led the campaign of intimidation against Croats in the village of Hrtkovci, was acquitted of all charges and returned to active political life in 2006.[10] After the kidnapping and murder of 19 ethnic Muslim passengers from the Belgrade-Bar railway at Štrpci in 1993, a low-ranking perpetrator was tried and sentenced by domestic courts but neither the commander of his unit nor officials of state and railway agencies were charged, despite evidence being raised against them at trial.[11] In the case of 17 ethnic Muslim passengers kidnapped from a bus and murdered in Sjeverin in 1992, investigation and prosecution of the case were delayed until 2003, when four people were convicted of torture and murder.

A few show trials were also conducted in the 1990s; in these trials para-military soldiers were charged but members of the regular military were not, and the prosecutions were often conducted in a way that assured the trials would not be carried to conclusion. One well publicized instance was the trial of the Vučković brothers in Šabac in 1994: the principal suspect was an alcoholic with a history of severe psychological illness who had been dismissed from the army in 1982. This established a distance between the military and the crimes, while also building a pretext for crimes to be traced to an unusual individual condition rather than to a political setting. While the trial dealt with individual crimes, it never raised the role of the Serbian Radical Party, which was part of the governing coalition, that had organized the paramilitary formation that included Vučković.[12]

The capacity for domestic prosecution was enhanced after 2000, with political changes in Serbia and Croatia. Vladimir Vukčević became the first special prosecutor for war crimes in Serbia in 2003, and Bosnia-Herzegovina's War Crimes Chamber began work in March 2005. While the Croatian parliament had made a declaration on the legitimacy of the state's military efforts in 2000, in response to pressure from the European Union special war crimes chambers were designated and the first cases began to be referred to them in 2005.

Early prosecutions in Croatia had been widely perceived as being selective. With the establishment of special chambers major cases began to be tried on a larger scale by domestic legal institutions. While the balance has favoured prosecutions of Croatian Serbs for violations committed as members of rebellious paramilitary forces, there have also been cases involving violations committed by Croat forces against civilians.[13] There are nonetheless dramatic instances of impunity in Croatia, including the continued untouchable status of paramilitary commander Tomislav Merčep, who is heavily implicated in kidnappings and killings in and around Pakrac in 1991–92 but remains an active political figure.[14] While the special war crimes chamber was established with the purpose of guaranteeing a level of objectivity and expertise in the conduct of trials, in practice the power of prosecutors to refer cases from the regular courts to this chamber is rarely used.

Since the special chamber for war crimes began work in Bosnia in 2005, 122 cases have begun in domestic courts.[15] The number of cases hardly corresponds, and probably never can do so, to the number of people who could potentially be charged with offences. There are barriers to prosecution imposed by basic political structures like the Dayton Peace Agreement: this achieved an end to armed conflict by assuring that power gained in the war would be maintained, and unsurprisingly many wartime figures continue to enjoy a protected status. There are also persistent issues of jurisdiction arising from the simultaneous operation of different judicial systems in the two entities and Brčko, as well as from ongoing confusion as to whether the applicable law derives from the Criminal Code of Yugoslavia, which was in force at the time of the conflict, or from the Criminal Code of Bosnia-Herzegovina, which addresses issues of war crimes in greater detail but did not come into force until 2003.[16]

Serbia faced both a large number of cases and huge challenges to prosecuting them. Some of the most prominent war crimes prosecutions since 2000 have involved the 'Scorpions' paramilitary group, members of which were convicted and sentenced in 2005 for a massacre of ethnic Albanian civilians in Podujevo, and in 2007 for participation in the Srebrenica genocide.[17] Aside from the question of crimes perpetrated, these cases raised the question of the role of military and state security services in the war; this presented a major portion of the legal strategy of nongovernmental advocacy groups in these cases. A more complicated picture emerges from the efforts to try the perpetrators of the Ovčara massacre near Vukovar in 1991. A conviction with harsh sentences was rendered in 2005, though this was subsequently overturned. The last word in the case may have been forfeited by the Serbian courts and could instead remain with ICTY, which convicted two of the main suspects in the massacre and released a third.[18]

In post-2000 Serbia a number of domestic murder cases remain unresolved. During the investigation of the murder of prime minister Zoran Djindjić in 2003, the 2000 murder of former president Ivan Stambolić was also solved and convictions were rendered against members of a disbanded 'special forces' unit in both cases. However the attempted murder in 2000 of politician Vuk Drašković has resulted in several convictions, all of which have been reversed on appeal, while nobody has been charged in the murder of newspaper editor Slavko Ćuruvija in front of his home in 1999. Suspicion remains that other unsolved killings, like that of journalist Radoslava (Dada) Vujasinović in 1994, can also be traced to regime-related forces but these cases remain unprosecuted.

Eight cases have been returned to domestic jurisdictions from ICTY. The case of killings of civilians in the Medak pocket has been transferred to Croatia. Most of the cases transferred from ICTY to domestic courts have been transferred to Bosnia-Herzegovina, where their conduct is closely monitored by the Tribunal.[19]

The close association between crimes committed in the course of the conduct of war and nearly all other types of major crime in the region has highlighted the persistent need for cross-border cooperation in prosecution and law enforcement. For instance, the Croatian politician and former paramilitary commander Branimir Glavaš was convicted of war-related murders and attempted to escape sentencing by fleeing to neighbouring Bosnia-Herzegovina where he holds citizenship. At Croatia's request he was quickly arrested by Bosnian police and prosecutors began to request his extradition. Though state prosecutors have made progress in assuring witness protection and allowing for testimony to be given remotely, serious obstacles remain to cross-border cooperation in trials, among them the legal ban on extradition which is shared by all of the states in the region.[20]

That the record of domestic prosecution should be mixed is hardly surprising. Domestic institutions – some new and untested, some old and burdened by legacies of subordination and complicity – took on a set of issues of extraordinary complexity and political sensitivity. They did so in an atmosphere of diminished trust in institutions, political uncertainty, uneven access to evidence, lack of clear jurisdiction and frequently hostile public sentiment, while simultaneously building institutional capacity and the capacity to collaborate and coordinate with their colleagues in states that were until recently hostile. Despite a record of disappointments and reversals along the way, important precedents are being set by domestic legal institutions.

The International Court of Justice

Governments in the region have also engaged on a smaller scale in efforts to request international courts to evaluate the behaviour of states. In two cases before the International Court of Justice (the ICJ) Serbia and its clients were charged with genocide.

The first time the ICJ was asked to make an intervention into the legal definition of genocide it affirmed the restrictive definition used by international criminal tribunals.[21] In its complaint against Serbia and Montenegro, Bosnia and Herzegovina asked the ICJ to determine that the conduct of campaigns against civilians in the war was genocidal, but the chamber maintained the position that only the 1995 Srebrenica killings constituted an 'act of genocide'. The court ruled in February 2007 that Serbia was guilty of failure to prevent and punish genocide but was guilty neither of genocide nor of complicity in genocide. Clearly, the ruling, which as the ICJ's first ruling on the crime of genocide was meant to create a precedent, sought to apply a narrow definition of the crime and a high standard of evidence. As a consequence the killings at Srebrenica in 1995 were found to constitute genocide but the intimidation and expulsion of civilians and the destruction of cultural property were not. They also established that direct and 'fully conclusive' evidence of intent was required rather than demonstrating intent through a 'pattern of acts' (paras. 76–81), and similarly required that the 'complete dependence' (paras. 138–52) of client paramilitary forces on their sponsors had to be demonstrated in order to establish the existence of relations of command and control. It would appear that in its decision the ICJ sought to reduce the number of genocide cases that could be brought before it. The ICJ ruling in the case is generally consistent with the narrow definition of the crime of genocide applied by ICTY.

Another genocide case, filed against Serbia by Croatia in 1999, has yet to be heard. The Serbian government has announced its intention to respond with a counter-complaint charging Croatia with genocide. While this development is likely to make the progress of the case more complicated, it may indicate at the same time the degree to which the filing of charges and counter-charges represents less a legal process and more a process of competition for political advantage. The continued stretching out of the time by which any pleadings before the court might begin could be thought of as the ICJ offering the opportunity for politicians to resolve a political dispute.

Non-judicial mechanisms: Attempts to create truth and reconciliation commissions

In addition to judicial mechanisms, there have also been several attempts since the late 1990s to create 'truth and reconciliation commissions' (TRCs) in the region. Three attempts at creating a commission in Bosnia took place between 1997 and 2006, one in 2001–3 in Serbia (then still officially united with Montenegro as the Federal Republic of Yugoslavia – FRY), and, since 2006, there has been an ongoing regional initiative by three NGOs from Bosnia, Croatia and Serbia. In Bosnia, decisions were also taken to establish two 'local' commissions – one on Srebrenica and one on Sarajevo – of which only the former completed its work and produced a report.

Overall, these attempts to create truth commissions have not produced any significant results. Although the current regional initiative is being undertaken very thoroughly, it is still too early to know whether it will actually lead to the establishment of a regional commission and many remain sceptical about the chances of its success.

There have been three principal reasons for the failure to create truth commissions until now: a lack of genuine political will among power-holders in the region to engage constructively with processes of confronting the recent past; a complicated relationship with international actors, including the ICTY, which have shaped domestic processes in ways that have not always been conducive to quests for 'truth and reconciliation'; and a deep and still enduring problem of divisive and fragmented visions of the recent past throughout the former Yugoslavia, encountered not only on an inter-ethnic level but even within civil societies of the same national group.

Bosnia and Herzegovina

The idea of a truth and reconciliation commission for the former Yugoslavia first appeared in the debates surrounding the creation of the ICTY in 1993. In the United States, those sceptical about the possibility of prosecuting war criminals in the former Yugoslavia argued that a better way forward was to create a UN-sponsored truth commission similar to the one that had recently completed its work on El Salvador.[22] The idea resurfaced two years later, when in side-letters to the Dayton Peace Agreement the parties to the Bosnian war agreed to establish an 'international commission of inquiry ... into the causes, conduct and consequences of the recent conflict' in the former Yugoslavia that was to include representatives of governments from the region along with 'distinguished international experts'.[23]

From the start, the organization that was most deeply involved in the process of creating a TRC for Bosnia was the United States Institute for Peace (USIP); according to some, it was the motor of the whole endeavour.[24] The USIP organized a number of meetings in the late 1990s with Bosnian political and religious leaders, justice officials and representatives of NGOs. One such meeting, led by Neil Kritz of the USIP, in Strasbourg in July 1997, explored the possibility of a truth and reconciliation commission.[25] The most enthusiastic domestic support for the initiative came from Jakob Finci, the president of Bosnia's Jewish Community and executive director of the country's Open Society Fund. Following the Strasbourg meeting, Kritz drafted a commission statute, which he then proposed to the three members of the Bosnian Presidency, religious leaders and civil society representatives.[26] According to Kritz, the main characteristics of such a truth commission were that it would not offer amnesties, but focus on fact-finding including establishing accurate numbers of people killed in the war. It would also be unique in documenting acts of heroism by ordinary citizens from all national groups – which was meant to 'help break down collective blame'.[27] However, when the Bosnian collective presidency rejected the initiative in spring 1998 the project came to a standstill. Later Kritz and Finci noted that ICTY officials had not supported the establishment of a Bosnian TRC at the time because it might conflict with the work of the Tribunal. They also explained that the Serb member of Bosnia's collective presidency, Momčilo Krajišnik, had insisted that he would personally select the Serb members of the commission and that the Bosnian Presidency would need to approve the TRC's final report prior to publication. As they noted, 'rather than agreeing to these crippling compromises, the TRC project was tabled'.[28]

In 2000, with Krajišnik extradited to The Hague and the ICTY deemed to have 'built a more solid foundation', the idea of a TRC for Bosnia was revived. A petition calling for a TRC was signed by over a hundred NGO and civil society representatives and a National Association for the Establishment of a Truth and Reconciliation Commission was created under Finci's direction. In February that year a round table in Sarajevo brought together some 80 members of various domestic and international organizations, who stated their support for the initiative. However, Gavin Ruxton, the ICTY representative, outlined the main objections to the TRC proposal, among which figured the fear that the TRC would interfere with the Tribunal's work: that there would be problems of overlap in the two bodies' investigative functions, that the TRC could undermine decisions by the ICTY (for example on whether 'genocide' had been committed), or that public hearings might jeopardize the Tribunal's witness protection programme or secret indictments.[29] In May 2001, the Tribunal's president Claude Jorda recognized in a speech in Sarajevo that the TRC was 'a national initiative and, as such, falls within your sovereign province', at the same time noting that such a body could not have autonomous investigative powers and had to provide the Tribunal with any information it acquired. It could, in fact, only deal with issues that were not a priority for the ICTY, such as reparations or 'the pedagogical and historical perspective of reconstructing the national identity'.[30] In other words, from the ICTY's perspective, a Bosnian truth commission could 'supplement and, if necessary, reinforce the International Tribunal in its mission of reconciliation', but not in any way represent a parallel and potentially rival institution, which would compete with the ICTY's work (or financing). Despite the TRC advocates' attempts to revise the proposed commission's mandate and reassure the ICTY, the latter's misgivings remained.

Finci and his associates also had to contend with a considerable domestic problem: the opposition of Bosnia's victim and missing persons associations. In 2002, following consultations with associations for missing persons of all three national groups, the Bosnian Ministry for Human Rights and Refugees rejected the draft law for a TRC submitted by Finci's association. As one participant later noted, 'everyone had a unanimous position … they rejected the idea of creating a commission, arguing that the only important thing for them was to find their missing family members'.[31] The victim associations' resistance to the idea of a national truth commission continued to represent a stumbling block. For victim groups, a truth commission was viewed as an elitist project pushed by 'professionalized' NGOs with strong links to international sponsors.[32] Victims' priorities were to be found elsewhere: achieving legal status for themselves or missing family members and thus being able to claim reparations, pensions, or inheritance; gaining knowledge about missing family members and locations of mass graves and speeding up exhumation and identification of bodies; and encouraging arrests and removal of perpetrators who were still in positions of power in their localities.[33] As one woman from Srebrenica put it: 'We don't need any more commissions or any other new institutions in addition to the ones we have. We only need those which already exist to carry out their work professionally and properly'.[34] From this perspective, the creation of a truth commission would only represent a distraction and postponement of more important action.

The final reason why attempts to create a Bosnian TRC came to nothing was a lack of political will to confront the recent past. A third attempt at creating a national truth commission in 2005–6, once again led by USIP (and its offshoot NGO in Bosnia called 'Dayton Project'), effectively sidelined Bosnian civil society and focused directly on political parties.[35] Under the auspices of the 'Dayton Project', a working group made up of representatives of the eight main parliamentary parties was formed to draft a law creating a truth commission as part of a larger package of constitutional amendments aimed at strengthening Bosnia's central institutions. These meetings were held behind closed doors and monitored by USIP's Neil Kritz and Donald Hays along with a representative from the UNDP, producing a draft that was largely based on the initial proposal drafted by Kritz and Finci in the late 1990s.[36] News of these meetings broke in March 2006, causing outrage in the Bosnian media and civil society because of the non-transparent and rushed nature of the process.[37] As one journalist put it: 'The fact is that truth and justice have long ago moved from the domain of fact-finding to the domain of politics, while thanks to our inert politicians, foreign organisations are supplying us with ready-made solutions to problems which for us are of existential importance'.[38] In the end, this initiative failed too: the working group agreed the draft law in May 2006, but the process ended there, sharing the fate of the wider initiative for constitutional change. The elections of October 2006 confirmed the deep divisions within the Bosnian political elite both in regard to visions of the past and those of the future.[39]

The only truth commission that actually came into being in post-Dayton Bosnia was the 'Commission for Investigation of the events in and around Srebrenica between 10 and 19 July 1995' (the 'Srebrenica Commission'), established by the Parliament of the Republika Srpska (RS) in December 2003.[40] This commission was not created voluntarily by the RS government, but rather as a response to a decision by Bosnia's Human Rights Chamber (a hybrid institution of eight foreign and six Bosnian judges set up by the Dayton Accords), following numerous requests from families searching for information about missing persons last seen in Srebrenica in July 1995. The RS government unsuccessfully appealed this decision and ultimately had no choice but to create a commission due to the direct intervention by the High Representative, Paddy Ashdown. Following long debates in the RS parliament concerning the Commission's mandate and membership, it finally began work in early 2004.[41] However, the Commission faced continuing obstruction by RS institutions which refused to provide documentation, as well as threats to its members and their public stigmatization as 'traitors' to their nation – provoking a second intervention by the High Representative in April 2004. Ashdown also redefined the commission's mandate on this occasion, narrowing the investigation of the events that took place in Srebrenica in July 1995 to focus on disclosing unknown locations of mass graves and compiling a list of missing persons.[42]

The commission's final report, produced in June 2004, provided the location of 32 mass grave sites, along with information concerning over 1,000 missing persons.[43] The report also gave an account of the role played in the killings by the RS army, police and the Ministry of the Interior, including confidential documents exposing 'Operation Krivaja' in which the attack on Srebrenica and the executions were planned. An addendum to the report provided in October 2004 contained a list of names of missing persons. In its session of 28 October, the RS Parliament adopted the report's conclusion that 'grave crimes had been committed in the Srebrenica region in July 1995 in violation of international humanitarian law' and made a formal apology to the families of the Srebrenica victims.[44] Finally, following yet another intervention of the High Representative in January 2005, a second working group was set up by the RS government to produce a list of 892 officials still employed by the institutions of the RS despite having been involved in the killings of July 1995. Some of the names from this confidential list were leaked to the Bosnian press.[45]

The significance of the Srebrenica Commission has been subject to very different interpretations. Whereas international representatives judged its report to be 'a historical and revolutionary event',[46] among Bosniaks the view prevailed that the report and the apology issued by the RS President were insincere and took place only 'because King [sic] Paddy Ashdown wielded his big stick'.[47] Among Bosnian Serbs, the commission was seen as imposed and it was not followed up by a distinctive change in policy towards the past.[48] Although the Commission report had taken over the ICTY's verdict in the case of General Krstić for its description of the context and the events in Srebrenica (which undermined the authority of the findings for many Bosnian Serbs, who view the ICTY as an anti-Serb institution), it did not also adopt the term 'genocide' for what had happened. In June 2005, the same RS President who had issued a formal apology to the victims of the massacre, Dragan Čavić, argued that 'there was no basis to speak of genocide', while RS officials continued to minimize and relativize the crime committed.[49] Indeed, it appears that for the RS government the Srebrenica Commission mainly served to enable a request for the creation of a similar commission to document the sufferings of Serbs in Sarajevo during the war.

The Sarajevo Commission was created in June 2006. International representatives refused to get involved in the project, denouncing it from the start as 'politicized'. Their reluctance was probably due to the fact that, in this instance, the main initiators were victim associations in the RS, many of which were linked to political parties in constant conflict with the Office of the High Representative. Resistance also came from Bosniak politicians reluctant to accept a highlighting of Serb sufferings in the capital and the creation of any 'symmetry' between Srebrenica and Sarajevo.[50] After two years of wrangling, Bosniak political leaders eventually compromised, but only after a boycott of the federal parliament by Serb members in May–June 2006 at the height of the negotiations on constitutional change. This compromise solution expanded the mandate of the commission to investigate the suffering not just of Serbs, but also of Croats, Bosniaks, Jews and others in Sarajevo during the war. The composition of the commission was criticized and the announcement of its creation was followed by delays and accusations of obstruction – this time by Bosniak politicians.[51] Finally, even those groups who had initially pushed for the commission stopped supporting it when its mandate was expanded beyond the fate only of the Sarajevo Serbs.[52] Like the projects for a national Bosnian commission, the Sarajevo Commission thus never got off the ground.

Serbia

The interplay of external factors, civil society divisions and the lack of political commitment also determined the fate of the FRY Truth and Reconciliation Commission. The commission was created in March 2001 by President Vojislav Koštunica, whose electoral victory over Milošević in September 2000 had led to regime change in Serbia. Ideologically, Koštunica defined himself as a 'democratic nationalist' – a label that reflected both his adherence to legal principles and democratic governance and his commitment to the idea of Serbian national unity and statehood.[53] Consistently critical of Western policy towards the Yugoslav conflict and outraged by NATO's 1999 bombing campaign against Serbia, Koštunica also never hid his disdain for the ICTY, which he viewed as a biased, American-dominated and anti-Serb institution.[54] It is likely that he envisioned a Yugoslav TRC as a body that would challenge the 'truth' represented by the Tribunal, or even possibly alleviate Western pressures for the extradition of Milošević to the ICTY which were stepped up in spring 2001, exactly at the time of the commission's creation.[55]

In 2001 there was very little interest among Western governments for any transitional justice mechanisms in Serbia other than the ICTY. The United States in particular continued to condition financial aid to Serbia through cooperation with the Tribunal, specifically on Milošević's extradition. External support for the TRC initiative came above all from Western NGOs, notably the newly created International Centre for Transitional Justice in New York and its president Alex Boraine, the former deputy chair of the South African TRC. Boraine was introduced to Koštunica in New York in November 2000, when the possibility of creating a truth commission was discussed. However, Koštunica set up the commission without further consultations with him – showing little consideration of external factors. Boraine remained committed to the project until the end of 2001, primarily advising the commissioners and trying to establish links between the commission and possible counterparts in the region. He organized a round table in Prague in October 2001, which brought together representatives of the commission and civil society representatives from Bosnia and Croatia. This meeting gave rise to sharp criticism of the commission's objectives by the other participants and ended up as a complete failure.[56] Boraine effectively withdrew from the project after Prague and did not attend the TRC's first public presentation of its work in May 2002.

Viewed very much as Koštunica's initiative, the commission soon became a victim of political infighting in the ruling Democratic Opposition of Serbia (DOS) coalition. Koštunica's main coalition partner, Prime Minister Djindjić, showed no interest in the commission or indeed in any 'truth-seeking' process. Djindjić made it clear that his priority was to re-establish links with the West, kick-start economic recovery, and turn Serbia into a modern, democratic country – putting the past behind as quickly as possible.[57] Other DOS party leaders were also reluctant to support the commission. Without government backing, the commissioners waited for months to get office space and a budget.[58] Over time even Koštunica appeared to lose interest in the commission. The commission's only subsequent contacts with Koštunica's office concerned its expansion to include new members and further financing. By the time the commission's fate was being decided in early 2003, Koštunica had clearly given up on the whole endeavour.

Along with the lack of sustained political support, the Yugoslav TRC also had to contend with deep hostility from within Serbia's civil society, particularly from those individuals and groups that had been the most active in the opposition to Serbian nationalism and Milošević's policy in the 1990s. For them, the idea of a truth commission – which had been discussed since 1999 and which had first been publicly raised shortly after Milošević's ouster by one of the politicians involved in these deliberations[59] – had effectively been hijacked by Koštunica, who had set up the TRC suddenly with no consultation. There were deep misgivings about some of the members chosen by Koštunica and considerable mistrust about its overall purpose.[60]

The commission's stated objective was: 'to investigate and determine causes and the course of conflicts which brought about the disintegration of the former state and the war, and led to horrifying human suffering and material destruction in the preceding decade'.[61] The emphasis was thus placed on historical inquiry into the causes of Yugoslavia's disintegration and wars. At an international conference held in May 2001 in Belgrade, some of the commissioners defended the project of examining the historical roots of the Yugoslav conflict, which also included the role played by international factors, arguing that the issue of war crimes was better left to the ICTY or domestic tribunals.[62] One of the commissioners, the economist Boško Mijatović, expressed hope that the commission would 'contribute to our understanding of the events of the past decade [and] help the world understand us and our behaviour and the circumstances that affected the misfortune of the former Yugoslavia'.[63]

According to the commission's critics, this smacked of an attempt to explain – even justify – Serbian actions during the 1990s to an international audience, rather than to present the Serbian public with evidence of their government's complicity in the crimes committed against other national groups.[64] And it was the latter that needed, in their view, to be the focus of any credible truth and reconciliation process. Almost immediately following the commission's creation, the law professor Vojin Dimitrijević and the historian Latinka Perović – two prominent anti-nationalist intellectuals – resigned from it, publicly expressing their deep scepticism towards the whole endeavour.[65]

The two resignations and the rejection of the commission by important segments of Serbian civil society proved to be insurmountable obstacles. The commission received almost no support or documentation from Serbian NGOs, nor from their counterparts in other parts of the former Yugoslavia. None of the commission's projects came to fruition. In February 2003, as the Federal Republic of Yugoslavia was replaced by Union of Serbia and Montenegro, the Montenegrin leadership refused to support the commission and nobody on the Serbian side fought for its preservation.[66] The commission thus drifted into oblivion, with debts outstanding and without ever having been officially notified of its demise.

Conclusion

Overall, the record of transitional justice initiatives in the region has been mixed. Judicial institutions have achieved some successes in apprehending and trying perpetrators, raising awareness and setting standards for human rights, creating a documentary record of crimes committed and enhancing the ability of domestic institutions to respond. Some of the more ambitious social and moral goals associated with legal initiatives have, however, proved elusive. The repeated false starts of 'truth seeking' initiatives underscore the point that it is easier to approach the past procedurally than it is to achieve a cathartic confrontation with it. Transitional justice initiatives have not bridged the cognitive divisions that undermine reconciliation in the region.

Several factors have interfered with the goals of reconciliation. In the first place, political elites in the region have for the most part participated in transitional justice unwillingly, seeking to satisfy internationally imposed conditions without alienating more nationalistic sections of the population. The institutions of civil society have been divided, both in terms of their goals and in terms of the means they saw as appropriate for achieving them. As time has passed since the end of armed conflict, economic concerns have come to appear to be more concrete than ones that seemed increasingly to be advocated by moralistically inclined intellectuals. Similarly, judicial institutions have been inconsistent. Domestic ones have not emerged completely from the legacy of subordination to political institutions, while international ones operate with a degree of distance and opacity that affords them little genuine authority in the region. Generally, domestic elites and institutions are not entirely prepared to embark upon the major work required to 'confront the past', while international actors often appear to have only a superficial interest in the question, reducing the sociocultural work of reconciliation to a series of concrete targets, like the delivery of suspects, without considering the multiple meanings of their initiatives in the public arena. A number of well-meaning international actors have, in the process of generating and encouraging initiatives, alienated potential participants by appropriating the process.

Does it follow that the goals of transitional justice are unattainable? Some of the dissatisfaction may derive from a lack of consensus as to what those goals are. Producing a documentary record and a criminal dossier do not involve the same motivations as catalyzing an open discussion of memory and responsibility. As Vojin Dimitrijević wrote on resigning from Serbia's abortive truth commission in 2001: 'I fear Great Historical Truths because great violence has been committed in their name and for their spread'.[67] To the degree that the product of 'confrontation' is a new consensus, this is all too familiar to people in societies emerging from authoritarian rule with its demands for ideological conformity.

It is possible that the contribution of criminal trials is limited to a narrowly defined field. A broader type of justice will call for different forms of engagement. In essence, the demand to 'confront' the past takes the shape of law and politics but is a demand involving far broader social and cultural processes. The role of the state is essential, but the state is better at generating compliance than at producing contributions of substance. It should not attempt to promote or suppress narratives but instead to encourage narrative activity. It is in the cultural process of understanding that versions of the past will be elaborated and compete with one another. Writers, filmmakers, artists and musicians are already developing new discourses and generating dialogues deployed to understand the past. These have received little official or international attention because they do not result in reports or convictions. But it is through these interventions that a new generation of political actors unburdened by complicity with the recent regimes will develop an approach to the past. Just ten years since the end of the last armed conflict, it is probably not surprising that this new understanding has not yet emerged. The legal and political initiatives of the last several years have helped offer a necessary if incomplete contribution to the development of new discourses. The shape of those discourses and the character of the debates they generate will take this contribution into account, but may not follow on from it in predictable ways.

Notes

1 The other major transitional justice initiatives that invite comparison would be 1) post-Second World War prosecutions of Nazis and fascist collaborators, 2) the array of trials and commissions established following the removals of military regimes from power in Central and South America, and 3) the post-civil war and post-apartheid initiatives engaged since 1990 in Africa. The Yugoslav cases are distinct from the first category in their temporal closeness to the events and the lack of a clear military victory, from the second category in the degree of international involvement, and from the third in the absence of a meaningful movement to consider culturally based alternatives or complements to judicial processes.

2 Full name: International Tribunal for the Prosecution of Persons Responsible for Serious Violations of International Humanitarian Law Committed in the Territory of the Former Yugoslavia since 1991.

3 See a letter by P. Robinson and S. Brammertz of 21 November 2008 and a report by Brammertz dated 24 November 2008 (http://www.icty.org/x/file/About/Reports%20and%20Publications/CompletionStrategy/Completion_Strategy_24nov2008_en.pdf).

4 The numbers cited are as of April 2009. ICTY maintains a running record: http://www.icty.org/sections/TheCases/KeyFigures

5 International Criminal Tribunal for the Former Yugoslavia, 'Some of the Tribunal's Achievements,' http://www.icty.org/sid/324.

6 Full details of the Čelebići and other cases mentioned below may be found at the Tribunal's website: http://www.un.org/icty.

7 The Karadžić indictment includes two charges of genocide: one for Srebrenica (paragraphs 41 to 47) and one identifying the destruction of population as an aim of the war (paragraphs 36 to 40).

8 See G. Bass, *Stay the Hand of Vengeance: The Politics of War Crimes Tribunals* (Princeton: Princeton University Press, 2001) and M. Kelly, *Nowhere to Hide: Defeat of the Sovereign Immunity Defense for Crimes of Genocide and the Trials of Slobodan Milošević and Saddam Hussein* (New York: Peter Lang, 2005).

9 P. M. Wald, 'Note from the Field: Dealing with Witnesses in War Crime Trials: Lessons from the Yugoslav Tribunal,' *Yale Human Rights and Development Law Journal*, vol. 5 (2002). In December 2008 Haradinaj became the first ICTY indictee to be profiled in the entertainment magazine *Vanity Fair*.

10 J. Zurković, 'Nije se Ostoja vratio, ali ima pravo da radi,' *Danas*, 20 March 2006.

11 Humanitarian Law Centre, 'Abduction at Štrpci – fifteen years on' (26 February 2008; http://www.hlc-rdc.org/saopstenja/800.en.html).

210   *Coming to Terms with the Past*

12 Unsigned, 'Vidovdanski masakr,' *NIN*, 12 July 2001, p. 20.
13 OSCE Mission to Croatia, *Background report: Domestic war crimes proceedings 2006* (Zagreb, 3 August 2007), p. 4.
14 A redacted US intelligence report on Merčep's activities can be found at http://www.foia. cia.gov/browse_docs.asp?doc_no=0001063835. See also D. Hedl, 'Croatia: Impunity prevails,' *Transitions Online*, 10 December 2005, http://www.legnostorto.com/index2.php? option=com_content&do_pdf=1&id=11239.
15 OSCE, 'War crimes cases started in January 2004–April 2009,' http://www.oscebih.org/ images/WC_Started_0409.jpg.
16 OSCE Mission to Bosnia and Herzegovina, *Moving towards a harmonized application of the law applicable in war crimes cases before courts in Bosnia and Herzegovina* (Sarajevo, August 2008), http://www.oscebih.org/documents/12615-eng.pdf.
17 'Massacre at Podujevo, Kosovo', CBC News, 29 March 2004, http://www.cbc.ca/news/ background/balkans/crimesandcourage.html; V. Perić Zimonjić, 'Serb "Scorpions" guilty of Srebrenica massacre', *The Independent*, 11 April 2007.
18 ICTY case no. IT-95-13/1-PT, 'The prosecutor of the Tribunal against Mile Mrkšić, Miroslav Radić and Veselin Šljivančanin.' All documents related to the case are available at http://www.icty.org/case/mrksic/4.
19 Monitoring of cases to Bosnia-Herzegovina is reported at http://www.oscebih.org/human_rights/ monitoring.asp?d=1.
20 OSCE Mission to Croatia, *Background report: Domestic war crimes proceedings 2006* (Zagreb, 3 August 2007), pp. 15–18.
21 All documents related to the case *Application of the Convention on the Prevention and Punishment of the Crime of Genocide (Bosnia and Herzegovina v. Serbia and Montenegro)* can be found online at http://www.icj-cij.org/docket/index.php?p1=3&p2=3&k=f4&case=91&code=bhy&p3=4.
22 See articles by H. Schwartz and A. Neier, *Human Rights Brief*, Spring 1994, vol. 1, no. 1, http://www.wcl.american.edu/hrbrief/01/1point.cfm.
23 Side letters to the General Framework of Agreement for Peace in Bosnia and Herzegovina, http://state.gov/p/eur/rls/or/dayton/52601.htm.
24 See Gavin Ruxton's comments at the roundtable 'Truth and Reconciliation: Imperative for the Future of Bosnia-Herzegovina', Sarajevo, 4 February 2000. http://www.angelfire.com/ bc2/kip/bosanski/conferences.htm.
25 'Cooperation Agreements in Bosnia', USIP *PeaceWatch*, August 1997, http://www.usip.org/ peacewatch/1997/897/bornia.html.
26 'Bosnia to Form a Single Truth Commission', USIP *PeaceWatch*, February 1998, http:// www.usip.org/peacewatch/1998/298/truth.html.
27 Kritz quoted in ibid.
28 N. J. Kritz and J. Finci, 'A Truth and Reconciliation Commission in Bosnia and Herzegovina: An Idea Whose Time has Come', *International Law Forum*, 2001, vol. 3, p. 56.
29 Ruxton in 'Truth and Reconciliation', op. cit.
30 C. Jorda, 'The ICTY and the Truth and Reconciliation Commission in Bosnia and Herzegovina' (12 May 2001, Sarajevo). ICTY Press Release, 17 May 2001, http://www.un. org/icty/pressreal/p591-e.htm.
31 Saliha Đuderija, quoted in 'Kredibilitet suda BiH je važan za građane BiH', Centar za istraživačko novinarstvo, 1 July 2005, http://www.cin.ba.
32 C. Jouhanneau, 'La recherché de la "vérité" entre langage international et categories morales locales: Réflexions sur la non-création d'une Commission Vérité et Réconciliation pour la Bosnie-Herzégovine', unpublished paper presented at conference on 'Politics of Reconciliation', Berlin, Centre Marc Bloch, October 27, 2007.
33 I. Delpla, 'In the Midst of Injustice: The ICTY from the Perspective of some Victim Associations', in X. Bougarel, E. Helms and G. Duijzings (eds), *The New Bosnian Mosaic: Identitites, Memories and Moral Claims in a Post-War Society* (Aldershot: Ashgate, 2007), pp. 211–34.
34 Adisa Tihić in 'Međunarodna Konferencija: Utvrđivanje istine u post-konfliktnom period: inicijative i perspective na zapadnom Balkanu', Sarajevo, 5–6 May 2006, pp. 47–48,

http://www.korekom.org/public/fck_files/file/Reg_%20forum%20za%20tran_pravdu-Sarajevo-5_i%206_maj%202006-transkripti.pdf.

35 The initiative and financing came from USIP and, according to some sources, the Bosnian parliament had no choice but to accept it (E. Hadžović, 'Truth Commission – concerting a story for $20 million', *Dani*, 10 March 2006).

36 This last point was noted by Mirsad Tokača in 'Medjunarodna konferencija', op. cit., p. 100.

37 See M. Tokača, J. Džumhur and E. Ramulić in ibid., pp. 89–100.

38 Hadžović, op. cit.

39 S. Mustajbegović, 'Bosnia: Constitution Setback', *Balkan Insight*, 25 January 2007, http://www.birn.eu.com/en/67/10/2141.

40 M. Picard and A. Zinbo, 'Sur le rapport du gouvernement de la Republika Srpska', *Cultures et conflits*, Spring 2007, no. 65, pp. 103–18.

41 The Commission had five Serb members (nominated by the RS government), one Bosniak representing the victims and one international representative (both nominated by the High Commissioner). The Office of the High Commissioner and the ICTY oversaw its work.

42 Picard and Zinbo, op. cit., pp. 112–13., pp. 78–79.

43 Vlada Republike Srpske, Komisija za istraživanje događaja u i oko Srebrenice od 10. do 19. Jula 1995, 'Događaji u i oko Srebrenice od 10. do 19 jula 1995', Banja Luka, 2004, http://www.forumtz.com/bos/imgDoc/Srebrenica.pdf.

44 'Vlada RS: Žaljenje zbog Srebrenice', B92, 10 November 2004.

45 Picard and Zinbo, op. cit., pp. 114–15.

46 Quoted in T. Topić, 'Otvaranje najmračnije stranice', *Vreme*, 1 July 2004.

47 Mirsad Tokača in the conference on 'Strategy for Transitional Justice in the former Yugoslavia', Belgrade, 1–2 October 2004, Humanitarian Law Centre, pp. 136–37.

48 Momčilo Novaković, MP for the Serbian Democratic Party in the BiH parliament, quoted in N. Ahmetašević, 'Komisije između istine i politike', *BIRN Justice Report*, 29 June 2006.

49 Picard and Zinbo, op. cit., p. 115.

50 See C. Jouhanneau, '"Si vous avez un problem que vous ne voulez pas régler, créez une Commission". Les commissions d'enquête locales dans la Bosnie-Herzégovine d'après-guerre', *Mouvements*, 2008, vol. 1, no. 53, pp. 166–74.

51 M. Buljugić, 'No Progress for Sarajevo Truth Commission', *BIRN Justice Report*, 20 February 2007, http://www.bim.ba/en/51/10/2327.

52 Ibid.

53 On Koštunica see A. H. Budding, 'From Dissidents to Presidents: Dobrica Ćosić and Vojislav Koštunica Compared', *Contemporary European History*, 2004, vol. 13, no. 2, pp. 185–201.

54 See *Vreme*, 5 July 2001, p. 16. In February 2001, Koštunica refused to meet the ICTY's chief prosecutor, Carla Del Ponte, on her visit to Belgrade, only reversing his position under pressure from his coalition partners.

55 Despite his disdain for the ICTY, Koštunica never publicly considered not cooperating with it. He acknowledged that this was Serbia's obligation, although he also stated that it was not a priority for his government. *Vreme*, 5 July 2001, pp. 16–17.

56 Interviews with commission members and other participants of the Prague workshop, Belgrade, November 2007 and May 2008.

57 Although Djindjić orchestrated Milošević's extradition to the ICTY, he justified it publicly in pragmatic terms – as a practical necessity for Serbia to obtain badly needed financial aid.

58 The commission received 1,300,000 dinars in 2001 and another 2,959,000 dinars in 2002, the equivalent of about $62,200 (document in possession of authors). This was considerably less than the norm, with TRC budgets ranging from $1 million for the Haiti commission to over $18 million per year in the case of the South African TRC. R. Kerr and E. Mobekk, *Peace and Justice* (Cambridge: Polity, 2007), pp. 132–33 and A. Chapman and P. Ball, 'The Truth of Truth Commissions: Comparative Lessons from Haiti, South Africa and Guatemala', *Human Rights Quarterly*, 2001, vol. 21, pp. 16–17.

59 Goran Svilanović, Yugoslavia's foreign minister and leader of the anti-nationalist Civic Alliance party. *Vreme*, 12 April 2001, p. 30.

60 For an overview of the main critiques, see D. Ilić, 'Jugoslovenska komisija za istinu i pomirenje, 2001-?' *Reč*, no. 73.19, October 2005.
61 Komisija za istinu i pomirenje, 'Osnovna pravila rada', document in possession of authors.
62 See Ilić, op. cit.
63 Quoted in *Vreme*, 12 April 2001, p. 30.
64 Ilić, op. cit., p. 65.
65 A third member also resigned, but without publicly criticizing the commission.
66 Interviews with commission members, Belgrade, November 2007 and May 2008.
67 A full English translation of the letter is available at http://listserv.buffalo.edu/cgi-bin/wa?A2=ind0202&L=JUSTWATCH-L&P=R83099&D=0&H=0&O=T&T=0.

Index

secession, right of 177, 185
Second World War: army in exile 102–3; cabinet
crises and King Peter 110–14; collapse and
occupation of Yugoslavia (1941) 82, 100, 101,
102, 103; D-Day 104; ethnic violence 77,
82–99; foreign policy 105–7; government in
exile 100–116; legacy for Croatia 118–21; Pact
with the Axis Powers 101; post-war rebuilding
123; prosecutions of Nazis 209; relations
between politicians and military 101–5;
Serb-Croat question 107–10; Yugoslav
resistance 103, 105; *see also četniks*; NDH:
partisans; *ustašas*
Seidler, Ernst von 32, 37
self-determination, principle of 13, 14, 16, 23,
35, 117, 125, 176,
185–86, 187
Self-Determination movement 184
self-management system 128, 144, 146, 150, 153
separatism 125, 133
Serb-Croat question 68, 107–10
Serb Cultural Club (SKK) 69, 74–76, 109
Serbia: and Battle of Kosovo (1389) 17, 19–22; as
bulwark against Austria and Germany 18, 19,
20–22; charged with genocide 200;
decentralized structure 148; as defender of
Christianity 17, 19, 22; democratization
movement 162, 164, 168, 170, 172;
dependence on Austria-Hungary in 19th
century 13–14; dispute with Slovenia on reform
156, 157; early relations with Bosnia-Herzegovina
14; effect of war on protests 171; elections
(1990s) 165–66, 167, 171, 172; elections
(2000) 161, 166, 171; extremism (influence on
Croatian Serbs) 140; in First World War 16,
18, 19, 20–22, 47; First World War disabled
veterans 48, 51, 52, 54, 55–56, 59; First
World War widows and orphans 51; genocide
complaint against Croatia 200; intellectuals
134; and Kosovo 177–80, 181, 183, 185, 186;
Kosovo Serbs' protests 148, 152–53, 164;
movement for abolition of 1974 Constitution
138; NATO bombings 171, 180, 205–6; new
generation of politicians (1980s) 135, 136,
137, 146; 1990 Constitution 165; *Otpor* 162,
167–68; popular protest and nationalism 155,
162–75; pro-government protests 169–70;
purge of liberals (1972) 129; referenda 165;
relations with Yugoslav Committee and
Yugoslavism 11, 12, 16; Second World War
German occupation 82, 84; state of uncertainty
in 172; statehood in socialist Yugoslavia 127;
student protests 154, 155, 166, 167, 168, 171;
symbols of 167, 169; television 166; territory

annexed by Bulgaria (1941) 82; and TRCs
201, 205–7, 208; university law (1998) 167,
168; war crimes trials in 197–98, 199;
workers' protests 150, 153–54, 155, 161–62;
see also Milošević, Slobodan
Serbian Academy of Arts and Sciences:
Memorandum (1986) 129
Serbian Democratic Party (SDS) 139
Serbian Orthodox Church 65, 66, 70, 76, 163,
168
Serbian Relief Fund 15
Serbs: in Austria-Hungary 12; campaign for
banovina 68, 69, 70; claim to Bosnian territory
69, 70; disatisfaction with interwar Yugoslavia,
and relations with Croats 62–80; divisions
within 63, 73; ethnic composition of partisans
119; nationalism 67, 74–75, 109, 136,
162–75; relations with government in exile
104, 107–10; secession movements (1939–40)
70–71; *see also* Bosnian Serbs; *četniks*; Croatian
Serbs; Kosovo Serbs
"Serbs, rally together" movement 69–70, 75
Šešelj, Vojislav 196, 197
Seton-Watson, R. W. 15
Šibinčić, Ostoja 197
Sigismund, Holy Roman Emperor 21
Sijerčić, Fehim 87–88
Simović, Dušan 100, 101, 102, 103, 107, 108,
112
Sisak: power plants 132
Sjeverin killings 197
SKH (Croatian League of Communists) 126, 127,
129, 130–31, 134, 135, 136–37
SKH-SDP 137, 139
SKJ *see* League of Communists of Yugoslavia
SKK *see* Serb Cultural Club
Skopje: disabled veterans 52; as potential capital
of Serbian *banovina* 68, 78; workers' protests
149
Slavonia 14, 38–39, 40, 119
Slovakia: democratization 170
Slovene Clericals 64
Slovenes: campaign for *banovina* 68, 76; and
declaration movement 32–37, 38, 39, 40, 41;
First World War campaign for Yugoslav state
28; government in exile and 109; Habsburg
reaction to dissent of 32, 34–35; hatred for
Magyars 29–30; military revolts (1917) 36;
position in socialist Yugoslavia 126;
resettlement in Second World War 84, 85;
support for Habsburgs 31, 33, 34
Slovenia: annexed by Axis powers 82;
anti-communist opposition 136; dispute with
Serbia on reform 156, 157; homogeneity 122;